Automated Essay Scoring:
A Cross-Disciplinary Perspective

Automated Essay Scoring:
A Cross-Disciplinary Perspective

Edited by

Mark D. Shermis
Florida International University

Jill Burstein
ETS Technologies, Inc.

LEA
LAWRENCE ERLBAUM ASSOCIATES, PUBLISHERS
2003   Mahwah, New Jersey   London

Lawrence Erlbaum Associates, Inc., Publishers
10 Industrial Avenue
Mahwah, New Jersey 07430

Cover concept by Barbara Ferguson
Cover design by Kathryn Houghtaling Lacey

Library of Congress Cataloging-in-Publication Data

Automated essay scoring : a cross-disciplinary perspective / edited by Mark D.
Shermis, Jill Burstein.
    p.   cm.
  Includes bibliographical references and index.
  ISBN 0-8058-3973-9 (alk. paper)
   1. Grading and marking (Students)–Data processing. 2. Educational tests and
measurements–Data processing. I. Shermis, Mark D., 1953- II. Burstein, Jill.

  LB3060.37 .A98 2002
  371.27'2–dc21

                                                        2002072221

Printed in the United States of America
10 9 8 7 6 5 4 3 2 1

TABLE OF CONTENTS

FOREWORD

Carl Bereiter, PhD

This is a coming-of-age book about automated essay scoring. Although still a young science, AES, as its practitioners call it, has passed an important transition and is ready to venture forth. Its youth was spent in demonstrating that a computer can do as well as human raters in the kind of scoring that is typically done in mass testing of writing ability—that is, scoring a large number of compositions produced under similar conditions in response to the same "prompt." Scoring such tests using human raters is an expensive business; achieving adequate reliability normally requires multiple raters, who have to be trained. Replacing even one rater by a machine would save substantial money, and so it is not surprising that funding for research on automating essay scoring has mainly been directed toward this very practical application. However, it was already demonstrated, in the pioneering research of Ellis Page in the 1960s, that a computer can yield scores that agree with human raters as well as they agree with each other. Performance gains since then have been incremental, even though the algorithms and the technology for executing them have become increasingly sophisticated. It seems that there are no new worlds to conquer as far as matching the human rater is concerned.

So what are the new worlds to be conquered? The most obvious, although it is only addressed obliquely in this book, is to do better than human raters. Human essay scorers are not perfect; if they were, it would be a first in the history of civilization. As human beings who have lives outside essay scoring, they are susceptible to quirks and biases carried over from their other lives. They are also susceptible to halo effects; the tendency, when something creates a generally favorable impression, to rate it highly on all counts. The correlation between ratings on style and content is probably a good deal higher than it deserves to be. Computer scoring ought to be able to overcome these human foibles. However, the question is, what do you use for a criterion if human raters are no longer taken as the standard? All the approaches to AES discussed in this book rely on training the system to match some external criterion.

One straightforward way of improving on ordinary human raters is to use experts' ratings to train the AES system; but what about the imperfections of the experts, who after all are human too? Commenting on the behavior of peer reviewers of manuscripts submitted to a scholarly journal (who are presumably as expert as you are going to get), the outgoing editor remarked that in his experience reviewers never recommended a badly written article for publication, yet they never gave bad writing as the reason for rejection. They always managed to find some content-related reason for rejection. The editor was concerned that this indicated a kind of negative halo effect: create a bad impression and you will be scored low on everything. Another approach to doing better than ordinary human raters would be to use expert writers rather than expert raters. Have reputable professional writers produce essays to the same specifications as the students and train the AES system to distinguish them. Sarah Friedman, in research carried out during the 1980s, found that holistic ratings by human raters did not award particularly high marks to professionally written essays mixed in with student productions. This indicates that there is room here for AES to improve on what raters can do.

A challenge that is receiving attention on several fronts is that of turning AES into a learning tool. Any time you have software that does something intelligent, there is the potential of using it to teach that something to those who lack it. The simplest use of AES in this regard is to give students the opportunity to score practice essays or preliminary drafts and thus, without guidance, work to improve their scores. However, in various chapters of this volume, we read of efforts to provide guidance. Depending on the design of the underlying AES system, it may point out grammar mistakes, content omissions, or discourse structure problems. A basic problem, well recognized by the authors, is that the learners are generally not competent to judge the validity of the advice. We have probably all had experience with the grammar and style checkers that come along with word processors. They often give bad advice, but to the person who is able to judge, it is at worst annoying. For the knowledgeable but careless writer, the errors they do catch probably make it worth the annoyance. However, for a naive writer, mistakenly flagging something as an error could be seriously miseducative. (So could mistakenly flagging something as laudatory, but that is not an issue, at least not at the present state of the art.) Accordingly, AES developers prefer to err on the side of letting errors slip by rather than marking things as errors when they are not; but it is impossible to design a system assertive enough to be useful without its erring to some extent in both ways. That means, probably, that the systems cannot be entirely self-instructional. In the context of a writing class, questions like "Is this an error or isn't it?" and "Would this essay really profit from saying more about such-and-such?"—prompted by feedback from the AES system—could provide worthwhile matter for discussion, and the butt of criticism would be a page of computer-generated output rather than a chagrined student.

The third challenge, which is already being hotly pursued by the Intelligent Essay Assessor group (Chapter 6), is to tackle essay examinations as distinguished from essay-writing tests. Although the two have much in common, the essay examination is supposed to be mainly testing content knowledge and understanding rather than composition skills. The essay exam has a long history; it is still widely used, especially in societies influenced by British education, and it is frequently recommended as a cure for the ills attributed to multiple-choice and other objective tests. However, the fact is that when essay examinations are used for mass testing, they contract most of the drawbacks attributed to objective tests. In the interests of reliability and speed, scorers are provided with a checklist of points to look for. This, along with time pressure, obliges them to score in a mechanical way that is more appropriate for a machine than for a fatigue-prone human. Thus, along with multiple-choice tests, they do not really answer the question, "What does this student know about X?" Instead they answer the question, "How many of the following list of Xs does the student know?" The second question is equivalent to the first only under the condition where the list of Xs represents an adequate sample of a domain. This is almost never the case, and in fact achievement tests are not generally aimed at statistical sampling at all. Instead, they are derived from judgments by teachers and subject matter specialists about what ought to be on the test. This has the unfortunate effect of encouraging students and teachers to focus their efforts on what they predict will be on the test rather than on objectives of more long-term value.

AES could help to break the mutual stranglehold that exists between tests and curricula, where the curriculum is constrained by what is on the tests and the tests are derived from what is conventionally taught. To do this, however, it is not enough that AES give students more leeway to show what they know; it can do that already. It has to yield usable results when students are not all answering the same question—when they may even be answering questions of their own invention. And it should be sensitive to indications of depth of understanding, not merely to the quantity of facts brought forth. If the cognitive learning research of the past quarter-century is destined to have any effect on education at all, it will likely be through a greatly increased emphasis on depth of understanding. AES not only needs to be there if this does happen, it could help to make it happen, by providing tools that can be used to evaluate depth. It appears this is a challenge that none of the AES research programs have met; however, as will become clear from the chapters in this book, researchers are developing algorithms and strategies that offer reason to believe it is a challenge that can be met.

I mention just one final challenge, which is one the research team I work with has undertaken, although its results are not at a stage that would warrant a place alongside the results presented in this volume. The challenge is applying the techniques of automatic text evaluation to online discourse. Online discourse is assuming increasing prominence in education as well as in various kinds of knowledge work. Not only is it central too much of distance education, it is increasingly taking over those portions of on-site education traditionally handled through discussion sections and short written assignments. Being in digital form to begin with, online discourse provides possibilities for more systematic evaluation than its nondigital predecessors. However, it also presents difficulties. It is more free-form than even the loosest essay assignments; the quantity of text produced by different students can vary greatly; and there are problems of reference or deixis when the discussion presupposes knowledge of shared experiences taking place offline. In addition—and this is where the really interesting challenge comes in— online discourse unfolds over time and therefore raises questions about assessing change. Is the discussion getting anywhere? Is there evidence of learning? Are there changes in belief or interpretation? What happens to new ideas as they enter the discourse? Monitoring online discourse is time-consuming for teachers, to much the same extent as marking papers, and so any help that technology might provide would be welcomed (by some). With this interest as background, I have read the contributions to this volume with great admiration for the quality of invention and with continual thought to where further invention might lead.

PREFACE

Research in the field of automated essay scoring began in the early 1960s. More recent advances in computing technology, along with the general availability and access to computers, has enabled further research and development in automated essay scoring and evaluation tools. Further, deployment of this capability has grown rapidly during the past few years.

As automated essay scoring and evaluation becomes more widely accepted as an educational supplement for both assessment and classroom instruction, it is being used in early education, and secondary and higher education. A primary challenge is to develop automated essay scoring and evaluation capabilities so that they are consistent with the needs of educators and their students. It is used widely in the public schools for state-wide assessment, as well as at the university level. Textbook publishers have also begun to integrate the technology to accompany their textbook instruction materials. Automated essay scoring and evaluation capabilities are now being used internationally.

Although there has been a growing literature in the area of automated essay scoring and evaluation, this is the first book to focus entirely on the subject. The development of this technology has met with many questions and concerns. Researchers' responses to these questions have guided the development of the technology. We have tried to address these questions in this book. Teachers typically want to know how the technology can supplement classroom instruction. They also want to understand how the technology works, and whether or not it will address relevant issues that will improve their students writing. Researchers in educational measurement typically have questions about the reliability of the technology. Our colleagues in computer science are interested in the various computing methods used to develop capabilities for automated essay scoring and evaluation tools. In compiling the chapters of this book, it was our intention to provide readers with as complete a picture as possible of the evolution, and the state-of-the-art of automated essay scoring and evaluation technology across these disciplines: teaching pedagogy, educational measurement, cognitive science, and computational linguistics. The chapters in this book examine the following: (a) how automated essay scoring and evaluation can be used as a supplement to writing assessment and instruction, (b) several approaches to automated essay scoring systems, (c) measurement studies that examine the reliability of automated analysis of writing, and (d) state-of-the-art essay evaluation technologies.

There are many people we would like to acknowledge who have contributed to the successful completion of this book. We first thank our families for continual humor, support and patience—Daniel Stern, Abby and Marc Burstein Stern, Sheila and Bernard Burstein, Cindy Burstein, the Altman, Barber, Nathan, Stern, and Weissberg families, Becky Shermis, and Ryan Shermis. We thank Gwyneth Boodoo for an introduction to Lawrence Erlbaum. We are grateful to the following people for their advice, collegiality, support, and enduring friendship: Slava Andreyev, Beth Baron, Martin Chodorow, Todd Farley, Marisa Farnum, Claire Fowler, Jennifer Geoghan, Bruce Kaplan, Claudia Leacock, Chi Lu, Amy Newman, Daniel Marcu, Jesse Miller, Hilary Persky, Marie Rickman, Richard Swartz, Susanne Wolff and Magdalena Wolska. We acknowledge our editors at Lawrence Erlbaum Associates, Debra Riegert and Jason Planer, for helpful reviews and advice on this book. We would like to thank Kathleen Howell for production work. We are very grateful to our talented colleagues who contributed to this work.

Mark D. Shermis
Jill Burstein

INTRODUCTION

Mark D. Shermis
Florida International University
Jill Burstein
ETS Technologies,Inc.

WHAT IS AUTOMATED ESSAY SCORING?

Automated essay scoring (AES) is the ability of computer technology to evaluate and score written prose. Most of the work to date has involved the English language, but models are currently being developed to evaluate work in other languages as well. All but the most enthusiastic proponents of AES suspect that there are forms of writing that will always be difficult to evaluate (e.g., poetry). However, for the 90% of writing that takes place in school settings, it should be possible to develop appropriate AES models.

THE TECHNOLOGY INFUSION PROBLEM

All researchers in automated essay scoring have encountered a skeptic or two who, in their best moments, are suspicious of the technology. These critics argue that the computer cannot possibly use the same processes as humans in making discerning judgments about writing competence. In fact, these same critics might assert that the aspects of a text being measured or evaluated by automated writing evaluation tools does not relate to true qualities of writing, namely those qualities likely to be specified in scoring guides.

Page and Peterson (1995) discussed the use of proxes and trins as a way to think about the process of emulating rater behavior. Trins represent the characteristic dimension of interest such as fluency or grammar whereas proxes (taken from approximations) are the observed variables with which the computer works. These are the variables into which a parser might classify text (e.g., part of grammar, word length, word meaning, etc.). In social science research, a similar distinction might be made between the use of latent and observed variables.

In terms of its present development, one might think of AES as representing the juncture between cognitive psychology and computational linguistics. The research documented throughout the following pages clearly demonstrates that AES correlates well with human-rater behavior, may predict as well as humans, and possesses a high degree of construct validity. However, the explanations as to why it works well are only rudimentary, subject to "trade secrets", and may not correspond well to past research. Skeptics often forget that although we seem to recognize good writing when we see it, we are often at odds when it comes time to articulating why the writing is good. This conundrum is often true with other technology infusions. Sometimes new technology offers an alternative method that allows us to achieve the same goal. Consider the following example:

If you ask a cook how to bake a potato, you will often get a response that suggests if you heat an oven to 400°, poke a few holes in the potato, place the potato in the oven and come back in an hour, your goal of a baked potato will be achieved. In the Southwest, one would go through the same procedure except that the oven would be replaced by a barbeque.

But what if some engineer said, "You know, I'm going to put this uncooked potato in a black box that generates no heat whatsoever, and in 15 minutes, you will have a baked potato." Would you believe this person? Probably not, because it would defy the general process with which you are most familiar. However, this is exactly how the microwave operates.

If you were to go back to the cooks and ask, "Which potato do you prefer?" your experts would invariably say that they preferred the one that was prepared in the oven. And they would point out that there are several things that your black box can't do. For example, it cannot really bake things like cakes and it cannot brown items. That was certainly true 25 years ago when microwaves were first introduced on a massive scale, but it is no longer the case today. The point is that the microwave may use a different set of physics principles, but the results are similar. There are narrow aspects of cooking that the microwave may never do, or do as well as the traditional oven, but innovation is tough to rein in once it has captured the minds of creative engineers and an enthusiastic public.

Another example: Lets suppose you wanted to measure the distance between where you are standing and the wall. The authentic approach to measurement for this task would be to have a colleague run a tape measure between you and the wall (assuming the tape measure was long enough). But what if we told you the same results could be obtained by placing a light pen in your hand, beaming it to the wall, and reading off the results in a digital display. You might object by asserting that there are some kinds of surfaces that would be particularly problematic (e.g., textured surfaces) for this new technology, ignoring that no matter what the circumstances, it would likely eliminate much of the measurement error that is inherent in using a tape measure.

Although not in its infancy automated essay scoring is still a developing technology. The first successful experiments were performed using holistic scores, and much of the recent work has been devoted to generating specific trait scores —that is, scores that measure specific aspects of writing, such as organization and style. As you will read in some of the chapters to follow, the direction of automated evaluation of student writing is beyond the automated prediction of an essay score. Specifically, the writing community is interested in seeing more analysis with regard to automated evaluation of writing. They have a growing interest in seeing automated feedback that provides information about grammaticality and discourse structure. For instance, with regard to grammar errors, there is interest in feedback about sentence errors such as fragments, and other errors such as with subject–verb agreement and commonly confused word usage (e.g., their, there, and they're). This kind of feedback has similar theoretical underpinnings to earlier, pioneering work in the development of the *Writer's Workbench* (MacDonald, 1982). The *Writer's Workbench* is software developed in the early 1980s that was designed to help students edit their writing. This software provided automated feedback mostly related to mechanics and grammar. Concerning the evaluation of discourse in student writing, instructors would like to see evaluations of the quality of a thesis statement, or relationships between two discourse elements, such as the thesis and conclusion. Analysis of both grammar and discourse is possible with the availability of computer-based tools that provide analyses of grammar and discourse structure (discussed in the Leacock & Chodorow, Chapter 12 and Burstein and Marc, Chapter 13). Generally speaking, instructors would like to see automated feedback that is similar to the types of feedback they typically include in their own handwritten comments to students. Both grammatical and discourse-based feedback could provide a useful aid to the process of essay revision.

You might think of the technology as being where microcomputers were during the early 1980s when writers still had a choice between the new technology and the typewriter. (Today, there is no longer an American manufacturer of typewriters.)

The fact that automated essay scoring is not yet perfect is both a blessing and a boon. It is a blessing insofar as the invitation is still open for all members of the writing community to become involved to help shape future developments in this area. It is also a boon because it is open to criticism about its current lack of features relevant to writing. Will the technology identify the next great writer? Probably not. But does it have the promise of addressing most of the writing in the classroom? Certainly.

We expect that automated essay scoring will become more widely accepted when its use shifts from that of summative evaluation to a more formative role. For example, Shermis (2000) proposed that one mechanism for incorporating AES in electronic portfolios is the possibility of having students "presubmit" their essays before actually turning the work into a human instructor. If this were incorporated as part of a writing class, then more instructors could view AES as a helpful tool, not a competitive one. If national norms were developed for some writing models then educational institutions could track the developmental progress of their students using a measure that was independent of standardized multiple-choice tests. A school could essentially document the value-added component of their instruction or experience.

WHY A CROSS-DISCIPLINARY APPROACH?

The development of automated essay evaluation technology has required perspectives from writing teachers, test developers, cognitive psychologists, psychometricians, and computer scientists. Writing teachers are critical to the development of the technology because they inform us as to how automated essay evaluations can be most beneficial to students. Work in cognitive psychology continues to help us to model our systems in ways that reflect the thought processes of students who will use the systems. As we continue to develop systems, psychometric evaluations of these systems give us essential information about the validity and reliability of the system. So, psychometric studies help us to answer questions about how the evaluative information from the systems can be compared to similar human evaluations, and whether the systems are measuring what we want them to. Computer science plays an important role in the implementation of automated essay evaluation systems, both in terms of operational systems issues and system functionality. The former deals with questions such as how best to implement a system on the web, and the latter with issues such as how natural language processing techniques can be used to develop a system. It is our intent in this book to present perspectives from across all of these disciplines so as to present the evolution and continued development of this technology.

REFERENCES

Page, E. B., & Petersen, N. S. (1995). The computer moves into essay grading: Updating the ancient test. *Phi Delta Kappan, 76*(7), 561-565.

Shermis, M.D. (2000). *Automateed Essay Grading for Electronic Portfolios.* Washington, DC: Fund for the Improvement of Post-Secondary Education (grant proposal).

MacDonald, N. H., Frase, L.T., Gingrich, P.S., & Keenan, S. A. (1982). The Writers Workbench: Computer Aids for Text Analysis. *IEEE Transactions on Communications, 3*(1), 105-110.

I. Teaching of Writing

1

What Can Computers and AES Contribute to a K–12 Writing Program?

Miles Myers
Institute for Research on Teaching and Learning (former Executive Director,
Edschool.com (Division of Edvantage Inc./Riverdeep), and former
Executive Director, National Council of Teachers of English)

Writing in a Washington Post column titled "Trying to Clear up the Confusion" (Mathews, 2001), Jay Mathews confessed that "what confuses me the most" is "How is it that these tests [the state and district mandated tests] are forcing so many good teachers to abandon methods they know work for their kids?" In writing and reading instruction, there are two reasons for the kindergarten through twelfth grade problem that troubles Mathews—one reason being the impact of state and district tests on public understanding and support of the schools and the other reason being the direct impact of these tests on subject matter goals. State and district mandated tests have two quite different and sometimes contradictory purposes—one contributing to social capital (public understanding) and the other contributing to human capital (student learning). State and district tests tend to emphasize the social capital goals of efficient reporting methods for the public and to ignore the human capital goals of academic learning in the classroom. In fact, some subjects require instructional methods that run counter to the methods imposed by many state- and district- mandated tests. Therefore, to achieve student success on some tests, teachers must abandon the methods they know are necessary in some subjects. This chapter argues that Internet–connected, computer–mediated instruction and assessment (Automated Essay Scoring) can make a substantial contribution to overcoming both the social capital problem of public understanding and the human capital problem of subject matter knowledge and instructional method.

INCREASING SOCIAL CAPITAL THROUGH COMPUTER MEDIATED ASSESSMENT

Since *Nation at Risk* (Gardner, 1983), policy analysts have generally agreed that two distinct social goals have been driving the reform of K–12 public education in the United States. These two social goals follow: first, an increase in the nation's human capital (Becker, 1964) through higher levels of literacy for all citizens (Reich, 1992) and, second, an increase in the nation's social capital (Coleman & Hoffer, 1987) through community devices for bridging and bonding in a pluralistic, multicultural society (Putnam, 2000). Each of these two social goals has had a direct impact on the K–12 curriculum, especially in the formation of the Standards for English (7–12) and English Language Arts (K–6) adopted by most states and

3

endorsed by various federal agencies. For example, many of these standards call for increasing the social capital in school communities (the networks and bonding in the community) by improving the communication between teachers and parents and by developing new lines of communication between home and school (Putnam, 2000). The purpose of social capital development is to build support for schools and to teach knowledge about citizenship through home–school interactions.

Social Capital: First Step

A possible first step in the social capital agenda is to professionalize K–12 subject matter teachers, using as one strategy the potential impact of Automated Essay Scoring (AES) on the professionalization of teachers. The communication between teachers and parents cannot be improved until the communication among teachers has been improved——until, in fact, teacher decision making ceases to be an isolated, individual act and is embedded within professionalized communities of teachers. In the literature on computerized scoring, from Ellis Page (Page & Paulus, 1968) onward, there is not one single mention of the powerful, potential impact of electronic scoring systems on the professionalization of K–12 teachers, who often teach 5 to 7 hours each day, often have more than 150 students each day, and rarely have time for extensive interactions with colleagues. After observing teachers in two projects (Los Angeles and the San Francisco Bay Area) use the internet to score papers and develop scoring guides, I have concluded that the potential impact of automated essay evaluation technology (AEET) on the professionalization of K–12 teachers may be one of AEET's most significant contributions.

What does AEET contribute to the following three foundations of a teaching profession: (a) cognitive expertise, defining what exclusive knowledge and skills are known by professionals; (b) normative procedures, defining how the effectiveness of a professional practice is to be measured and how client results are to be judged; and (c) service ideals—defining how professionals report the purposes, results, and ethics of their practices to clients and to themselves (see Larson, 1977, for an analysis of professionalization)? The first two must precede the third.

Notice that these three elements of a profession are, in fact, the three critical elements of an assessment system: validity (what is authentic knowledge in a profession?), reliability (do professionals agree on results?), and accountability (do professionals report clearly and accurately to the public? (Linn, Baker, & Dunbar, 1991). Validity tells us what is worth measuring or, put in professional terms, tells us what knowledge and skills define the cognitive expertise of a profession. The reliability question tells us the acceptable range of score consistency from one rating to another or, put in professional terms, tells us what normative procedures describe merit and mastery in the profession. Finally, the accountability question tells us how testing results are to be reported to the public or, put in professional terms, explains a profession's service ideals, particularly its purposes, accomplishments, and ethics.

At present, the K–12 teaching community has rare, now–and–then, face–to–face meetings on these issues, but teachers do not have the resources for adequate, consistent follow–up. What can be done? The computer, internet–connected and equipped with the automated essay scorer, can add any–time, any–place connectivity and follow–up to the rare face–to–face professional meetings, enabling teachers to continue together the design of topics, the writing of rubrics, the scoring of papers, the writing of commentaries, and so forth. In the typical process of AES, teachers submit a sample of scored student papers covering all score points, and the software of AES uses this sample to fine–tune the scoring around whatever features appear to be valued in the sample. Thus, the AES results represent the normative trends of some of the features valued by the teacher, or the teacher community scoring the papers. For example, Diederich gives us the following example of how teachers handled the problem of priority among the primary features of composition——Ideas, Organization, Wording, Flavor, and so forth:

> "At first the numbers ran from 1 to 5, but since their courses concentrated on Ideas and Organization, they [the teachers] persuaded us to give double weight to those ratings by doubling the numbers representing each scale position. This weighing had no basis in research, but it seemed reasonable to give extra credit for those qualities these teachers wished to emphasize." (Diederich, 1974, p. 54).

It is obvious that the automated essay scorer makes it possible to begin to make visible some of the scoring trends within many groups of teachers and, as a result, make visible both some of the critical interpretive problems and the range of scores in the field. Score differences can enliven the professional discussion. While reliability is an objective in measurement circles, it is not an appropriate goal for professionalization. Healthy professions need some internal differences. Not so many differences that the profession loses all coherence ——Starch and Elliot (Starch & Elliot, 1912) argued that the variation in grading practices was enormous——but some difference is desirable. A scoring session without any differences is a profession gone dead. K–12 teaching has become deprofessionalized partly because of this misguided use of measurement reliability, partly because teachers rarely observe each other teach, and partly because teachers rarely observe each other's scores, rubrics, and commentaries. Computerized scoring can help correct these problems by giving us ready access to scoring information from across the country.

Combined with an electronic portfolio system, an extended automated scorer and responder could also make available a wide range of topics and lesson assignments, models of student writing, and different representations of knowledge (e.g., graphs, charts, maps, tapes, videos), all adding to our available knowledge about what kinds of tasks meet the profession's tests for validity and merit.

In summary, the internet–connected computer with automated evaluation technology can help solve the problem of teacher–connectivity (teachers have limited time to get together) and the problem of portability (students and teachers can quickly retrieve scores and feature lists for use, and for criticism and analysis, for modification and new trials). These are key contributions to the professionalization of K–12 composition teachers.

Social Capital: Second Step

A possible second step in the social capital agenda is to use the computer, internet–connected and AES–equipped, to establish a new approach to the home–school connection. In an age when both parents often work full time, when many students are not attending neighborhood schools, and when very few K–12 schools have serious parent education programs, the school–home connection, the source of much of the social capital supporting the K–12 school, has become dangerously frayed (Putnam, 2000)—to the point that multiple–choice test scores in the local newspaper are the single most effective message parents receive. Because very few K–12 schools meet with parents more than 2 or 3 times each year, there is no parent education program about the curriculum beyond the barest simplicities. In addition, the state and the district tend to adopt multiple–choice tests that keep the message to parents simple. The adopted tests represent the curriculum and, at the same time, shape both the curriculum and parental expectations. Perhaps, setting aside some AES prompts for students and parents to access on the internet from home, including the opportunity to submit essays for scores and analysis, is one way to begin to communicate to parents and students a much more informative portrait about what composition classes are trying to teach and why most state-mandated tests do not report much about the composition program.

However, computerized scoring alone is not enough. In addition, as I proposed in the past, to make clear to parents and the public what schools are doing, we need to set aside rooms in all of our K–12 schools and in many public places to exhibit student performance on a range of tasks. I add to this proposal that schools should make available for examination on the internet a wide range of student work from the local school site, accompanied by teacher commentaries on selected pieces. The computer can help us build the home–school connection around composition and literature instruction in a way that multiple–choice test results never have and never could.

INCREASING HUMAN CAPITAL THROUGH COMPUTER MEDIATED INSTRUCTION

In addition, to social capital goals, almost all of the standards adopted for English Language Arts (K–6) and English (7–12) have proposed increasing the nation's human capital goals by developing a three–part academic curriculum (National Council of Teachers of English and the International Reading Association, October, 1995, 1996): (a) learning the basic skills in reading (decoding) and writing (spelling and usage); (b) learning cognitive strategies in lower and higher order thinking skills (Resnick, 1987), in writing processes, and in literary and critical reading strategies (Scholes, 1985); and (c) learning a deeper knowledge of the subject matter domains in English courses (literature, composition, language, methods of representation; Myers, 1996). In general, the state- and district-adopted tests primarily use a multiple–choice format, emphasize the basic skills curriculum, and de–emphasize the learning of cognitive strategies and the deeper knowledge of the subject matter domains. For example, to ensure a focus on basic skills, California has mandated that state money can only be used to fund staff development emphasizing decoding and that all bidders for staff development funds must sign a "loyalty oath" promising not to mention "invented spelling" in their programs (Chapter 282, California Statutes of 1998). "Invented spelling" is, among other things, a code word for "constructed response" and is a common feature of composition instruction.

Why has the state intruded into the issues of instructional method? Because, the argument goes, some of the most effective instructional methods for teaching cognitive strategies and subject matter depth—for example, the Project method and constructed responses— have not been the most effective instructional methods for teaching the basic skills, the Basic Skills Method emphasizing explicit drills and multiple choice. States have generally opted for the Basic Skills Method, leading to improved basic skills and low scores in literary understanding and written composition. In California, reading scores go up from second to third grade and then drop as comprehension becomes more important than decoding through eleventh grade. This chapter argues that computer-mediated instruction, internet-connected and AES-equipped, can solve the traditional problems of the Project method and various versions of the Method of Constructed Response by providing for the integration of basic skills instruction into the Project method.

Evidence of a Score Gap

Several researchers suggested that multiple–choice tests of overall achievement, especially when they are combined with high stakes incentives for teachers and students, inevitably damage some parts of the curriculum (Shepard, 2000; Whitford & Jones, 2000; Resnick & Resnick, 1992).

However, what is the evidence that basic skills curriculum policies have led to a decline in the quality and frequency of composition and literature instruction? First, in some states, basic skills instruction and testing have often turned written responses into formulaic writing, a form of writing-by-the-numbers. Teaching formulas, not substance, is one way to get scores up. For example, during the early years of the Kentucky Instructional Results Information System (KIRIS), reading scores on KIRIS increased rapidly, and scores on the National Assessment of Educational Progress (NAEP) and American College Testing (ACT) rose much more slowly (Koretz, McCaffrey & Hamilton, 2001) In fact, in the first 6 years of Kentucky's KRIS test, Kentucky's NAEP scores on fourth-grade reading ranged from just below 60% to slightly more than 60% of the students at basic or above, but during the same period, the percentage of Kentucky students at apprentice or above on the KRIS test (basic skills) ranged from nearly 70% to over 90% (Linn & Baker, 2000). Both KIRIS and NAEP have constructed responses, but, clearly, these two types of tests were not measuring the same thing. For example, in the Kentucky test, teachers "may have engaged in...teaching students strategies to capitalize on scoring rubrics" (Koretz, McCaffery, and Hamilton, 2001, 116). George Hillcocks, in fact, has concluded that state tests of composition have often locked-in formulaic writing, producing a harmful effect on the quality of composition instruction (Hillocks, 2002) but often increasing the state scores valuing formula.

These differences in what tests measure has also produced the pervasive "fourth grade reading gap," sometimes known as the "secondary school drop." In international comparisons of performance on reading assessments, U.S. fourth graders perform close to the top on fourth grade tests, and U.S. eleventh graders perform close to the bottom on eleventh grade tests (Rand Reading Study Group, 2001). The former tends to emphasize the curriculum of basic skills (spelling, punctuation, decoding, usage, basic who–what–where comprehension), and the latter tends to emphasize the curriculum of metacognition, interpretation and some domain knowledge. In group comparisons within the U.S., reading scores often drop "after fourth grade, when students are required to master increasingly complex subject–based material" (Manzo, 2001). Says Catherine Snow, chair of the Rand Reading Study Group, "... real problems emerge in middle school and later grades, even for children who it turns out are doing fine at the end of grade 3" (Manzo, 2001). To address these contradictions, some have suggested that these different types of tests should be referred to by different names—the early grade tests being labeled "reading tests" and the later tests being labeled "language" or "vocabulary" or "curriculum–based" tests (Hirsch, 2000). Others have suggested that the national focus on early reading has been disguising a "core problem" of ignoring and even misunderstanding comprehension, "skillful reading," and interpretive skills (RRSG, 2001). In a study funded by the U.S. Office of Education, the Rand Reading Study Group identified at least five distinctive components of "comprehension" and interpretive reading programs: (a) Cognitive and metacognitive strategies and fluency, (b) Linguistic and discourse knowledge, (c) Integration of graphs and pictures into text, (d) Vocabulary and world knowledge, and (e) Clarity of goal–construction ("purposeful reading") (Rand Reading Study Group, 2001: 10–17). These components of comprehension are most frequently tested by constructed responses (NAEP, Scholastic Aptitude Test II, College Board English Achievement Tests), requiring great skill in written composition and in literary interpretation.

In fact, these Rand Reasoning Study Group components of "Comprehension" in reading are a mirror image of the essential components of process and content in Composition programs: (a) Writing strategies, both in the writing of the text (Applebee, 1986; Emig, 1971; Perl, 1980) and in the writer's external scaffolds for writing (reference books, networks, response groups, computers); (Collins, Brown, & Newman, 1989; Elbow, 1973); (b) Knowledge of Point of View toward Subject (I–You–It), and Audience/Community (Bruffee, 1984; Moffett, 1968; Ede &

Lunsford, 1984); (c) Knowledge of Modes (Narrative, Description, Persuasion, Expository) and Text Structure (chronology, contrast–comparison, sequence, cause–effect, thesis–evidence–conclusion) (Kinneavy, 1971); (d) Knowledge of Spectator and Participant Roles for shifting Stance from Transactional to Poetic, from Fiction to Non–Fiction and visa versa (Britton & Pradl, 1982; Ong, 1982); (e) Processes for the integration of media into text and for the translation of non–print sign system (pictures, graphs, oral tapes) into text (Jackendoff, 1992); and (f) Knowledge of sentence construction and writing conventions (Christensen & Christensen, 1978; Strong, 1973).

A quick review of these features of composition instruction should make clear that the nationwide emphasis on basic skills, including formulaic writing, has ignored much of the knowledge needed for competency in written composition. When NAEP assesses composition achievement, the results are similar to the results in advanced comprehension beyond basic skills: Only 23% of U.S. fourth graders and 22 % of U.S. twelfth graders were at or above the proficient level in written composition in 1998 (NAEP 1998). In summary, in both reading and writing on emphasis on basic skills drives down scores on interpretation and constructed response.

The Problem of the Project method

How do we teach both basic skills and interpretation? In addition to having a specific set of processes (strategies and skills) and content (sentence, discourse, and domain knowledge), composition instruction has a specific set of successful instructional methods encompassing specific principles of lesson design. In fact, George Hillocks, according to Shulman, argued that the content of composition instruction, one's conception of the subject itself, "carries with it an inherent conception of its pedagogy" (Shulman, 1999). If one is looking for a way to improve student learning, says Stigler (Stigler & Hiebert, 1999), one should focus on lesson design: It "could provide the key ingredient for improving students' learning, district by district, across the United States ... " (pp. 156–157).

What kinds of lesson designs are most effective in the teaching of writing? Greg Myers (Myers, 1986) identified his own best practice as a combination of two methods: case assignments based on actual writing situations and small student response groups collaborating on each other's writing. George Hillocks, after an extensive review of the research literature on instructional method in composition teaching, identified the Environmental Mode as the best method among four: Presentational (lectures, teacher presentations and drills), Natural (teacher as facilitator, free writing, peer group response), Environmental, (specific projects), and Individualized (tutorials). This Environmental method, which includes case assignments and group response, is another name for both the Workshop Method, a common method among teacher consultants of the National Writing Project, and for the Project method, derived from Dewey (Hillocks, 1986). Myers also traces the case method and group response to Dewey, specifically to the "Dewey inspired English education textbook, *English Composition as a Social Problem* (p. 154)," written by Sterling Andrus Leonard in 1917.

Hillocks uses a meta–analysis of experimental studies of best practices to establish the effectiveness of the Environmental Mode: "On pre–to–post measures, the Environmental Mode is over four times more effective than the traditional Presentational Mode and three times more effective than the Natural Process Mode" (Hillocks, 1986, p. 247). In addition, Hillocks argued that the "description of the better lessons" in Applebee's study of the best writing assignments in 300 classrooms (Applebee, 1981) "indicates clearly that those lessons [Applebee's best practices] have much in common with the Environmental Mode" (Hillocks, 1986, p. 225). One reason for this effectiveness, says Hillocks, is that the Environmental Mode "brings teacher, student, and materials more nearly into balance" (Hillocks, 1986, p. 247).

The arguments against the Project method (and progressive education) are that it ignores the importance of drill and memorization, and the importance of explicit (not tacit) learning for learning's sake (not for some instrumental purpose) (Bagley, 1921). It is difficult to read the debates about the Project method (See TCRecord.org for Bagley's articles on this debate) without coming to two conclusions: First, the Project Method may be uniquely effective in composition instruction (and possibly some kinds of literary instruction, as well) because a composition assignment must always have some kind of instrumental purpose (sending a message to an audience or understanding the structure of a subject), must go beyond whatever has been memorized in some rote fashion, and must include both a micro framework (word, sentence, example) and a macro framework (discourse, idea) framework for directing attention.

Nevertheless, there are four critical problems that have limited the success of the Project method in composition instruction in many classrooms: (a) The need for a variety of audiences (how does one reach out to different audiences to create portability for student work within a publication network connected to the classroom?); (b) The need to make Composition Knowledge—sentence structure, discourse patterns, and conventions—visible, explicit and concrete (how does one insert drill, memorization, and explicit knowledge into an activity sequence without losing the overall shape of the activity?); (c) The need for an assessment system which is storable, portable, and, most importantly, socialized and professionalized (How does one reduce the management and scoring problems in the Project method?); and (d) the need for a professionalized teaching staff to make the Project method work (how does one begin to professionalize the teaching staff?). Adding computers, internet–connected and AES–equipped, helps solve these four critical problems in the project method in composition instruction, K–12.[1]

---

[1] Robert Romano and Tom Gage first proposed that computer software could be used to solve the problems of the print–based Project method in Moffett's Interaction series. Professor Gage, Humbolt State University, introduced Robert Romano to James Moffett, and Romano, working with Moffett, built a software company (Edvantage, Inc.) to try these ideas out in the classroom. Edvantage is now part of Riverdeep, Inc.

Need for Audiences From Outside the Classroom

The internet and computer–mediated connections have the unique capability of solving the problem of finding a way to publish student work easily and cheaply for a diverse audience responsive to student work. Networks for finding and developing diverse, responsive audiences for student work are already widely available and growing. In fact, AES is itself an internet connection to an audience which will provide a score and possibly some other evaluative responses. In current classrooms, the claim is often made that "the isolated blind are leading the isolated blind" in the peer response groups of the Project method. If each student has an internet–connected computer, this claim is no longer valid.

Need For Explicit Instruction

The second criticism of the Project method is that the basic structure of Composition Knowledge is not made explicit in the Project method, leaving students to discover things for themselves during the activity cycle of the Project. In the typical text–bound classroom, when direct, explicit instruction is placed within a Project sequence, the Project itself often gets lost in the Presentational materials. When choices of topics are introduced at several points in the Project sequence, the organization of Projects becomes even more complicated and opaque for the average secondary teacher with 150 or more students in five or six classes daily.   All of these problems of management and explicit instruction undermined Houghton–Mifflin's Moffett Interactive Series (Moffett, 1973), which was an inventive attempt, using predominately text–materials (large and small cards, booklets, posters, games) and some audio cassette tapes, to organize composition instruction around the Project method and the ideas of James Moffett.

It is important to recognize that the Project method evolved during the time of the Village Economy when the work of adults was visible to every child (Myers, 1996). In the Village Economy of face–to–face oral literacy, the child could watch each explicit step in the blacksmith's work or the farmer's workday. In today's World Economy of Translation Literacy, work has become more mediated and informational and, thus, more opaque to the child.   As a result, the child cannot see the explicit steps of informational work without substantial help from the home and school.   Diane Ravitch (Ravitch, 2000) argued that the Project method ("progressive education") has too often ignored the importance of the explicit transmission of knowledge and, as a result, has seriously harmed the education of poor and minority students who did not receive this knowledge at home. Similarly, Lisa Delpit reports that Direct Instruction (Distar), a Presentational Method of instruction, was a successful reading program "because it actually taught new information to children who had not already acquired it at home" (Delpit, 1995, p. 30).

It is clear that the Presentational Method, exemplified by Distar, can teach students to do reasonably well on multiple–choice tests of Language and Composition Knowledge, but it does not effectively teach students to write. On the other hand, when explicit presentations are inserted inside activity, the presentational method often swamps the environmental or project method. Yet without presentational approaches, the project method can fail to be effective with many students, especially poor and minority students. What is the solution to this dilemma?

In classrooms using well–designed software, the internet–connected computer appears to solve this dilemma by embedding explicit knowledge within a stable, still–dominant framework of instrumental activity. How is this done? By exploiting four capacities that, it seems to me, are unique to the computer—creation of Instant links, Virtual Toys, Second Chances, and Materials Portability. In software Lesson Design, the key problems in writing instruction, other than formatting, screen–appearance, and technical issues in the code, seem to focus on the use of these four computer capabilities: (a) Where to put the Instant links, (b) How to design the Virtual Toys, (c) When to provide Second Chances (for more practice or for closure on a particular section), and (e) How to drop, store, retrieve, list, and add texts, various other instructional materials, and student work (materials portability). Consider the problem of Instant links. If a student needed to learn something about composition knowledge at some point in the activity sequence leading to a finished composition, one could insert in the software a banner or drop-down menu providing the options of an instant link to an exercise on an explicit piece of composition knowledge—say, punctuation, spelling, capitalization, discourse transitions, thesis sentences, and so forth. In addition, the software could add Second Chances (and third, fourth, or fifth) with new exercises for students who did not do well the first time and need another try.

The instant links need not be limited to composition knowledge. Some could link to the subject knowledge underlying the composition topic, including charts of information, concept maps, pages of highlighted text, interviews with experts on the subject, and references to other print and internet sources. In addition, instant links can, if the teacher desires, enable students to jump ahead in the activity sequence or to go back if they need a second chance to do better. The instant links are arranged then as clusters of activities, exercises, or references at various points in an overall sequence. Not all parts of the activity cycle or series are a required sequence, although the software can allow teachers to set the program so that all or part of the activity cycle could become a required sequence for some students. The central point here is that the instant links in computer mediated lesson design does not swamp the activity sequence of the project method, which is often what happens when teachers must stop an activity sequence for the transmission of knowledge to a group of students in a paper-bound class.

One of the problems in the use of Instant links on the computer is that students will forget where they left off in the activity sequence when they decided to link to sources of explicit knowledge. Thus, there need to be concrete reminders of the overall structure of the project, which is itself abstract and for many students opaque. One typical reminder of project structure is the ever–present Virtual Toy—for example, showing the student's location as a rabbit, a figure, a blinking light, or whatever on a map of the overall activity sequence. After completing the work at any Instant link, the student can refer to a visual map–stepladders, hiking trails, highways–showing the student where he or she is, once again entering the activity sequence.

These rabbits, figures, stepladders, and hiking trails illustrate one of the most powerful capabilities of computers in composition instruction: the creation of Virtual Toys for bridging from the abstract to the concrete, for turning ideas into toys. The fundamental idea comes from Celeste Myers, who 40 years ago built a preschool around the idea (Myers, 1967) or Jerome Bruner who wrote a book on the subject (Bruner, et al., 1976) or Vygotsky who was one of the first to notice (L. S. Vygotsky, 1962). However, the importance of the idea of Virtual Toys as a computer capability comes from Alan Kay, vice–president of research and development at the Walt Disney Company and one of the original architects of the personal computer. He described his own discovery of Virtual Toys as a computerized bridge from the abstract to the concrete when he looked at Seymour Papert's Logo: "He [Papert] realized that computers turn abstraction in math into concrete toys for students. He allowed them to make things that were mathematical…." (Kay, 2000). The same principle is at work in numerous software programs that use Virtual Toys to teach such things as the explicit structure of discourse or physics (Taylor, Poth, & Portman, 1995).

The computer also offers an unusual range of opportunities for them which are a critical addition to the Project method because they enable students to pace their practice and second efforts to fit their own needs. The average secondary teacher, teaching grades 7 to 12, has a student load each day of 150 or more students. In a book–bound classroom, without computers, the management and cursory monitoring (What does a quick look tell me?) of the special needs of students for information and practice in Composition Knowledge is a nearly impossible task. The computer helps the teacher monitor and manage Second Chances. And it is Second Chances which, according to Marshall Smith (Smith, 2000), may be one of the key (but hidden) strengths of the U.S. K–12 school system. Computers, Internet–connected and AES–equipped, help make more Second Chances even more possible in the K–12 classroom. AES allows students at any time (and several times) to submit their work for scoring and response, and, in addition, AES prompts, which can be integrated into any Project, provide clear reporting for easy management and monitoring by teachers.

Following is a final word about Materials Portability. When the Moffett Interaction Series came on the market, there were constant complaints from Houghton Mifflin sales representatives about the weight and size of the package. Sales representatives did not want to lug the series up the steps to my classroom at Oakland High School in 1973, for example, and for teachers who were doing classroom preparation at home, all of the materials could not be hauled back and forth daily. In addition, teachers who had to move from one room to another often found the package impractical. In addition, because students were often checking out one piece or another to take home, teachers had to spend time on preventing materials from getting lost. Computer software made the materials of the Interaction Series portable for the first time.

Need for an Assessment System

The third limitation of the Project method is the absence of an overall testing system that works within curriculum–based activities of the Project method. Although, the usual multiple–choice tests work fine for linked exercises on explicit knowledge, these tests do not work for assessments of the overall achievement of students in written composition and literary interpretation. Resnick and Resnick (1992) argued that a curriculum of "higher order thinking skills"—for example, the curriculum of a composition program–requires new kinds of tests. They claim that old tests have decomposed skills to small bits of behavior within a tightly sequenced curriculum of basic skills, but the new assessments of "higher order thinking skills" will need performance, exhibition, and whole enactments of authentic problem solving, often in projects like composition where reading, speaking, and listening are integrated into the writing sequence.

Why have so many states turned to multiple–choice tests to measure such things as writing? First, using predictive theories of validity, psychometricians hired by the states have argued that multiple-choice tests are " highly valid" measures of writing because scores on multiple choice tests and scores on writing samples have had fairly high correlations (.70) (Godshalk, Swineford, & Coffman, 1966). However, the use of correlations to argue the validity of multiple–choice measures of composition achievement has, today, almost no serious support.

Two other reasons are certainly cost and time. Every on–demand "authentic assessment" or constructed response in composition has to contend with how much time the test takes, how much money and time is spent on the scoring process, and what are the costs of storage and reporting. In one sense, the selection of an on–demand "authentic" task requires one to balance off the high cost and high validity of authentic assessments against the low cost and low validity of multiple–choice tasks, as the following scale of increasing verisimilitude and authenticity makes clear (adapted from Shavelson, Gao, & Baxter, 1993): (a) A True/False Test, (b) A Multiple Choice Test, (c) A 15-minute limit on a constructed response giving an opinion, and (d) One hour to write an editorial on a topic.

This scale makes clear that problems, especially length of time, are inevitable in on–demand tasks. In the New Standards Project, we found that our one–week tasks in written tasks were alright for some classes and too long for others. NAEP, one of our best On–Demand tasks, has not solved the time problem. In 1986, NAEP measured writing in Grades 4, 8, and 12 with a 15-minute writing sample; but, because of professional pressure, in 1988, NAEP increased the time on some tasks to 20 minutes for Grade 4 and 30 minutes for Grades 8 and 12. By 1992, NAEP was allowing 25 minute for fourth grade and either 25 or 50 minute for grades 8 and 12. My understanding is that more and more districts, now adding more state tests with incentives attached, have dropped NAEP testing because the NAEP tests take too much time. To get more samples and to reduce costs, NAEP has been once again reducing the time given to students to take the test.

Generalizability is also a problem for teachers estimating student performance on a particular kind of task. NAEP is an on–demand test for estimating group (national) performance in three different modes of written composition (narrative, information, persuasion). But to get an estimate of how an individual student is developing as a writer, given the variability of student performance in many cases, teachers need more than one sample per mode and may need to sample a variety of modes (research paper, directions, biography, autobiography, critical analysis, letter). Shavelson, et al. reports that generalizability across tasks is a big problem in assessment: "Regardless of the subject matter (science or mathematics) or the level of analysis (individual or school), large numbers of tasks are needed to get a generalizable measure of achievement. One practical implication of these findings is that assuming 15 minutes per CAP task, for example, a total of 2.5 hours of testing time would be needed to obtain a generalizable measure (.80) of student achievement" (p. 229).

AES can help K–12 teachers overcome these difficult problems of time, cost, and generalizability in assessment, especially if AES technology is designed to inform K–12 teachers about sampling in different modes, generalizability, score variability, and so forth. There are good data on how well AES technology matches the scores of human raters (see later chapters), and there are considerable data on how practical AES systems are especially their cost–effectiveness. Educational Testing Service (ETS) uses the ETS developed *e-rater*® automated scoring system and one human reader to evaluate the essay portion of the Graduate Management Admissions Test, and College Board uses WritePlacer, an application of Intellimetric™ developed by Vantage Technologies, in College Board's placement program, accuplacer on–line. AES could certainly help to reduce the backbreaking load that secondary teachers of composition must carry if they assign and respond to frequent writing by their students. This load is a "permanent" problem in secondary schools, not just a concern that might "become permanent and structural" if computer scoring is allowed in the classroom (Herrington & Moran, 2001). Yes, there are strategies for coping: some writing can be left for peer response groups, and some left unread (checked off). However, computer–scored (and analyzed) essays, using one of the automated essay scorers, can produce a score and some analysis in a few seconds, and for a secondary student looking for a first or second opinion on an essay, computer–scored essays is a very helpful and a relatively cheap addition. By making it possible to provide a greater variety of scored samples, this addition to the classroom not only helps reduce the teacher's paper load but also provides a way of attacking the teacher's assessment problems outlined previously.

In addition, programs like e–rater are useful in teacher conferences and student response groups. At a recent conference examining the problems of assessment, one teacher commented that e–rater potentially provided a third voice at teacher–student conference about a piece of writing. The teacher said the following (paraphrase):

> "The student and I can together consult the *e–rater*® scoring and analysis of the essay, giving us a third party with whom we can agree or disagree. The *e–rater*® score and analysis can make clear that there is something in the world called Composition Knowledge, that evaluating essays is not just a personal whim in my head" (Myers & Spain, 2001, p. 34).

Finally, computers provide easy storage and easy retrieval for the five–part assessment sets that can accompany each topic: (a) The topic and any special testing conditions (time–materials–task sequence); (b) Six point rubrics for the specific topic, (c) Six anchor/model papers for each score point; (d) Six commentaries describing the relation between the rubric and the anchor papers at each score point; and (e) Six brief teacher notes, which highlights what the student in a given anchor paper needs to focus on in instruction. In addition, electronic portfolios could with some design modification, provide easy storage and retrieval for each student's work during the project sequence, including exercise sheets showing student work on some problem of explicit knowledge. Every review I have read of electronic scoring programs has ignored the contribution that these AES technologies can make to a practical (storable, retrievable, portable) portfolio serving both the K–12 classroom and other institutional levels. My own view is that at the moment we do not have even the bare bones of a good electronic Portfolio that can connect to AES technology and some of the good instructional software available.

The Need for Professionalization

The fourth limitation of the Project method is that it requires professional teachers so does AES. To achieve their potential as contributors to K–12 writing programs, computers, internet–connected and AES–equipped, must be embedded in an instructional system (project method), an assessment system (electronic portfolios tied to classroom assignments and external tests), and a social network within an institutionalized professional community. The computer revolution, described in part earlier, has not happened in K–12 schools, and it will not happen without a long, overdue recognition of the importance of teacher professionalization and the "Social Life of Information" (Brown & Duguid, 2000) in teacher communities. Similarly, Lawrence Cremin (Cremin, 1965) argued that the Project method and "progressive education ... demanded infinitely skilled teachers, and it failed because such teachers could not be recruited in sufficient numbers, p. 56" and Alan Kay has argued that Seymour Papert's program Logo "failed because elementary teachers were unable to understand what this was all about" (Kay, 2000, p. 23). In a recent review of the impact on instruction of state writing assessments, George Hillocks reported that although the scoring of actual samples of student writing increases the number of times that writing tasks are assigned, the quality of composition instruction suffers from the failure to invest in K–12 teacher knowledge about composition instruction. Says Hillocks, "Certainly, testing assures that what is tested is taught, but tests cannot assure that things are taught well" (Hillocks, 2002). AEET could help provide the professional connectivity that teachers need to deepen their knowledge, subject matter and pedagogy in the Project method. The AEET now available has made an important contribution to assessment and K–12 curriculum reform, but the various product designs suggest that AEET has not, fully appreciated its pedagogical responsibilities in the education of teachers. Nevertheless, as discussed earlier in this chapter Jay Mathews (Mathews, 2001) would find that the experience of writing an essay for an AES teaches him far more about writing a composition than taking one of the state-mandated multiple–choice tests.

REFERENCES

Applebee, A. N. (1981). *Writing in the secondary school*. Urbana, IL: National Council of Teachers of English.

Applebee, A. N. (1986). Problems in process approaches: Toward a reconceptualization of process approaches. In D. Bartholomae (Ed.), *The teaching of writing* (Vol. 85th Yearbook, p. 95-113).

Bagley, W. (1921). Dangers and difficulties of the project method and how to overcome them: Projects and purposes in teaching and learning. *Teachers College Record, 22*(4), 288-297.

Becker, G. S. (1964). *Human capital*. Chicago, IL: University of Chicago Press.

Britton, J. N., & Pradl, G. M. (1982). *Prospect and retrospect: Selected essays of James Britton*. Montclair, NJ: Boynton/Cook Publishers.

Brown, J. S., & Duguid, P. (2000). *The social life of information*. Boston, MA: Harvard Business School Press.

Bruffee, K. (1984). Collaborative learning and the conversation of mankind. *College English, 46*, 635-652.

Bruner, J., Jolly, A., & Sylva, K. (Ed.). (1976). *Play, its role in development and evolution*. New York: Basic Books.

Christensen, F., & Christensen, B. (1978). *Notes toward a new rhetoric: Nine essays for teachers* (2nd ed.). New York: Harper and Row.

Collins, A., Brown, J. S., & Newman, S. E. (1989). Cognitive apprenticeship: Teaching the craft of reading, writing, and mathematics. In L. B. Resnick (Ed.), *Knowing, learning, and instruction: Essays in honor of Robert Glaser*. Hillsdale, NJ: Lawrence Erlbaum Associates, Inc.

Cremin, L. (1965). *The transformation of the school: Progressivism, in American education, 1876-1957*. New York: McGraw-Hill.

Delpit, L. (1995). *Other people's children*. New York: McGraw-Hill.

Diederich, P. (1974). *Measuring growth in English*. Urbana, IL: National Council on Teachers of English.

Emig, J. (1971). *The composing process of twelfth graders*. Urbana, IL: National Council on Teachers of English.

Gardner, D. (1983). *Nation at risk: The imperative for educational reform*. Washington, DC: U.S. Department of Education.

Godshalk, F., Swineford, F., & Coffman, W. (1966). *The measurement of writing ability*. New York: College Board.

Herrington, A., & Moran, C. (2001). What happens when machines read our students writing? *College English, 63*, 480-499.

Hillocks, G. (1986). *Research on written composition: New directions for teaching*. Urbana, IL: National Council of Teachers of English.

Hillocks, G. (2002). *The testing trap: how state writing assessments control learning*. New York City, NY: Teachers College Press.

Hirsch, E. D. (2000). The tests we need. *2001 Editorial Projects in Education (Education Week), 19*, 1-9.

Jackendoff, R. (1992). *Language of the mind*. Cambridge, MA: MIT Press.

Kay, A. (2000). *Keynote*. Paper presented at New Directions in Student Testing and Technology, APEC 2000 International Conference. University of Clalifornia, Los Angeles.

Kinneavy. (1971). *Theory of discourse*. Englewood Cliffs, NJ: Prenctice Hall.

Koretz, D., McCaffrey, D. F., & Hamilton, L. S. (2001). *Toward a framework for validating gains under high stakes conditions*. Paper presented at the Annual Conference of the National Council on Measurement in Education, Seattle.

Larson, M. S. (1977). *The rise of professionalism*. Berkeley, CA: The University of California Press.

Linn, R. L., Baker, E. L., & Dunbar, S. B. (1991). Complex performance-based assessment expectations and validation criteria. *Educational Researcher, 20*(8), 15-21.

Linn, R. L., Baker, E. (2000). *Assessment challenges—Technology solutions*. Paper presented at the APEC Conference. University of California, Los Angeles.

Mazo, K. K. (2001). Panel urges study of reading comprehension. *2001 Editorial Projects in Education (Education Week)*, 1-3.

Mathews, J. (2001). Trying to clear up the confusion. *The Washington Post*, A6.

Moffett, J. (1968). *Teaching the universe of discourse*. Boston: Houghton Mifflin.

Moffett, J. (Ed.) (1973). *Interaction: A student-centered language arts and reading program*. Boston: Houghton Mifflin.

Myers, C. (1967). *Learning is child's play: The vision of circle preschool*. Oakland, CA: Circle Pre-School, Alpha Plus Corporation.

Myers, G. (1986). Reality, consensus, and reform in the rhetoric of composition teaching. *College English, 48*, 154-171.

Myers, M. (1996). *Changing our minds: Negotiating English and literacy*. Urbana, IL: National Council of Teachers of English.

Myers, M., & Spain, A. (2001). *Report of the conference chairs on the Asilomar Conference on testing and accountability.* Paper presented at the Asilomar Testing and Accountability Conference, Asilomar, CA.

NAEP (1998). *The 1998 NAEP writing report card.* Washington, DC: National Assessment of Eduational Progress. U.S. Department of Education and the National Assessment Governing Board.

National Council of Teachers of English and the International Reading Association. (1995). *Standards for English language arts (draft).* Urbana, IL: National Council of Teachers of English.

National Council of Teachers of English and the International Reading Association. (1996). *Standards for English language arts.* Urbana, IL: National Council of Teachers of English

Ong, W. (1982). *Orality and literacy.* New York: Methuen.

Page, E., & Paulus, D. (1968). *The anlaysis of essays by computer.* Sorrs, CT: University of Connecticut, ERIC, and the U.S. Office of Education.

Perl, S. (1980). *A look at basic writers in the process of composing, basic writing: A collection of essays for teachers, researchers, and administrators.* Urbana, IL: National Council of Teachers of English.

Putnam, R. D. (2000). *Bowling alone.* New York: Simon and Schuster.

Ravitch, D. (2000). *Left back.* New York: Simon and Schuster.

Reich, R. (1992). *The work of nations: Preparing ourselves for 21ˢᵗ century capitalism.* New York: Vintage.

Resnick, L. B. (1987). *Education and learning to think.* Washington, DC: National Academy Press.

Resnick, L. B, & Resnick, D. P. (1992). Assessing the thinking curriculum: New tolls for educational reform. *Changing assessments: Alternative views of aptitude, achievement, and instruction* (pp. 9-35). Boston, MA: Kluwer Academic Publishers.

RRSG. (2001). *Reading for understanding: Towards an R&D program in reading comprehension.* RAND Reading Study Group, OERI, U.S. Department of Education.

Scholes, R. (1985). *Textual power: Literacy theory and the teaching of English.* New Haven, CT: Yale University Press.

Shavelson, R. J., Gao, X., & Baxter, G. P. (1993). Sampling variability of performance assessments. *Journal of Educational Measurement, 30,* 215-232.

Shepard, L. A. (2000). The role of assessment in a learning culture. *Educational Researcher, 29*(7), 4-14.

Shulman, L. (1999). Foreword. In G. Hillocks (Ed.), *Ways of thinking, ways of teaching* (pp. vii-x). New York: Teachers College Press.

Smith, M. (2000). *Using data for multiple purposes.* Paper presented at the New Directions in Student Testing and Technology, APEC 2000 International Assessment Conference, University of California, Los Angeles.

Starch, D., & Elliott, E. C. (1912). Reliability of grading high school work in English. *School Review, 21,* 442-457.

Stigler, J., & Hiebert, J. (1999). *The teaching gap*. New York: Free Press.

Strong, W. (1973). *Sentence combining: A composing book*. New York: Random House.

Taylor, B. A. P., Poth, J., & Portman D. J. (1995). *Teaching physics with toys: Activities for grades K-9*. New York: Terrific Science Press.

Vygotsky, L. S. (1962). *Thought and language*. Cambridge, MA: MIT Press.

Whitford, B. L., & Jones, K. (Eds.) (2000). *Accountability, assessment, and teacher commitment: Lessons from Kentucky's reform efforts*. Albany: State University of New York Press.

II.   Psychometric Issues in Performance
Assessment

2

Issues in the Reliability and Validity of Automated Scoring of Constructed Responses

Gregory K.W.K. Chung and Eva L. Baker
University of California, Los Angeles
National Center for Research on Evaluation, Standards,
  and Student Testing

For assessment results to be useful and trustworthy, they must meet particular expectations of quality. Quality criteria for traditional assessments of academic achievement include validity, fairness, and reliability. This chapter will explore the concepts of validity (with fairness as a subtopic) and reliability as they apply to computer-assisted scoring of student essays or other student-constructed responses.

When new developments occur in technology, it is common to say that they cannot be compared sensibly to the "old way" of doing things. For example, comparing word processing to typewriters was ultimately an unproductive enterprise because word processing provided many more functions than a simple typewriter, rendering any direct contrast of results partial and unconvincing. It is also true that technologists may themselves resist applying quality criteria to their new enterprises. For some, creating a proof of concept equals a proof of value. For example, in the 1980s, it was sufficient to demonstrate that an artificial intelligence (AI) system "ran" as opposed to its achieving high degrees of accuracy in its analysis. AI researchers were unwilling to consider evaluating the impact of their work in part because the process of making the system seemed as important as its potential outcomes. In fact, much of new technology has not been systematically evaluated by scientific methods, a process largely bypassed because of the speed of change and the expanding consumer market (Baker & Herman, in press).

As the computer extends its incursion in the testing field, should we expect to make comparative quality judgments? When achievement tests evolve to a wholly different style, eschewing broad sampling of content for deep and intensive simulation, it is likely that standards for judging their quality will necessarily evolve and that there will be a lag between the innovation and the development of credible evaluation methodology. However, at the present time, most computer-supported testing does not reflect a radical change in how learning is to be measured. Rather, it serves to make our present procedures more efficient, whether we are considering item generation, administration, or as in the case of this chapter, computer-assisted essay scoring. Therefore, it is reasonable to argue that essay scoring by computer can be readily judged by applying extant standards of quality.

Let us start with standardization. Underlying the application of any quality criteria is the expectation that tests have been both administered and scored in known ways: the examination is timed or untimed; additional resources are prohibited or prescribed; help is given or withheld. The conditions apply equally to all students, and specified exceptions occur only for approved reasons. In the determination of scoring, we similarly need to be reassured about the standardization of the process. An answer key is provided for multiple-choice responses. Constructed responses can receive a fixed range of scores. Raters use similar criteria for judging essays. Unless we know the conditions of test administration and the rudiments of scoring procedures, we are sure to be stymied in our interpretation of test results.

VALIDITY

Validity, on the other hand, depends on standardized procedures, but has itself far greater requirements. To judge the degree of validity, we must understand the intended use of test results. In contrast to the common interpretation, validity is not a known attribute of a test. Rather, it is a property of the inference drawn from test results, and depends on what uses will be made of the findings: For example, she is a good enough writer to graduate from high school; he has mastered algebra sufficiently well to skip a basic course; or this school has children with poor reading results and needs to revise its instruction. This definition of validity, expanded in detail by Messick (1989), is at the heart of the recent revision of the Standards for Educational and Psychological Testing (American Educational Research Association [AERA], American Psychological Association [APA], and National Council of Measurement in Education [NCME], 1999). These standards link valid inferences to the purpose for which a test is being employed. As a result, it would be inappropriate to claim that a given test "is valid" without knowing the intended uses of test results. Two implications flow from this definition. One is that any discussion of the validity of test results, including those generated through the use of automated essay scoring, is necessarily conditioned by the use of results. We must know in advance what uses will be made of the test results. To draw a conclusion that there is sufficient evidence to support or to design studies that bear on validity interpretations, there must be a clear and shared understanding of test purposes. A second implication is that if new purposes are attached to existing tests, additional validity evidence will need to be sought. Common purposes for tests in an academic setting include the following: to select students for admissions, to place students in special programs, to provide feedback to students to increase their achievement, to provide feedback to teachers to improve their instruction, to evaluate organizations or special programs, to assign grades or other rewards and sanctions, and to monitor individual or institutional performance over time. Consider this simple example: We would want to determine whether a test that was intended to help improve instruction actually provided a level of information that would cue teachers to performance attributes needing attention. A system developed to select the best writers would be less likely to be useful for the instructional improvement purpose.

Several additional formulations of validity criteria have been developed (Baker, O'Neil, & Linn, 1993; Linn, Baker, & Dunbar, 1991). These include some attention to characteristics intended to support fairness, such as whether the prompts (or other stimuli) are written to avoid unnecessary linguistic hurdles, such as peculiar word choice, syntax, or discourse structure. A more difficult area, and one particularly important for tests used for individual or institutional accountability, is to demonstrate that the test is sensitive to instruction. Using a set of writing prompts that were impervious to instruction would violate this criterion.

RELIABILITY

Reliability is a necessary attribute of valid interpretation. Reliable in lay terms means consistent. It implies that for an individual or for a group (depending on the test), repeated administrations of the same or comparable tests would yield a similar score. In simple terms, this means that if Fred could take a 100-item multiple-choice test 6 times, we could estimate how much each score would vary from Fred's "true" or theoretically accurate score. In writing assessments, and in the testing of other constructed responses, in addition to the scores of examinee Fred, scores could vary among the raters or judges of Fred's response. If we used two judges, then we would want to estimate the reliability of the raters (the consistency of scoring between raters) and the agreement among sets of raters. Therefore, two sets of scores would be analyzed—those of the examinees and those of the raters. Reliability studies will require us to estimate the degree to which student and rater variations occur.

Although when considering multiple-choice test items, the consistency of performance among items is thought to be a reliability issue, in a writing assessment, consistency of performance among different writing prompts can be conceived as a validity issue as well. Validity enters into the discussion because it is often the case that only one or two "items" are given to a student because of time constraints. Thus, it is important to assure that these items, or prompts, are comparable. When prompts vary in their degree of difficulty (i.e., in the degree to which they are good representatives of the domain of interest), it is possible to be misled by results. For instance, if a state administers an easy writing prompt in 2002, followed by a prompt that has more stringent requirements in 2003, the public might incorrectly infer that writing competence had dropped in the state or that the specific preparation of a set of candidates was inferior to that of candidates in the prior year. Looking at empirical differences (i.e., average scores) is clearly insufficient to make this judgment. Qualitative analyses would need to be conducted to determine the degree to which the questions: (a) evoked comparable responses, (b) depended upon common cognitive demands [e.g., type of argument], (c) elicited comparable discourse structures, and (d) had about the same requirements for student prior knowledge. Generalizability studies have been able to estimate the error due to student, rater, and task variables and their interactions (Shavelson & Webb, 1991). In general, the student-by-task interaction has consistently been the largest source of variance, suggesting that many tasks are required for adequate domain coverage (Brennan & Johnson, 1995). The demand for a high number of tasks may impose a practical limitation to the use of constructed response assessments.

Finally, reliability may very well need to be judged in terms of the classification accuracy provided by the measure. For example, we could obtain a high reliability coefficient for a test, but find that when that test is used to classify students into four or five categories of proficiency, the probability of misclassification is unacceptably high (Jaeger & Craig, 2001; Rogosa, 1999a, 1999b, 1999c).

Of prime importance to the validity of score inferences for the common purposes of testing is whether the scores for students substantially reflect their proficiency on the domain being measured. Good writers should score better than poor writers (as judged by a reasonable external criterion) across prompts asking for the same type of writing (e.g., persuasion). High scores should not be obtained by illicit means, such as figuring out the algorithm used in the scoring or other gaming strategies. Furthermore, models upon which score values are derived need to be robust over rater groups and tasks. In the following sections we use these definitions of validity and reliability to examine typical methods of validation, and provide examples from the literature that serve as models for validation.

LEARNING FROM VALIDITY STUDIES PERFORMANCE ASSESSMENT

Extrapolating from traditional forms of testing to automatically scored essays is likely to be of only limited value to an analysis of validity. In this section, in an effort to heighten relevance, we will revisit the context of performance assessment, that is, assessment that depends on extended, constructed responses by students.

Performance assessment has a number of typical characteristics. Assessment requiring a performance component is usually intended to demonstrate the examinee's ability to invoke different types of learning, to process information, and to display multi-step solutions. The time demands for performance assessment are high, often requiring many times the test administration time of a short-answer or multiple-choice formatted test. The extended time is usually thought to increase fidelity of the task to the criterion or real-life application. The trade-off is that the greater amount of time required for a single examination task reduces the degree to which a domain of content can be broadly sampled. This reduction of domain coverage can result in inappropriate inferences and raise questions about fairness. For example, in history essays, it may make a very big difference if the question focuses on the Depression period or the post-World War II era in the 20th century. Teaching may have covered these topics to a different degree, students may have systematically varying stores of relevant prior knowledge, and as a result, performance might differ from one task to another. It is misleading to describe such differences as difficulty differences. Such variations probably occur because the domain is neither well specified nor adequately sampled. In the area of writing, for example, a similar difference could occur if persuasive tasks were used to measure elementary school programs that emphasize narrative writing.

Specifications for performance tasks, including writing, should focus on the particular task demands, explicit prior knowledge requirements, process expectations, and details of the scoring criteria.

Scoring may emphasize processes, product, or both. Ephemeral process responses (that is, processes that occur in real time) may be captured by judges or recorded by media for evaluation at a later time. Product responses represent the "answer," solution, or project created by the student. These are also made available to judges or raters. Both process and product responses are most typically judged by the application of general criteria, although in some cases, particular elements of an answer are sine qua non. For example, in the aforementioned Depression writing task, it may be an absolute requirement that the student include a discussion of "New Deal" palliatives.

Validity inferences for performance assessments therefore, have additional requirements to those expected in traditional testing. First, constructs need to be redefined as domains for adequate sampling. Broad-based ability constructs, such as mathematics proficiency, will not work well, as there are too many different ways in which such a construct might be operationalized, a particular problem in the light of restricted task sampling. This situation makes the possibility of mismatch between intentions, actual examination, and generalization, highly probable. If adequate sampling is not possible, because of testing burden for individuals or cost, then inferences must be limited to the content and processes sampled. Because performance assessments are thought to increase the fidelity of the examination to the setting or context of application, performance assessment designers and scorers must create specifications that map to the conditions under which the skill is to be used. Second, because domain definition is extremely important, it is similarly wise to link validity inferences for many instructionally relevant purposes to evidence that the students have been provided with reasonable opportunity to learn the desired outcomes. The application of generalizability models, in the absence of explicit information about instructional exposure, may very well mislead interpreters to conclude that a domain is well-sampled, when in fact, the explanation for a high coefficient is that all tasks are tapping general intellectual capacity as opposed to instructed content and skills.

CURRENT METHODS OF VALIDATING AUTOMATED SCORING OF CONSTRUCTED-RESPONSE ASSESSMENTS RARELY GATHER VALIDITY EVIDENCE IN THE APPLICATION CONTEXT

A simplified validation process for an automated scoring system is illustrated in the block diagram in Figure 2.1. The boxes denote the major processes and the arrows denote the process flow. There are three major stages: (a) validation of the software system, (b) validation of the scoring system independent of the application context, and (c) validation of the scoring system used in the application context. As we argue, much of the evidence gathered in numerous studies of automated scoring tends to focus on the second stage, score validation. Rarely is the system performance evaluated in the application context.

Score validation applies primarily to the evaluation of the scores produced by an automated scoring system against a gold standard. In applications where the automated scoring system is intended to replace human scoring or judgment (e.g., for reasons of cost, efficiency, throughout, or reliability), scores assigned by humans are considered the gold standard, although it is well known that human ratings may contain errors. This evaluation method is common standard practice across a variety of disciplines (e.g., text processing, expert systems, simulations), including the evaluation of automated essay scoring performance (e.g., Burstein, 2001; Burstein, Kukich, Wolff, & Lu, 1998; Cohen, 1995; Landauer, Foltz, & Laham, 1998; Landauer, Laham, Rehder, & Schreiner, 1997; Page, 1966, 1994; Page & Petersen, 1995). Indexes of interrater agreement and correlations between pairs of raters are typical metrics used to demonstrate comparability. High levels of adjacent agreement (but not exact agreement) and high correlations have consistently been reported regardless of scoring system. The assumption behind these analyses is that scores from human and automated systems are interchangeable.

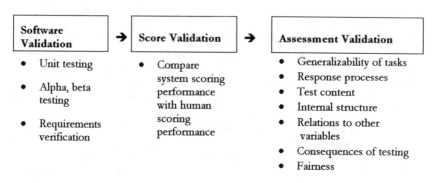

FIG. 2.1. Validation process.

However, these reliability estimates may not be sufficient evidence for the interchangeability of scores. Agreement statistics provide information on the absolute agreement between raters and correlation statistics provide information on relative agreement between raters (i.e., the degree to which raters' scores result in similar rank orderings of papers). Neither index takes into account variation due to task, rater, and their interaction.

One way to address these issues is to examine these data within a generalizability framework. As Clauser (2000) suggested, an automated scoring system not susceptible to within-task variance should demonstrate similar generalizability of scores as human raters. For an example of conducting a generalizability study to address this issue, see Clauser, Swanson, and Clyman (1999). In that study, Clauser et al. provided an example of such an analysis and provided guidance in estimating the degree to which the true scores underlying the automated scoring system is the same as that measured by the human ratings.

The recognition that the rating process is complex and subject to bias suggests the need to demonstrate that systematic bias is not introduced into the scoring model by way of bias inherent in the human ratings. Baker and O'Neil (1996) identified five characteristics of raters that may impact raters' scoring of an examinee's essay: rater training, relevant content and world knowledge, linguistic competency, expectations of student competency, and instructional beliefs. Baker (1995) and Baker, Linn, Abedi, and Niemi (1995) attributed low domain knowledge of the essay topic as contributing to low reliability between raters when scoring student written responses for prior knowledge and misconceptions. Similarly, there is some evidence that hints that automated scoring of essays may be sensitive to limited English proficiency (LEP) examinees. Using the earlier 1999 version of e-rater®, Burstein and Chodorow (1999) found a significant language by scoring method (human, automated scoring) interaction. The automated scoring system scores and human rater scores differed on essays from two of five language groups (although the agreement analyses found no such interaction).

Summary

High reliability or agreement between automated and human scoring is a necessary, but insufficient condition for validity. Evidence needs to be gathered to demonstrate that the scores produced by automated systems faithfully reflect the intended use of those scores. For example, automated essay scoring for the purpose of improving instruction should yield information that is usable by teachers about students who need improvement. Similarly, automated scoring for the purpose of assessing students' progress in writing competency should detect changes in writing as a result of instruction. In either case, the scoring system should not be unduly influenced by variables unrelated to the construct being measured (e.g., typing skill). The issue is less whether high reliability can be achieved and more one of whether substitution of human ratings with automated ratings results in a decrease of validity (Clauser, 2000). In the next section we examine methods that we believe can be used to validate automated scoring systems.

VALIDATING AUTOMATED SCORING SYSTEMS FOR CONSTRUCTED-RESPONSE ASSESSMENTS

Assessment validation is the most comprehensive means of establishing validity. Assessment is a process that begins with identifying the goals of the assessment and ends with a judgment about the adequacy of the evidence to support the intended use of the assessment results. As discussed in the previous section, demonstrating reliability is a necessary but insufficient condition to satisfy assessment validation. To the furthest extent possible, assessments need to be validated in the context that they will be used. This means administering the assessments to a sample of participants drawn from the population of interest, using standardized administration procedures, and evaluating the assessment results with respect to its intended use.

Kane, Crooks, and Cohen (1999) described a chain of inferences that need to be substantiated at each step of the validation process. The scores resulting from the assessment need to be interpreted in light of the evidence gathered to support inferences about the extent to which (a) scoring of responses is adequate, (b) the tasks offer sufficient domain coverage, and (c) the assessment result can be extrapolated to the target domain of interest. Each set of inferences at each stage have particular requirements. At the scoring stage, evidence is required to demonstrate that the scoring procedure has been applied as intended. Evidence also needs to be gathered to demonstrate that the set of tasks chosen for the assessment provides sufficient coverage of the universe of possible tasks. Finally, evidence needs to be gathered to show that the scores from the assessment are likely to be representative of the target performance. For example, such evidence can be of the form of criterion-related validity evidence or an evaluation of the overlap between the demands of the assessment tasks and the expected demands in the target domain. In the following section, we present examples of work, drawn from diverse fields within and without the automated scoring systems literature, that illustrate assessment validation process.

Validation Processes in Mission Critical, Complex Systems

One of the clearest examples of the validation process is in the practices used to validate large and complex engineering systems (e.g., satellite systems, defense systems, transportation systems, financial systems). For example, testing of satellites is comprehensive and occurs at multiple levels (from a functional test of a black box to a comprehensive system test). At the system level, analogous to assessment validation, the satellite is subjected to tests that approximate space conditions. Thermal cycling simulates the temperature swings that occur in orbit and vacuum tests simulate the zero-atmosphere conditions of space. Tests of satellite performance are repeated across these different conditions to gather evidence that the satellite is operating as expected. During each test, every signal path is tested for continuity through the primary and redundant switches, and every amplifier is power cycled. Incomplete validation testing can be disastrous—as evidenced by numerous failures of complex systems (Herrmann, 1999).

Although an extreme case, this example illustrates the point that system testing in the application context (or as close as possible) is an essential component of the validation process. The goal of such testing is to validate system performance under the range of conditions in which the system is expected to operate. The rationale of this approach is to achieve the highest level of confidence possible about the interpretations and inferences drawn from the results of the test. In the following sections, we present some methods to gather validity evidence in an automated scoring context.

Example 1: Expert-Derived Scoring Criteria

In contexts closer to education, one method to establish criteria for scoring is to base the dimensions of a scoring rubric on expert performance. Experts possess a set of skills and knowledge that are distinct from those of novices, and the continuum of skill separating novice from expert serves as a useful way of characterizing competency. The ingenuity of using experts is twofold. First, by definition, an expert possesses the requisite knowledge and skills for the domain of interest and is able to differentiate important from less important information (Chi, Glaser, & Farr, 1988). Developing a scoring rubric based on an expert's explication of the central concepts is an efficient way to capture the most important and salient content of a domain.

The second aspect of using expert-derived scoring rubrics is that experts possess the desired end-state of academic and other training not only in terms of content, but also in terms of cognition—how they solve the task. Thus, the process of how an expert solves a task provides a benchmark against which to measure student performance.

Baker, Freeman, and Clayton (1991) pioneered the development of this approach over 15 years ago initially in their assessments of history knowledge. In subsequent studies, the method was refined and tested in numerous domains (e.g., chemistry, geography, mathematics, general science). To illustrate the process, Baker et al. (1991) gathered think-aloud data from participants of differing expertise in history to examine what experts did rather than what they said they did. Nine participants (three advanced graduate students, three history teachers, and three Advance Placement history students) responded to a history prompt and talked aloud during the task. Baker et al. (1991) found that the history graduate students (considered experts) and some teachers all used the following processes during their response: (a) they used a strong problem or premise to focus their response; (b) they drew on prior knowledge of principles, facts, and events to bolster their response; (c) they referred to specific parts of the supplied text; and (d) they explicitly attempted to show the relations among the principles, facts, and events. The less experienced participants (the Advanced Placement students and some teachers) relied on the text in terms of paraphrasing or restating the text, and attempted to cover all elements in the text instead of distinguishing between important and less important elements.

Relationship to Automated Scoring Systems. The use of expert-derived scoring rubrics in an automated scoring context has been largely unexplored in education, to the best of our knowledge. That is, given a task or prompt, typical scoring rubrics are developed based on what experts perceive as important and of value, not what experts actually do on the given task. Baker et al. (1991) speculated that in the development of their scoring rubrics, experts compiled the set of criteria that may have been an outcome of the experts' desire to be comprehensive and thoughtful.

One example that has its roots in expert-derived scoring methods is the use of experts to define the specific content demands of a knowledge or concept map task

(Herl, Niemi, & Baker, 1996). Domain experts define the set of terms and links for the mapping task. The task is then administered to one or more experts, and the set of expert maps is used as the scoring criteria for student maps. This approach is particularly suited for automated scoring applications. The use of experts in the development of the task, and in the scoring itself, has the same benefits outlined before. In numerous studies across age, content, and setting, the use of expert-derived referent knowledge maps has shown to be related significantly to learning outcomes (Chung, Harmon, & Baker, in press; Herl et al., 1996; Herl, O'Neil, Chung, & Schacter, 1999; Klein, Chung, Osmundson, Herl, & O'Neil, 2001; Osmundson, Chung, Herl, & Klein, 1999). In all cases, understanding of the concepts and relations contained in the knowledge map is assumed to be important. The degree to which students' knowledge maps convey expert-like understanding (as measured by scoring student maps against expert maps) has consistently been related to the learning outcomes of the task, of which successful performance is assumed to be contingent on an understanding of the concepts and links used in the knowledge maps. Further, under conditions where learning was expected, the expert-derived scoring method demonstrated sensitivity to instruction (i.e., higher post-instruction scores compared to pre-instruction scores). This sensitivity is of critical importance in settings where change is expected.

Example 2: Response Process Measure

As assessments move toward being sensitive to cognitive demands, evidence needs to be gathered to substantiate claims that the task evokes the presumed cognitive processes. Confirmation of the existence of these processes increases trustworthiness of the results of the assessment. Uncovering unrelated or construct-irrelevant processes undermines the validity of any interpretations about task performance. For example, the inference that high performance on a problem-solving task is the result of using efficient problem-solving strategies needs to be substantiated with evidence that examinees are using problem-solving strategies and not test-taking or gaming strategies.

Evidence of response processes in computer-based constructed response assessments can be gathered by a variety of means: (a) measuring task performance at the end of the assessment or repeatedly over the duration of the assessment, (b) measuring online computer activity (i.e., what the user is doing during the task), (c) measuring online cognitive activity (i.e., what the user is thinking as he or she engages in the task), and (d) triangulating relations among task performance, online computer activity, and online cognitive activity. For the purposes of validating an assessment that claims to be cognitively demanding, convergent evidence from all four measures would strengthen the validity argument considerably.

One example of integrating online computer activity with task performance is in a series of studies examining the utility of online behavioral measures as indicators of problem solving. In a study reported by Schacter, Herl, Chung, Dennis, and O'Neil (1999), the authors integrated a web-searching task with a knowledge-mapping task. Students first created a knowledge map on the topic of environmental science based on their existing prior knowledge of the subject. After completing the initial knowledge map, the maps were scored in real-time and general feedback was given to the students about which concepts "needed work." At that point, students were given access to web pages on environmental science and instructed to improve their maps by searching the World Wide Web for relevant information. During this phase of the task, students could search for information, modify their knowledge maps, and request feedback on the quality of their map.

The task outcome measure was students' final knowledge map score. Online behavioral measures were derived from the searches students conducted during the task such as simple browsing among pages, focused browsing (browsing among pages that were highly relevant to a concept in the knowledge map), and use of feedback. Significant relations were found between these online behaviors and students' knowledge map scores. Other studies that examined web search strategies in greater depth supported the choice of these process measures (e.g., Klein, Yarnall, & Glaubke, 2001; Schacter, Chung, & Dorr, 1998).

Relationship to Automated Scoring System. Evidence based on response processes may be particularly suited for automated scoring systems. Response process evidence is one of five sources of validity evidence discussed in the Standards for Educational and Psychological Testing (AERA, APA, NCME, 1999). Presumably, in automated scoring systems, response process evidence will be derived from computer-based data sources.

The example illustrates two points with respect to validity. First, the inference drawn about students' problem solving — those students who demonstrated higher knowledge map scores engaged in better problem solving — is strengthened considerably by the response process evidence (i.e., online process measures). Students who engaged in productive searches as measured by the relevance of the information to concepts in the students' knowledge map were more likely to construct higher scoring knowledge maps. Although this finding is unsurprising and consistent with the general findings in the literature, its importance lies in its support of the interpretation of student problem-solving performance.

The second point is that the online behavioral measures were derived directly from theoretical conceptions about information seeking. Search was conceptualized as an inherent cognitive activity, and thus the online behaviors that were targeted for measurement were those that would most likely reflect effective searching and would differentiate between students possessing high and low search skills.

Summary. Two examples of gathering validity evidence for constructed-response assessments in an automated scoring context were presented. The use of domain experts to develop scoring criteria was presented as a way to efficiently capture domain content. Using expert-derived criteria is an attractive method because domain experts embody a set of skills and knowledge that serves as a desirable outcome of education and training. A second approach discussed, suited to automated scoring systems, is the use of construct-derived measures to provide evidence of expected response processes. The evidential utility of this approach was discussed with respect to providing evidence of the existence of processes presumably underlying performance, thus strengthening the validity of inferences drawn about performance.

DISCUSSION

We are at the beginning of the move toward the deployment and adoption of systems that perform automated scoring of constructed-response performance. With respect to essay scoring, it is clear that the scoring technology is feasible, and it is also clear that such systems can score essays as reliably as human raters. In the broader context, computer-based assessments offer new and exciting means to measure aspects of human performance that cannot be done feasibly outside of computational means.

What is less clear is how these systems work in the field for different purposes. We know little about three components that may have critical bearing on the validity of inferences drawn about student performance on these assessments. First, for those scoring methods that model human ratings, there is little work on the extent to which biases that exist in human raters are captured into the model. Second, it is unclear to what extent the algorithms underlying automated scoring are traceable to theoretical models of human learning and cognition. Assessments that claim to be sensitive to cognitive demands need to provide evidence of such sensitivity. Automated scoring that demonstrates high agreement with human raters is desirable but does not necessarily provide compelling validity evidence. Finally, and most importantly, there has been little reported in the way of validating the performance of automated scoring systems in an applied context. Do automated scoring systems work as intended in an educational context, free of biases and unintended consequences? The history of testing suggests that these issues and others not yet conceived will surface as automated systems are fielded.

Toward Construct-Centered Scoring Systems

Increasingly, the limitations of using human raters as the gold standard are being exposed. Human rating of complex performance requires complex judgment, which is subject to biases and inconsistencies. For these reasons, some researchers suggest a move away from the exclusive reliance on human raters as the gold standard (Bennett & Bejar, 1998; Clauser, Margolis, Clyman, & Ross, 1997; Clauser et al., 1995; Williamson, Bejar, & Hone, 1999). Scoring models that are derived from human raters (e.g., regression models that use human ratings as the dependent variable, or process models that operationalized human judgment) may capture biases inherent in raters.

The issues raised earlier can be addressed partially by focusing on validity. First, for the reasons discussed earlier, the adoption of expert-based scoring criteria seems particularly attractive. Experts possess the skills and knowledge expected of competent performance in a given domain, and thus using experts as exemplars seems a reasonable approach.

Second, the use of cognitively-derived process and performance measures seems justified as assessments become increasingly grounded in cognitive psychology (Baker et al., 1991; Baker & Mayer, 1999; Embretson, 1998; Williamson et al., 1999; Bennett, 1993a, 1993b). The cognitive demands of the task will suggest a set of examinee operations that will yield evidence of use (or not) of particular cognitive process and competency (or not) on particular outcomes. This area may hold the greatest potential to advance automated scoring but is subject to task, interface, and examinee constraints (Bennett & Bejar, 1998).

One example that expresses this idea is in the development of *e-rater®*. The measures in *e-rater®* directly are traceable to the construct of writing competency (Burstein, 2001; Burstein, Kukich, Braden-Harder, Chodorow, Hua, Kaplan, et al., 1998; Burstein, Kukich, Wolff, et al., 1998; Burstein, Wolff, & Lu, 1999). Burstein and colleagues have embedded algorithms into the design of e-rater® that are intended to reflect the criteria used for scoring essays. This is a major characteristic that distinguishes e-rater® from other essay scoring systems. The importance of this is that in addition to exposing the scoring methodology to public inspection, the algorithm is attempting to capture elements of writing that are directly related to writing competency. In contrast, other essay scoring methods analyze surface features (e.g., Page, 1966, 1994; Page & Petersen, 1995) or match documents (e.g., Landauer et al., 1998; Landauer et al., 1997).

We are currently exploring the idea of construct-centered scoring of problem solving with IMMEX (Interactive Multimedia Exercises; Stevens, Ikeda, Casillas, Palacio-Cayetano, & Clyman, 1999). IMMEX is a promising computer-based tool for the assessment of problem solving. We have gathered, synchronized, and integrated a comprehensive set of response process evidence (i.e., online activity and cognitive activity) with task outcomes and measures of individual differences. Preliminary analyses suggest strong convergent evidence among the behavioral processes, cognitive processes, and task performance. We are currently designing software to operationalize problem-solving processes based on participants' characteristics and moment-to-moment task performance (i.e., individual difference and current and past activities in the assessment). We will examine our approach with respect to cognitive response processes and relations to external criteria (Chung, de Vries, Cheak, Stevens, & Bewley, in preparation).

Implications for Reliability

The implications for reliability of adopting a construct-centered scoring approach are twofold. First, the reliability of raters will no longer be an issue. In place of rater reliability may be generalizability of scoring algorithms, particularly to evaluate the performance of different scoring implementations (e.g., regression vs. expert-based comparisons), or to evaluate the impact of changes to an algorithm (abduction studies). Second, the cognitive focus may require taking into account differences in students and tasks when considering generalizability (Nichols & Kuehl, 1999; Nichols & Smith, 1998; Nichols & Sugrue, 1999). It is not necessarily the case that when two tasks appear the same on the surface that they demand the same kinds of skills (e.g., persuasive vs. expository essays).

Implications for Validity

Interestingly, the adoption of automated scoring may increase the quality of assessments by requiring more rigor in the assessment development process (e.g., Almond, Steinberg, & Mislevy, 2001; Mislevy, Steinberg, Almond, Breyer, & Johnson, 1999; Mislevy, Steinberg, Breyer, Almond, & Johnson, 2001; O'Neil & Baker, 1991). Improvements may be realized in task design, scoring approach, and specification of and gathering of validity evidence. Finally, computer-based constructed response tasks may provide the opportunity to measure the construct of interest more directly than other means (Baker & Mayer, 1999). The demand for evidence to support score interpretation and the methods outlined earlier may well result in higher quality assessments (e.g., scoring algorithms and task designs). The result should be assessments whose scores are defensible, traceable to cognitive theory, subject to inspection, and interpretable with respect to a well-defined criteria.

AUTHOR NOTE

We would like to thank Joanne Michiuye for her help with the preparation of this chapter, and Bill Bewley and Christy Kim-Boschardin for their reviewing an earlier draft of this chapter.

The work reported herein was supported under the Educational Research and Development Centers Program, PR/Award Number R305B60002, as administered by the Office of Educational Research and Improvement, U.S. Department of Education. The findings and opinions expressed in this report do not reflect the positions or policies of the National Institute on Student Achievement, Curriculum, and Assessment, the Office of Educational Research and Improvement, or the U.S. Department of Education.

Correspondence concerning this article should be addressed to Gregory K. W. K. Chung, UCLA CSE/CRESST, 301 GSE&IS, Box 951522, Los Angeles, CA 90095–1522. Electronic mail may be sent to greg@ucla.edu.

REFERENCES

Almond, R., Steinberg, L., & Mislevy, R. (2001). *A sample assessment using the four process framework* (CSE Tech. Rep. No. 543). Los Angeles: University of California, National Center for Research on Evaluation, Standards, and Student Testing (CRESST).

American Educational Research Association, American Psychological Association, and National Council for Measurement in Education. (1999). *Standards for educational and psychological testing.* Washington, DC: American Educational Research Association.

Baker, E. L. (1995). Learning based assessments of history understanding. *Educational Psychologist, 29*, 97–106.

Baker, E. L., Freeman, M., & Clayton, S. (1991). Cognitive assessment of history for large-scale testing. In M. C. Wittrock & E. L. Baker (Eds.), *Testing and cognition* (pp. 131–153). Englewood Cliffs, NJ: Prentice–Hall.

Baker, E. L., & Herman, J. L. (in press). Technology and evaluation. In G. Haertel & B. Means (Eds.), *Approaches to evaluating the impact of educational technology*. New York: Teachers College Press.

Baker, E. L., Linn, R. L., Abedi, J., & Niemi, D. (1995). Dimensionality and generalizability of domain-independent performance assessments. *Journal of Educational Research, 89*, 197–205.

Baker, E. L., & Mayer, R. E. (1999). Computer-based assessment of problem solving. *Computers in Human Behavior, 15*, 269–282.

Baker, E. L., & O'Neil, H. F., Jr. (1996). Performance assessment and equity. In M. B. Kane & R. Mitchell (Eds.), *Implementing performance assessment: Promises, problems, and challenges* (pp. 183-199). Mahwah, NJ: Erlbaum.

Baker, E. L., O'Neil, H. F., Jr., & Linn, R. L. (1993). Policy and validity prospects for performance-based assessment. *American Psychologist, 48*, 1210–1218.

Bennett, R. E. (1993a). On the meaning of constructed response. In R. E. Bennett & W. C. Ward (Eds.), *Construction versus choice in cognitive measurement: Issues in constructed response, performance testing, and portfolio assessment* (pp. 1–27). Hillsdale, NJ: Lawrence Erlbaum Associates, Inc.

Bennett, R. E. (1993b). Toward intelligent assessment: An integration of constructed-response testing, artificial intelligence, and model-based measurement. In N. Frederiksen, R. J. Mislevy, & I. I. Bejar (Eds.), *Test theory for a new generation of tests* (pp. 99–123). Hillsdale, NJ: Lawrence Erlbaum Associates, Inc.

Bennett, R. E., & Bejar, I. I. (1998). Validity and automated scoring: It's not only the scoring. *Educational Measurement: Issues and Practice, 17*(4), 9–17.

Brennan, R. L., & Johnson, E. G. (1995). Generalizability of performance assessments. *Educational Measurement: Issues and Practice, 14*(4), 9–12.

Burstein, J. (2001, April). *Automated essay evaluation with natural language processing*. Paper presented at the annual meeting of the National Council on Measurement in Education, Seattle, WA.

Burstein, J. C., & Chodorow, M. (1999, June). Automated essay scoring for nonnative English speakers. In *Computer-mediate language assessment and evaluation of natural language processing*. Joint symposium of the Association of Computational Linguistics and the International Association of Language Learning Technologies, College Park, MD.

Burstein, J., Kukich, K., Braden-Harder, L., Chodorow, M., Hua, S., Kaplan, B., et al (1998). *Computer analysis of essay content for automatic score prediction: A prototype automated scoring system for GMAT analytical writing assessment* (RR–98–15). Princeton, NJ: Educational Testing Service.

Burstein, J., Kukich, K., Wolff, S., & Lu, C. (1998, April). *Computer analysis of essay content for automated score prediction*. Paper presented at the annual meeting of the National Council on Measurement in Education, San Diego, CA.

Burstein, J., Wolff, S., & Lu, C. (1999). Using lexical semantic techniques to classify free-responses. In E. Viegas (Ed.), *Breadth and depth of semantic lexicons* (pp. 227–246). New York: Kluwer.

Chi, M. T. H., Glaser, R., & Farr, M. J. (Eds.). (1988). *The nature of expertise*. Hillsdale, NJ: Lawrence Erlbaum Associates, Inc.

Chung, G. K. W. K., de Vries, L. F., Cheak, A. M., Stevens, R. H., & Bewley, W. L. (in press). Process measures of problem solving. *Computers in Human Behavior.*

Chung, G. K. W. K., Harmon, T. C., & Baker, E. L. (2001). The impact of a simulation-based learning design project on student learning. *IEEE transactions on Education, 44,* 390–398.

Clauser, B. E. (2000). Recurrent issues and recent advances in scoring performance assessments. *Applied Psychological Measurement, 24,* 310–324.

Clauser, B. E., Margolis, M. J., Clyman, S. G., & Ross, L. P. (1997). Development of automated scoring algorithms for complex performance assessments: A comparison of two approaches. *Journal of Educational Measurement, 34,* 141–161.

Clauser, B. E., Subhiyah, R. G., Nungester, R. J., Ripkey, D. R., Clyman, S. G., & McKinley, D. (1995). Scoring a performance-based assessment by modeling the judgments of experts. *Journal of Educational Measurement, 32,* 397–415.

Clauser, B. E., Swanson, D. B., & Clyman, S. G. (1999). A comparison of the generalizability of scores produced by expert raters and automated scoring systems. *Applied Measurement in Education, 12,* 281–299.

Cohen, P. R. (1995). *Empirical methods for artificial intelligence.* Cambridge, MA: MIT Press.

Embretson, S. E. (1998). A cognitive design system approach to generating valid tests: Application to abstract reasoning. *Psychological Methods, 3,* 380–396.

Herl, H. E., Niemi, D., & Baker, E. L. (1996). Construct validation of an approach to modeling cognitive structure of U.S. history knowledge. *Journal of Educational Research, 89,* 206–218.

Herl, H. E., O'Neil, H. F., Jr., Chung, G. K. W. K., & Schacter, J. (1999). Reliability and validity of a computer-based knowledge mapping system to measure content understanding. *Computers in Human Behavior, 15,* 315–334.

Herrmann, D. S. (1999). *Software safety and reliability: Techniques, approaches, and standards of key industrial sectors.* Piscataway, NJ: IEEE Computer Society.

Jaeger, R. M., & Craig, N. (2001). An integrated judgment procedure for setting standards on complex, large-scale assessments. In G. J. Cizek (Ed.), *Setting performance standards: Concepts, methods, and perspectives* (pp. 313–338). Mahwah, NJ: Lawrence Erlbaum Associates, Inc.

Kane, M., Crooks, T., & Cohen, A. (1999). Validating measures of performance. *Educational Measurement: Issues and Practice, 18*(2), 5–17.

Klein, D. C. D., Chung, G. K. W. K., Osmundson, E., Herl, H. E., & O'Neil, H. F., Jr. (2001). *Examining the validity of knowledge mapping as a measure of elementary students' Scientific understanding* (Final deliverable to OERI). Los Angelses: University of California, National Center for Research on Evaluation, Standards, and Student Testing (CRESST).

Klein, D. C. D., Yarnall, L., & Glaubke, C. (2001). Using technology to assess students' Web expertise (CSE Tech. Rep. No. 544). Los Angeles: University of California, National Center for Research on Evaluation, Standards, and Student Testing (CRESST).

Landauer, T. K., Foltz, P. W., & Laham, D. (1998). An introduction to latent semantic analysis. *Discourse Processes, 25,* 259–284.

Landauer, T. K., Laham, D., Rehder, B., & Schreiner, M. E. (1997). How well can passage meaning be derived without using word order? A comparison of latent semantic analysis and humans. *Proceedings of the 19th annual meeting of the Cognitive Science Society, USA,* 412–417.

Linn, R. L., Baker, E. L., & Dunbar, S. B. (1991). Complex, performance-based assessment: Expectations and validation criteria. *Educational Researcher, 20*(8), 15–21.

Messick, S. (1989). Validity. In R. L. Linn (Ed.), *Educational measurement* (3rd ed., pp. 13–103). New York: Macmillan.

Mislevy, R. J., Steinberg, L. S., Breyer, F. J., Almond, R. G., & Johnson, L. (1999). A cognitive task analysis with implications for designing simulation-based performance assessment. *Computers in Human Behavior, 15,* 335–3374.

Mislevy, R., Steinberg, L., Almond, R., Breyer, F. J., & Johnson, L. (2001). *Making sense of data from complex assessments* (CSE Tech. Rep. No. 538). Los Angeles: University of California, National Center for Research on Evaluation, Standards, and Student Testing (CRESST).

Nichols, P. D., & Kuehl, B. J. (1999). Prophesying the reliability of cognitively complex assessments. *Applied Measurement in Education, 12,* 73–94.

Nichols, P. D., & Smith, P. L. (1998). Contextualizing the interpretation of reliability data. *Educational Measurement: Issues and Practice, 17*(3), 24–36.

Nichols, P. D., & Sugrue, B. (1999). Contextualizing the interpretation of reliability data. *Educational Measurement: Issues and Practice, 18*(2), 18–29.

O'Neil, H. F., Jr., & Baker, E. L. (1991). Issues in intelligent computer-assisted instruction: Evaluation and measurement. In T. B. Gutkin & S. L. Wise (Eds.), *The computer and the decision-making process* (pp. 199-224). Hillsdale, NJ: Lawrence Erlbaum Associates, Inc.

Osmundson, E., Chung, G. K. W. K., Herl, H. E., & Klein, D. C. D. (1999). *Concept mapping in the classroom: A tool for examining the development of students' conceptual understandings* (CSE Tech. Rep. No. 507). Los Angeles: University of California, National Center for Research on Evaluation, Standards, and Student Testing (CRESST).

Page, E. B. (1966). The imminence of grading essays by computer. *Phi Delta Kappan, 47,* 238–243.

Page, E. B. (1994). New computer grading of student prose, using modern concepts and software. *Journal of Experimental Education, 62,* 127–142.

Page, E. B., & Petersen, N.S. (1995). The computer moves into essay grading: Updating the ancient test. *Phi Delta Kappan, 76,* 561–565.

Pfleeger, S. L. (1998). *Software engineering: Theory and practice.* Upper Saddle River, NJ: Prentice Hall.

Rogosa, D. (1999a). *Accuracy of individual scores expressed in percentile ranks: Classical test theory calculations.* (CSE Tech. Rep. No. 509). Los Angeles: University of California, National Center for Research on Evaluation, Standards, and Student Testing (CRESST).

Rogosa, D. (1999b). *Accuracy of year-1, year-2 comparisons using individual percentile rank scores: Classical test theory calculations.* (CSE Tech. Rep. No. 510). Los Angeles: University of California, National Center for Research on Evaluation, Standards, and Student Testing (CRESST).

Rogosa, D. (1999c). How accurate are the STAR national percentile rank scores for individual students? An interpretive guide. Palo Alto, CA: Stanford University Press.

Schacter, J., Chung, G. K. W. K., & Dorr, A. (1998). Children's Internet searching on complex problems: Performance and process analyses. *Journal of the American Society for Information Science, 49,* 840–849.

Schacter, J., Herl, H. E., Chung, G. K. W. K., Dennis, R. A., & O'Neil, H. F., Jr. (1999). Computer-based performance assessments: A solution to the narrow measurement and reporting of problem solving. *Computers in Human Behavior, 15,* 403–418.

Shavelson, R. J., & Webb, N. M. (1991). *Generalizability theory: A primer.* Newbury Park, CA: Sage.

Stevens, R., Ikeda, J., Casillas, A., Palacio-Cayetano, J., & Clyman, S. (1999). Artificial neural network-based performance assessments. *Computers in Human Behavior, 15,* 295–313.

Williamson, D. M., Bejar, I. I., & Hone, A. S. (1999). 'Mental model' comparison of automated and human scoring. *Journal of Educational Measurement, 36,* 158–184.

III. Automated Essay Scorers

3
Project Essay Grade: PEG

Ellis Batten Page
Duke University

This chapter describes the evolution of Project Essay Grade (PEG), which was the first of the automated essay scorers. The purpose is to detail some of the history of automated essay grading, why it was impractical when first created, what reenergized development and research in automated essay scoring, how PEG works, and to report recent research involving PEG.

The development of PEG grew out of both practical and personal concerns. As a former high school English teacher, I knew one of the hindrances to more writing was that someone had to grade the papers. And if we know something from educational research it is that the more one writes, the better writer one becomes. At the postsecondary level where a faculty member may have 25 to 50 papers per writing assignment, the task of grading may be challenging, but manageable. However, in high school, where one writing assignment often results in 150 papers, the process is daunting. I remember many long weekends sifting through stacks of papers wishing for some help. The desire to do something about the problem resulted, seven years later, in the first prototype of PEG.

In 1964, I was invited to a meeting at Harvard, where leading computer researchers were analyzing English for a variety of applications (such as verbal reactions to a Rorschach test). Many of these experiments were fascinating. The meeting prompted me to specify some strategies in rudimentary FORTRAN and led to promising experiments.

EARLIEST EXPERIMENTS

The first funding to launch this inquiry came from the College Board. The College Board was manually grading hundreds of thousands of essays each year and was looking for ways to make the process more efficient. After some promising trials, we received additional private and Federal support, and developed a program of focused research at the University of Connecticut.

By 1966 we published two articles (Page 1966a, 1966b), one of which included the Table shown later (see Table 3).

TABLE 3.1
Which one is the Computer?

Judges

	A	B	C	D	E
A		.51	.51	.44	.57
B	.51		.53	.56	.61
C	.51	.53		.48	.49
D	.44	.56	.48		.59
E	.57	.61	.49	.59	

Most numbers in Table 3.1 are correlations between human judges, who independently graded a set of papers. Judges correlated with each other about .50. In the PEG Program, "Judge C" resembled the four teachers in their correlations with each other. In that sense, the experiment met Alan Turing's famous criterion related to artificial intelligence that an outside observer could not tell the difference between performance on the computer and human performance.

Although Table 3.1 suggested that neither humans nor computers produced stellar results, it also led to the belief that computers had the potential to grade as reliably as their human counterparts (in this case, teachers of English).

Indeed, the mid-1960s were a remarkable time for new advances with computers, designing humanoid behavior formerly regarded as "impossible" for computers to accomplish. Thus, PEG was welcomed by some influential leaders in measurement, in computer science, schooling, and government, as one more possible step forward in such important simulations.

The research on PEG soon received federal funding and one grant allowed the research team to become familiar with "The General Inquirer," a content analytic engine developed in the early 60s. A series of school-based studies that focused on both style and content (Ajay, Tillett, & Page, 1973; Page & Paulus, 1968) was also studied. PEG set up a multiple-classroom experiment of junior- and senior-high classes in four large subject-matter areas. The software graded both subject-knowledge and writing ability. Combining appropriate subject-matter vocabulary (and synonyms) with stylistic variables, it was found that PEG performed better by using such combinations than by using only one or the other. Those experiments, too, provided first-ever simulations of teacher content-grading in the schools.

Despite the early success of our research, many of our full-scale implementation barriers were of a practical nature. For example, data input for the computer was accomplished primarily through tape and 80-column IBM punched cards. At the time, mainframe computers were impressive in what they could do, but were relatively slow, processed primarily in batch mode, and were not very fault-tolerant to unanticipated errors. Most importantly, access to computers was restricted from the vast majority of students either because they did not have accounts or they were unwilling to learn the lingua franca of antiquated operating systems. The prospect for students to use computers in their own schools seemed pretty remote. Thus, PEG went into "sleep mode" during the 1970s and early 1980s because of these practical constraints and the interest of the government to move on to other projects. With the advent of microcomputers in the mid 1980s, a number of technology advances appeared on the horizon. It seemed more likely that students would eventually have reasonable access to computers, the storage mechanisms became more flexible (e.g., hard drives and floppy diskettes), and computer programming languages were created that were more adept at handling text rather than numbers. These developments prompted a re–examination of the potential for automated essay scoring.

During the "reawakening" period, a number of alternatives were formulated for the advanced analysis of English (Johnson & Zwick, 1990; Lauer & Asher, 1988; Wical & Mugele, 1993). Most of these incorporated an applied linguistics approach or attempted to develop theoretical frameworks for study of writing assessment. In the meantime, we turned our attention to the study of larger data sets including those from the 1988 National Assessment of Educational Progress (NAEP).

These new student essays had been handwritten by a national sample of students, but were subsequently entered into the computer by NAEP typists (and NAEP's designs had been influenced by PEG's earlier work). In the NAEP data set, all students responded to the same "prompt" (topic assignment). For the purposes of this study, six human ratings were collected for each essay. Using these data, randomly-selected formative samples were generated which predicted well to cross-validation samples (with "r"s higher than .84). Even models developed for the one prompt predicted across different years, students, and judge panels, with an "r" hovering at about .83. Statistically, the PEG formulations for reliability now surpassed two judges which matched the typical number of human judges employed for most essay grading tasks.

BLIND TESTING —THE PRAXIS ESSAYS

Because of their emerging interest in the topic of automated essay scoring, the Educational Testing Service (ETS) commissioned a blind test of the Praxis essays using PEG. In this experiment, ETS provided 1,314 essays typed in by applicants for their Praxis test (the Praxis program is used in evaluating applicants for teacher certification). All essays had been rated by at least two ETS judges. Moreover, four additional ratings were supplied for 300 randomly-selected "formative" essays, and the same number of 300 "cross-validation" essays.

The main outcomes are shown in Table 3.2 (Page & Petersen, 1995). Table 3.2 presents the prediction of each separate judge with the computer (PRED column). Furthermore, the PEG program predicted human judgments well—better even than three human judges.

In practical terms, these findings were very encouraging for large-scale testing programs using automated essay scoring (AES). Suppose that 100,000 papers were to be rated, and PEG developed a scoring model based on a random sample of just 1,000 of them. Then, for the remaining 99,000 papers, computer ratings could be expected to be superior to the usual human ratings in a striking number of ways:

1. The automated ratings would surpass the accuracy of the usual two judges. (Accuracy is defined as agreeing with the mean of judgments.)
2. The essays would be graded much more rapidly, because fewer human readings would be required.
3. Machine-readable protocols would be graded more economically, saving 97% of the grading costs.
4. Essay results could be described statistically in many different ways, and used to study group differences, yearly trends, teaching methods, and a host of other important policy or research questions. (Such reports from human graded efforts are often time-consuming and costly.)
5. For individual accuracy of writing abilities, scores would be much more descriptive than the ordinary ratings results from two human judgments.
6. Validity checks could be built-in to address potential biases (computer or human).

TABLE 3.2
Correlation of Computer Ratings with Six Human
Judges (JS) (n essays=300)

Judge	PRED	JS1	JS2	JS3	JS4	JS5
JS1	.732					
JS2	.778	.649				
JS3	.740	.748	.585			
JS4	.748	.705	.684	.674		
JS5	.737	.596	.656	.643	.666	
JS6	.716	.550	.668	.594	.649	.635
Avg.	.742			.646		

Note. Data were from the Educational Testing Service test sample of its Praxis writing assessment, n = 300 The computer ratings (PRED) were based on analysis of 1,014 other essays from Praxis, and are applied to this test sample. Table used by permission.

CONSTRUCT VALIDITY OF PEG

The test results for Praxis showed many that the Praxis was a good proving ground for the status of PEG as a truly "valid" test of writing. When we say a test has construct validity, we mean that the data "make sense" with other scores and key data. Keith (Chapter 9) provided extensive evidence for the validity of PEG with regard to both predictive and construct validity. Basically, he showed that the scores from PEG align well with objective tests, the weights from one PEG model predict well scores with other PEG models, and that PEG scores predict writing outcomes (e.g., course grades). The reader is referred to the Keith chapter for more details.

HOW THE COMPUTER JUDGES ESSAYS

Certain underlying principles of PEG remained consistent across the three decades of research on automated essay grading. There was an assumption that the true quality of essays must be defined by human judges. Although individual judges are not entirely reliable, and may have personal biases, the use of more and more judges permits a better approximation to the "true" average rating of an essay. The goal of PEG is to predict the scores that a number of competent human judges would give to a group of similar essays. A human judge reads over an essay, forms an opinion of its overall quality, and decides on a score. The judge then assigns that score to the essay and moves on to read another. Holistic scoring is the usual way papers are judged in large programs, because more detailed scoring will be very expensive. What influences this human judge? In other experiments, PEG has studied the scores that judges give to certain traits in an essay. These traits are likely to be on anyone's list of important qualities of an essay (e.g., content, organization, style, mechanics, and creativity). Because a computer is not human, some would claim it cannot actually "read" an essay, or "analyze" its grammar in the same way as an English teacher. Yet most people would concede that the computer is able to identify approximations for instrinsic characteristics in much the same way as social scientists use observed and latent variables (see Shermis & Burstein, Preface-this volume).

The recent gains in accuracy from PEG ratings represent a large movement from the crudest early approximation, toward measures that are closer to the underlying intrinsics. Current programs explore complex and rich variables, such as searching a sentence for soundness of structure, and weighing such ratings across the essay. One area of excitement about such work is the constant effort to close the gap between trins and proxes, between computer programs and the human judges.

COMPARISONS OF PREDICTIONS

Just how well does PEG now simulate human judges? The answer hinges on correlations: first between human judges, and then between the human judges and PEG. One classic way of making such comparisons involves a form of multiple-regression analysis: the prediction of a criterion (average judge rating) from the ideal weighting of the independent variables (chosen from what the computer can measure in the essay). Those variables that best predict human ratings are commonly said to be "included" in the overall computer scoring. Because typical

PEG models include 30 to 40 variables, it would be hard to "coach" a writer on all of them simultaneously. In fact, if a writer had mastery of all such variables, it is quite likely that we would conclude that he or she was a good writer.

TRAITS REVISITED

In the earliest PEG work, one promising approach was to study traits, such as those mentioned earlier: content, organization, style, mechanics, and creativity. How do human judges behave, when asked to grade such entities? Based on our work, there tends to be a high correlation among the traits. Many judges administer homogenous "overall" opinions of an essay. Thus, the best use of traits may be to apply them ipsatively, that is, comparing the traits as measured within the student. So, for instance, a more diagnostic result would be to find that Johnny seems stronger in one trait (or trait cluster) than in another. This has been explored within PEG and shown to be in some ways practical (Page, Poggio, & Keith, 1997).

THE CLASSROOM CHALLENGE AND WRITE AMERICA

Concerned with improving writing practice and performance, PEG research has concentrated on how to improve student writing and simultaneously relieve the pressure of the extra work for teachers to grade such work. Could PEG meet the "classroom challenge" in terms of being used as a practical tool in student writing?

The result from the publicity generated by the NAEP and Praxis experiments was an outpouring of interest from English teachers in both secondary and postsecondary settings to use some version of the software. English teachers often felt stretched-out by what was expected of them—and what they demanded from themselves. Nevertheless, schools do not assign much writing. In 1988, for example, 80% of sampled 12th graders reported less than one paper per week across all courses they were taking (Applebee, Langer, Jenkins, Mullis & Foertsch, 1990, p. 44).

In one study using PEG, hundreds of classroom essays were drawn from two states (Connecticut and North Carolina). It was found that PEG did a credible job in making predictions of teacher ratings. Other experience provided additional reasons for optimism about PEG in the classroom:

1. The ETS blind test actually wrote on 72 different topics (the Praxis topics were in part a study of prompts). Thus, different topics haven't necessarily been a threat to classroom grading and use.
2. Models built on one dataset could be applied to other data sets with similar results (see also Keith, this volume). For instance, we could use formulas from NAEP to predict the judgments from the Praxis study. Such predictions were above .80 — very high for different test conditions.
3. Most reassuring of all was our study of construct validity (Page, et al, 1997). We appeared to be tapping into the writers' underlying skills.

These considerations led to the inauguration of a new experiment aimed at the classroom called "Write America!" (WA). The target for WA was a profile that included a wide range of student abilities (both across classes and within classes), and a wide range of classroom conditions, topic choices, study strategies, and time allowance. In short, WA was more concerned for sampling classroom realism than it was for assuring experimental control.

WA aimed at measuring essay quality within the usual classroom. Thus, WA teachers were encouraged to do their "usual" activities for such essays. Some assigned students to type the results of a research project. For example, one class might have a writing session, with new topics or assigned topics which might be specific to the class.

As data collection proceeded, there was little likelihood for the regular teachers to have contacts with the other teacher-readers (who were from a different state). PEG's success would be measured by how well PEG predicted each of the test ratings (teacher and second reader), and their standardized average.

On average, the two judges correlated about .50 with each other, rating the essays within a class. For the WA experiment, there was no extra penalty or reward for the students in these classes because any grade received would depend directly on the teacher, and the teacher was blind to the second rating.

SCORING FOR WRITE AMERICA

Again, we ran multiple tests with 80% and 20% samples (formative and validation essays) to see how well the mean scores within that 20% validation sample were predicted. After repeated trials, a mean prediction was achieved for the validation sample of .69. When the Spearman–Brown Prophecy Formula was applied, it produced an equivalent to three teacher raters. This seemed like a powerful enough aid for teachers who wanted to help their students learn to write. Thus, the results suggested that PEG could be effectively used as a "Teacher's Helper" for the classroom.

College teachers often use assistants for such grading, however for primary and secondary schools, such help is rare. Indeed, it is unlikely that one grading assistant would be as accurate as the multiple-prediction obtained through the WA experiment. Table 3.3 summarizes the results of this effort.

MORE RECENT WORK WITH PEG

In 1993, PEG was modified in several significant ways. The project acquired several parsers and various dictionaries. In addition, the software now incorporated special collections and classification schemes. A number of tests explored these additions to determine if they provided distinctions among levels of writing ability. The results were reported during various professional meetings and in the research literature (Page, 1994).

TABLE 3.3
Correlations Between Judges and Write-America Predictions

| | Teacher | Teachers | | Write America | | Computer |
		Reader2	MeanJudge	Pred_Tch	Pred_R2	Pred_Mean
Teacher	.481	.857		.621	.611	.613
Reader 2	.481			.588	.581	.686
MeanJudge	.857	.858		.679	.686	.686
Pred_Tch	.621	.538		.679	.954	.977
Pred_R2	.611	.581	.686	.954		.987
Pred_Mean	.613		.576	.686	.977	.987

Note. Teachers=the regular teachers in each class, who assigned essays and graded them for their own students; Reader2's = were other teachers who graded students they did not know; MeanJudge = the standardized average of the two raters; Pred_Tch = Predicted Teacher; Pred_R2 = Predicted R**2 where **2 is the square of R; Pred_Mean = Number of essays – 3,651. In this experiment, Write America is equal to three or more teacher-advisers. The key result is how well PEG (the computer) predicted these teachers and their average ratings. Used by permission.

PEG GOES ON THE WORLD WIDE WEB

Shermis, Mzumara, Olson, & Harrington (2001) reported on the first work with PEG employing a web-based interface. That experiment examined the use of an automated essay system to evaluate its effectiveness for the scoring of placement tests (a "low stakes test") as part of an enrollment management system. The design was similar to those of other PEG experiments. Approximately 1,200 essays were scored holistically by four raters. Of the 1,200 essays, 800 were used for model formation and approximately 400 were used as a validation sample. Although human judges correlated with each other at .62, the PEG system correlated with the judges at .71. Also, the speed of the new interface meant that about three essays were graded every second. Furthermore, the cycle time, from the submission of the essay to producing a report, was about two minutes. PEG turned out to be a "cost-effective means of grading essays of this type (Shermis, Mzumura, Olson & Harrington, 2001, p. 247)."

INFLUENCE OF PROMPTS

Shermis, Rasmussen, Rajecki, Olson, & Marsiglio (2001) obtained PEG scorings of essays, and made useful discoveries about prompts: Both human and machine raters "tended to higher scores for analytic and practical themes, and lower scores for those involving emotion" (p. 154). This research could help increase the awareness of the need for "fairness" in such prompts or at least engender greater care in the generation of prompts. The researchers also suggested that some thought might be given to weighting prompts much in the same way that dives are weighted in a swimming competition—harder dives are given greater weights. AES could be a mechanism by which such weights are assigned (Shermis, Rasmussen, Rajecki, Olson, & Marsiglio, 2001).

PEG AND TEACHERS

Although most of the research with PEG has concentrated on evaluating it with regard to its reliability and validity, a few researchers have focused on central questions of PEG's potential, especially in the schools.   Most of these studies analyzed teacher intentions and probable behaviors, assuming they could get access to an automated essay scorer like PEG (Truman 1994, 1995, 1996, 1997, 1998). Research concluded the following:

> English and language arts teachers have made it clear that they would welcome some assistance when it comes to evaluating and grading essays They report feeling that they should make more writing assignments, but are not doing so because of the time required to evaluate and provide feedback (p5)."

But the researchers also caution: "…it is almost certainly the case that, at this stage, using PEG in the classroom is more complicated than teachers and administrators think it will be".

HAS COMPUTER GRADING NOW BEEN "ACCEPTED?"

Has computer grading now been "accepted?" This may seem, to some, a startling question. Lack of acceptance has been circulating around since the mid-1960's when PEG was first developed, and even since the rigorous blind tests in the mid-90's (and the advent of other competing AES systems), the notion has still been strongly resisted. However, perhaps it is useful to consider the question of AES acceptability within a broader context. All important testing does a job that is inherently unpopular. It differentiates among individuals, and often ties these differences to major decisions — admission to selective programs, professional advancement, licensing, and certification. Just as multiple-choice testing still has many critics, we can expect that computerized grading of essays will continue to be problematic for some. Here we consider what objections may be especially interesting: there are the humanist objections, the defensive objections, and the construct objections.

Humanist objections

The humanist objections go back to the beginning of the computer revolution. It was asserted that certain choices require "human" knowledge and background wisdom, whereas the computer will do "only what it is programmed to do." It will not "understand" or "appreciate" an essay, critics said, and so it cannot measure what a human judge measures. Its judgments should be flatly rejected.
   Such arguments were so common 50 years ago that Alan Turing (1912–54), a very gifted British computer scientist, devised a response in the form of his classic

"difference game" — still widely known as the "Turing Test," referred to at the beginning of this chapter. Imagine, Turing asked, that you have a person behind one door and a computer behind another, and that you don't know which is which. You are allowed to slip notes under the door, read the printed responses, and try to determine which door hides the computer. If you are unable to find a relevant question that will reveal which is the machine the computer wins the game.

However, suppose we play a newer version of this game. We now have seven doors, with human raters behind six of them and a computer behind the seventh. We pass essays under all seven doors and get back a score (or set of scores, if we're rating traits). We examine the scores and continue to pass essays and collect ratings. Can we tell which door hides the computer? When we study the results with 300 essays, we find that we can easily identify the computer. PEG agrees best with the other judges!

Where does this leave the humanist objection? PEG has shown the world one solution to the Turing Test.

Defensive Objections

Defensive objections boil down to questions about the assumptions of the essay environment. What about playful or hostile students? A mischievous student might do anything to belittle or embarrass the testing program. Our research on the Praxis Series essays has been conducted only on "good-faith" efforts — written by motivated students eager to receive good scores. In the "real world," we would need to defend against writers who generate essays under "bad-faith" conditions.

A number of strategies could be undertaken to protect against such possibilities, and most of the AES systems have subroutines that attempt to flag such efforts. For example, PEG has one subroutine that alerts the system to common vulgarities that are often associated with "bad-faith" essays. I use this as an example of one of the many subroutines that might be employed. The PEG subroutines are so rich in descriptive variables that bizarre elements could be flagged in many ways, and the odd essay marked and set aside for human inspection. Such setting-aside of essays is already common in large-scale, human-judge assessments. It is done when essays are judged as off-the-subject or unreadable — or when differences between the judges' ratings are unacceptably large. Thus, it might be possible to identify a large proportion of "bad-faith" essays. Although it has not been demonstrated that PEG could do this comprehensively, it is a welcomed research challenge.

In the meantime, the question is moot for the majority of AES applications. Most operations require at least one parallel human reading for high-stakes situations (as contrasted with classroom and other routine uses).

Construct Objections

Construct objections focus on whether the computer is counting variables that are truly "important." These detractors are looking for the trins, not the proxes. These critics don't accept the correlations that are typically provided in AES research because the grading engines might be still measuring the wrong things which are "merely statistical" as they relate to writing quality.

However, one must ask the following in return: How do we tell that human judges are qualified? In any large-scale assessment, there will be human judges who are not invited to return. Which ones are they? Generally the answer is, "Those whose correlations with other judges are unacceptably low." Perhaps the one "really qualified" judge is the one who is dropped, but one will never know because the standard way of measuring a judge's accuracy is to correlate an individual's ratings with those of other judges.

Why, then, isn't such a comparison appropriate for the computer program? Surely the reason can't be the absence of human brain cells, and if we accept the criterion for evaluating the computer that we already use for evaluating humans, it is pretty clear from the research that one judge asked back for next year's assessment will be — the computer program.

Today, with the kinds of proof in this summary, and with the citation of so many successful trials — we do appear to have reached the sort of proof that makes clear a functioning, versatile, effective, intellectual system. Obviously, we have a new intellectual system, for the future of mental measurement. In one form or another, the underlying, traditional PEG is bound to have a bright future, whatever the divergent, minor, and major forms it will pursue in the future.

REFERENCES

Ajay, H.B., Tillett, P., & Page, E.B (1973). *Analysis of essays by computer (AEC–II)*. Final Report to the National Center for Educational Research and Development Washington, DC: Office of Education, Bureau of Research.

Applebee, A. N., Langer, J. A., Jenkins, L. B., Mullis, I. V. S., Foertsch, M.A (1990) *Learning to write in our nation's schools: Instruction and achievement in 1988 at grades 4, 8, and 12* (Rpt No 19–W–02). Washington, DC: National Assessment of Educational Progress.

Johnson, E., & Zwick, R. (1990) Focusing the new design: The NAEP technical report (Research Report 19–TR–20). Princeton, NJ: Educational Testing Service.

Lauer, J., & Asher, J. W. (1988) *Composition research: Empirical design.* New York: Oxford University Press.

Page, E. B. (1966a). The imminence of grading essays by computer. *Phi Delta Kappan, 48,* 238–243.

Page, E. B. (1966b). Grading essays by computer: Progress Report Invitational Conference on Testing Problems (pp. 86–100). Princeton, NJ: Educational Testing Service.

Page, E. B. (1994). Computer grading of student prose, using modern concepts and software. *Journal of Experimental Education, 62(2),* 127–142.

Page, E. B., Fisher, G. A., & Fisher, M. A. (1968). Project essay grade: A FORTRAN program for statistical analysis of prose. *British Journal of Mathematical and Statistical Psychology, 21,* 139.

Page, E. B., & Paulus, D. H. (1968). *The analysis of essays by computer.* Final Report to the U.S. Department of Health, Education and Welfare Washington, DC: Office of Education, Bureau of Research.

Page, E. B., & Petersen, N. S (1995) The Computer moves into essay grading: Updating the ancient test. *Phi Delta Kappan, 76*(6), 561–566.

Page, E. B., Poggio, J. P., & Keith, T. Z. (1997) *Computer analysis of student essays: Finding trait differences in the student profile.* Symposium given at American Educational Research Association meetings, Chicago.

Shermis, M. D., Rasmussen, J. L., Rajecki, D. W., Olsen, J., & Marsiglio, C. (2001). All prompts are created equal, but some prompts are more equal than other prompts. *Journal of Applied Measurement, 2*(2), 154–170.

Truman, D.L (1994). *"Teacher's Helper" and the high school classroom: Some promising early results.* Symposium conducted at the annual meetings of the South Atlantic Modern Language Association, Baltimore.

Truman, D. L. (1995) *"Teacher's Helper": Applying Project Essay Grade in English classes.* Symposium conducted at the annual meeting of the American Educational Research Association, San Francisco.

Truman, D. L. (1996, April). Tracking progress in Student Writing: Repeated PEG Measures? Symposium conducted at the annual meeting of the National Council of Measurement in Education. New York, N.Y.

Truman, D. L. (1997, March). *How classroom teachers may track student progress in writing.* Symposium conducted at the annual meeting of the American Educational Research Association. Chicago, IL.

Truman, D. L. (1998, April). *Tracking student progress in essay writing.* Symposium presented at the annual meeting of the American Educational Research Association. San Diego.

Wical, K., & Mugele, R. (1993, January). Power Edit analysis of prose: How the system is designed and works Paper presented at the annual meetings of NCARE, Greensboro, NC.

4

A Text Categorization Approach to Automated Essay Grading

Leah S. Larkey
W. Bruce Croft
University of Massachusetts, Amherst

Researchers have attempted to automate the grading of student essays since the 1960s (Page, 1994). The approach has been to define a large number of objectively measurable features in the essays, such as essay length, average word length, and so forth, and use multiple linear regression to try to predict the scores that human graders would give these essays. Even in this early work, results were surprisingly good. The scores assigned by computer correlated at around .50 with the English teachers who provided the manually assigned grades. This was about as well as the English teachers correlated with each other. More recent systems consider more complex features of essays, for example, work at ETS (Educational Testing Service) has attempted to simulate criteria similar to what a human judge would use, emphasizing sophisticated techniques from computational linguistics, to extract syntactic, rhetorical, and content features (Burstein, et al. 1998). The Intelligent Essay Grader (IEA) attempts to represent the semantic content of essays by using features that group associated words together via singular value decomposition (SVD) (Landauer, 2000).

The present approach to automated essay grading involves statistical classifiers. Although this approach was a new way to attack the essay grading problem when we first reported it (Larkey, 1998), it is widely used in information retrieval and text categorization applications. Binary classifiers were trained to distinguish "good" from "bad" essays, and the scores output by these classifiers were used to rank essays and assign grades to them. The grades based on these classifiers can either be used alone, or combined with other simple variables in a linear regression. This research measures how well these classifier-based features compare and combine with other simple text features.

BACKGROUND CONCEPTS FROM INFORMATION RETRIEVAL AND TEXT CATEGORIZATION

Any technique for automatically assigning numbers to text must first represent documents in terms of component features, and define measures (of quality, of similarity between documents, of probability of class membership, etc.) based on those representations. This work uses the simple "bag of words" representation of text, common in information retrieval and text categorization research. Text (a document, or a set of documents) is characterized by the set of words it contains regardless of the order in which the words occur. Often words are stemmed, to equate regular singular and plural forms of nouns (e.g., dog, dogs), and different inflections of regular verbs (jump, jumps, jumped, etc.). Sometimes slightly more complex units like word bigrams are included in the "bag."

Such representations often take into account the number of times each stem occurs, representing text as a vector where each component of the vector is a word (or stem), whose weight is some function of the number of times the word occurs in the document. An extremely successful form of weighting, widely used in information retrieval, is known as $tf\,idf$ weighting. In its simplest form, a $tf\,idf$ weight is the product $\log(tf) \times idf$, where tf is the number of times the word occurs in a document, and $idf = \log(N\,/\,df)$, where N is the total number of documents in the (training) collection, and df is the number of documents containing the term. Thus, a word receives more weight if it occurs more times in the document, but it receives less weight if it occurs in a large number of documents. In practice, one usually uses a version of $tf\,idf$ which includes some smoothing and normalization (Robertson and Walker, 1994).

Such simple representations have been highly successful in information retrieval and text categorization tasks. One can retrieve documents by computing distances between query and document vectors (Salton, 1989), and classify documents by computing distances between document vectors, or between document vectors and document class vectors.

These vector representations are also the starting point for probabilistic models of information retrieval, which estimate the probability that a document satisfies a query (Turtle, 1991; van Rijsbergen, 1979) and probabilistic models for text categorization, which estimate the probability that a document belongs to a class (e.g. (Lewis, 1992b, and McCallum, 1998) and see (Mitchell, 1997) for many examples). The language models now dominating information retrieval research (Ponte & Crofts 1998; Miller, 1999) are also based on these simple vector representations of documents.

ESSAY GRADING AS CATEGORIZATION

The starting point for this research is a conception of essay grading as a text categorization problem. Crudely put, does an essay belong to the class of "good" essays? From a training set of manually categorized data, derive a mathematical function called a classifier, whose output can be interpreted as measuring how well an essay fits the "good" category. It may seem strange to treat grading as a binary classification problem (good" versus "bad" rather than an n-way problem, that is, a choice among n>2 alternatives, with a class for each possible numeric grade, 1 through 6. However, poorly written essays with the same grade do not necessarily resemble each other. Pilot studies performed for this project showed better performance in training a classifier to recognize a good essay, than in training classifiers to identify bad versus fair versus mediocre, etc. essays.

BAYESIAN INDEPENDENCE CLASSIFIERS

Bayesian independence classifiers are one of many similar kinds of probabilistic classifiers which estimate the probability that a document is a positive exemplar of a category, given the presence of certain features (words) in the document. First proposed by Maron (1961), they are examples of general linear classifiers (see the excellent overview in (Lewis, 1996)). Fuhr (1989) and Lewis (1992b) have explored improvements to Maron's model. The current model is similar to Lewis's, and has the following characteristics: First, a set of features (terms) is selected separately for each classifier. Bayes theorem is used to estimate the probability of category membership for each category and each document. Probability estimates are based on the co-occurrence of categories and the selected features in the training corpus, and some independence assumptions (Cooper, 1991).

In particular, The Bayesian classifier estimates the log probability that the essay D belongs to the class of "good" documents:

$$\log P(C \mid D) = \log P(C) + \sum_i \begin{cases} \log(P(A_i \mid C)/P(A_i)) \\ \quad \text{if } D \text{ contains feature } A_i \\ \log(P(\overline{A_i} \mid C)/P(\overline{A_i})) \\ \quad \text{if } D \text{ does not contain feature } A_i \end{cases}$$

Where $P(C)$, is the prior probability that any document is in class C, the class of "good" documents, $P(A_i \mid C)$ is the conditional probability of a document having feature A_i, given that the document is in class C. $P(A_i)$ is the prior probability that a randomly chosen document would contain feature A_i. $P(\overline{A_i} \mid C)$ is the conditional probability that a document does not have feature A_i given that the document is in class C, and $P(\overline{A_i})$ is the prior probability that a document does not contain feature A_i. This is based on Lewis's binary model (Lewis, 1992), which assigns zeros or "1"s for feature weights depending on whether terms are present or absent in a document, rather than using the number of times the term is present. These probabilities are estimated in the obvious way; for example, $P(A_i)$ is the number of documents containing feature A_i divided by the total number of documents (with some smoothing).

There are more sophisticated models that take term frequencies into account (see (Mitchell, 1997), for some possibilities), but the simpler form works well, especially with so little training data.

k-NEAREST-NEIGHBOR CLASSIFICATION

In addition to the classification approach described earlier, this study also includes k-nearest-neighbor classification, one of the simplest methods for classifying new documents (essays) based on a training set. This method first finds the k essays in the training collection that are most similar to the test essay using some similarity measure. The test essay then receives a score which is a similarity weighted average of the grades that were manually assigned to these k retrieved training essays (Duda & Hart, 1973). This approach is a more conventional application of n-way classification to the essay grading problem, in that it asks the question whether an essay is more like essays which received a grade of 1, 2, and so forth.

THE EXPERIMENTAL DATA

Five data sets were obtained from Educational Testing Service. Each essay in each set had been manually graded. The sets varied in the number of points in their grading scale and the size of the data sets. They covered widely different content areas and were aimed at different age groups. The first set, Soc, was a social studies question where certain facts were expected to be covered. The second set, Phys, was a physics question requiring an enumeration and discussion of different kinds of energy transformations in a particular situation. The third set, Law, required the evaluation of a legal argument presented in the question. The last two questions sets, G1 and G2, were general questions from an exam for college students who want to pursue graduate studies. G1 was a very general opinion question intended to evaluate how well the student could present a logical argument. G2 presented a specific scenario with an argument the student had to evaluate. All the questions except G1 required the student to cover certain points. In contrast, a good answer to G1 would be judged less by what was covered than by how it was expressed.

For the first three sets, Soc, Phys, and Law, we received one manual score per training essay, based on an unknown number of graders. The last two sets, G1 and G2, were manually scored by two graders. In addition to the scores assigned by the two graders, each essay was assigned a "final" score, which was usually, but not always, the average of the two graders' scores summarizes the characteristics of each data set. The columns headed *Train* and *Test* indicate the number of manually graded essays in each subset of documents for each type of essay. The column headed *Grades* indicates the number of points in the grading scale for that essay.

TABLE 4.1
Data Sets Used in Automatic Essay Grading Experiments

	Train	Test	Grades
Soc	233	50	4
Phys	586	80	4
Law	223	50	7
G1	403	232	6
G2	383	225	6

A standard technique in training statistical classifiers is to set aside part of the training data as a tuning set to avoid overfitting and to choose parameters and methods based on the results on the tuning set. This tuning is more likely to generalize to the test data. However, preliminary work with different divisions of one of these data sets showed better results when all the training data were used in all phases of training, due to the small size of all these data sets. It should be noted that no test sets were used for any tuning or selection of parameters. All tuning, including finding thresholds, was carried out on the training set.

EXPERIMENT 1

Experiment 1 concerned the first three sets of essays, Soc, Phys, and Law. Bayesian classifiers and k-nearest-neighbor classifiers were trained and their performance was compared with the linear regression approach using text-complexity features. Finally, everything was combined by using the two types of classifier outputs as variables in the linear regression, along with the text-complexity features. In all cases, thresholds were derived to divide up the continuum of predicted scores into the appropriate number of each grade.

The two phases of training, feature selection and training of coefficients, were carried out in manner similar to that of (Larkey & Croft, 1996), and are described more fully later.

Bayesian Classifiers. Several binary Bayesian independence classifiers were trained to distinguish better essays from worse essays, dividing the set at different points. For example, for essays graded on a 4-point scale, a binary classifier was trained to distinguish "1"s from "2"s, "3"s, and "4"s, another to distinguish "3"s and "4"s from "1"s and "2"s, and another to distinguish 4's from "1"s, "2"s, and "3"s.

Feature Selection. First, all occurrences of 418 stopwords were removed from the essays. The remaining terms were stemmed using the *kstem* stemmer (Krovetz, 1993). Any stemmed terms found in at least three essays in the positive training set were feature candidates. The selection of features from this set was carried out independently for each binary classifier as follows.

Expected mutual information (EMIM) (van Rijsbergen, 1979) was computed for each feature, and the features were rank ordered by EMIM score. From this set, the final number of features chosen for the classifier was tuned on the training data. Classifier scores were computed for a range of feature set sizes, for each document in the training set. The feature set size which produced training document scores yielding the highest correlation with the manual scores was considered optimal.[1]

k-nearest-neighbor classifiers. In this implementation of *k*-nearest-neighbor, the similarity between a test essay and the training set was measured by the Inquery retrieval system, a probabilistic retrieval system using *tf idf* weighting (Callan, et al., 1995). The entire test document was submitted as a query against a database of training documents. The resulting ranking score, or belief score, was used as the similarity metric. The parameter *k*, the number of top-ranked documents over which to average, was tuned on the training set, to choose the value producing the highest correlation with the manual ratings. This process yielded values of 45, 55, and 90, for the *Soc, Phys,* and *Law* essay sets.

---

[1] A criterion of average precision for the binary classifier yielded very similar results.

Text-Complexity Features. The following eleven features were used to characterize each document:

1. The number of characters in the document (*Chars*)
2. The number of words in the document (*Words*).
3. The number of different words in the document (*Diffwds*).
4. The fourth root of the number of words in the document, as suggested by Page (Page, 1994) (*Rootwds*).
5. The number of sentences in the document (*Sents*).
6. Average word length (*Wordlen* = *Chars/Words*).
7. Average sentence length (*Sentlen* = *Words/Sents*).
8. Number of words longer than five characters (*BW5*).
9. Number of words longer than six characters (*BW6*).
10. Number of words longer than seven characters (*BW7*).
11. Number of words longer than eight characters (*BW8*).

Linear Regression. The SPSS (Statistical Package for the Social Sciences) stepwise linear regression package was used to select those variables which accounted for the highest variance in the data, and to compute coefficients for them. Regressions were performed using three different combinations of variables: (a) the 11 text-complexity variables (b) just the Bayesian classifiers, and (c) all the variables - the 11 text-complexity variables, the k-nearest-neighbor score, and the scores output by the Bayesian classifiers.

Thresholds. Using the regression equation derived from the training data, a predicted score was calculated for each training essay, and the essays were rank-ordered by that score. Category cutoffs were chosen to put the correct number of training essays into each grade. This technique is known as *proportional assignment* (Lewis, 1992). These cutoff scores were then used to determine the assignment of grades from scores in the test set. For the individual classifiers, cutoff scores were derived the same way, but based on the k-nearest-neighbor and Bayesian classifier scores rather than on a regression score.

Measures. For this first experiment, three different measures capture the extent to which grades were assigned correctly. The Pearson product-moment correlation (r), the proportion of cases where the same score was assigned (Exact), and the proportion of cases where the score assigned was at most one point away from the correct score (Adjacent). Unlike the correlation, these measures capture how much one scoring procedure actually agrees with another scoring procedure. Of particularly interest in these experiments was to compare our algorithm's performance on these three measures with the two human graders. Individual judges' grades were available only for the last two data sets, G1 and G2, which are discussed in Experiment 2.

Results

Tables 4.2, 4.3, and 4.4 show the results on the first three data sets, Soc, Phys, and Law. The column labeled *Variable* indicates which variable or group of variables contributed to the score. *Text* indicates the linear regression involving the text-complexity variables listed above. *Knn* indicates the *k*-nearest-neighbor classifier alone. *B1*, *B2*, and so forth indicate the individual Bayesian classifiers trained on different partitions of the training essays into "good" and "bad." *All Bayes* indicates the composite grader based on linear regression of the Bayesian classifiers. *All* is the grader based on the linear regression using all the available variables. When there is a number included in parentheses next to the variable name, it shows the value of the parameter set for that variable. For Knn, that parameter is the number of training documents that contribute to the score. For the Bayesian classifiers, the parameter is the number of terms included in the classifier. The columns labeled *Exact*, *Adjacent*, and *r* show results using the measures described above. The column labeled Components shows the variables that the stepwise linear regression included in the regression equation for that combination of variables. Only conditions involving linear regression have an entry in this column. (Note, the results for all five data sets are summarized in Figure 4.1).

TABLE 4.2
Results on *Soc* Data Set

Variable	Exact	Adjacent	r	Components
Text	.56	.94	.73	BW6, Rootwds, Wordlen
Knn (45)	.54	.96	.69	
B1 (200)	.58	.94	.71	
B2 (180)	.66	1.00	.77	
B3 (140)	.60	1.00	.77	
B4 (240)	.62	.98	.78	
All Bayes	.62	1.00	.78	B2, B3
All	.60	1.00	.77	Sents, B2,B3

Note. Knn = *k*-nearest-neighbor classifier; B1 = A binary Bayesian classifier trained to distinguish essays which received a score of 1 from all other scores; B2 = A binary Bayesian classifier trained to distinguish essays which received a score of 2 and above from essays which received scores below 2; B3 = A binary Bayesian classifier trained to distinguish essays which received a score of 3 and above from essays which received scores below 3; B4 = A binary Bayesian classifier trained to distinguish essays which received a score of 4 and above from essays which received scores below 4; BW6 = Number of words longer than 6 characters; Rootwds = The fourth root of the number of words in the document ; Wordlen = Average word length *(Chars/Words)*; All Bayes = Score based on stepwise linear regression of all the Bn's (Bayesian classifiers) above; Sents = The number of sentences in the document.

TABLE 4.3
Results on *Phys* data set

Variable	Exact	Adjacent	r	Components
Text	.47	.91	.56	Sents, Wordlen, Rootwds
Knn (55)	.44	.90	.53	
B1 (320)	.51	.90	.61	
B2 (480)	.50	.89	.59	
B3 (420)	.55	.90	.63	
B4 (240)	.49	.89	.61	B1,B3
All Bayes	.50	.89	.63	B1,B3
All	.47	.93	.59	B2, B3, B4, BW7, Diffwds, Wordlen, Rootwds

Note. Knn = *k*-nearest-neighbor classifier; B1 = A binary Bayesian classifier trained to distinguish essays which received a score of 1 from all other scores; B2 = A binary Bayesian classifier trained to distinguish essays which received scores of 2 and above from essays which received scores below 2; B3 = A binary Bayesian classifier trained to distinguish essays which received scores of 3 and above from essays which received scores below 3 ; B4 = A binary Bayesian classifier trained to distinguish essays which received scores of 4 and above from essays which received scores below 4; BW6 = A binary Bayesian classifier trained to distinguish essays which received scores of 6 and above from essays which received scores below 6; Rootwds = The fourth root of the number of words in the document; Wordlen = Average word length (*Chars/Words*); All Bayes = Score based on stepwise linear regression of all the Bn's (Bayesian classifiers) above; BW7 = A binary Bayesian classifier trained to distinguish essays which received scores of 7 and above from essays which received scores below 7; Diffwds = The number of different words in the document.

TABLE 4.4
Results on *Law* data set

Variable	Exact	Adjacent	r	Components
Text	.24	.66	.57	Rootwds
Knn(90)	.40	.66	.61	
B1 (50)	.36	.54	.60	
B2 (120)	.32	.72	.75	
B3 (300)	.28	.72	.74	
B4 (300)	.28	.84	.76	
B5 (120)	.36	.82	.76	
B6 (160)	.42	.86	.79	
B7 (160)	.32	.78	.78	
All Bayes	.32	.84	.79	B2, B3,B6
All	.36	.84	.77	B2, B3,B6, Knn, BW6

Note. Knn = *k*-nearest-neighbor classifier; B1 = A binary Bayesian classifier trained to distinguish essay which received a score of 1 from all other scores; B2 = A binary Bayesian classifier trained to distinguish essays which received scores of 2 and above from essays which received scores below 2; B3 = A binary Bayesian classifier trained to distinguish essays which received scores of 3 and above from essays which received scores below 3; B4 = A binary Bayesian classifier trained to distinguish essays which received scores of 4 and above from essays which received scores below 4; B5 = A binary Bayesian classifier trained to distinguish essays which received scores of 5 and above from essays which received scores below 5; B6 = A binary Bayesian classifier trained to distinguish essays which received scores of 6 and above from essays which received scores below 6; B7 = A binary Bayesian classifier trained to distinguish essays which received scores of 7 and above from essays which received scores below 7; All Bayes = Score based on stepwise linear regression of all the Bn's (Bayesian classifiers) above.

Performance on the *Soc* data set appears very good; the *Phys* set is less so. Both were graded on a 4-point scale, yet all three measures are consistently lower on the *Phys* data set. Performance on the *Law* set is also quite good. Although the Exact and Adjacent scores are lower than on the *Soc* data set, one would expect this on a seven-point scale compared to a four-point scale. The correlations are in roughly the same range. Some generalizations can be made across all three data sets, despite the differences in level of performance. First, the Bayesian independence classifiers performed better than the text-complexity variables alone or the *k*-nearest-neighbor classifier. In the Text condition, *Rootwds*, the fourth root of essay length, was always selected as one of the variables. In the *All* condition, in which all available variables were in the regression, the length variables were not as obviously important. Two of the three sets included a word length variable (*Wordlen, BW6, BW7*) and two of the three sets included an essay length variable (*Sents, Diffwds, Rootwds*). In the All condition, at least two Bayesian classifiers were always selected, but the *k*-nearest-neighbor score was selected for only one of the three data sets. Finally, the performance of the final regression equation (*All*) was not consistently better than the performance using the regression-selected Bayesian classifiers (*All Bayes*).

Discussion of Experiment 1. The performance of these various algorithms on automatic essay grading is varied. Performance on the Soc data set seemed very good, although it is hard to judge how good it should be. It is striking that a certain fairly consistent level of performance was achieved using the Bayesian classifiers, and that adding text–complexity features and *k*-nearest-neighbor scores did not appear to produce much better performance. The additional variables improved performance on the training data, which is why they were included, but the improvement did not always hold on the independent test data. These different variables seem to measure the same underlying properties of the data, so beyond a certain minimal coverage, addition of new variables added only redundant information. This impression was confirmed by an examination of a correlation matrix containing all the variables that went into the regression equation.

These results seem to differ from previous work, which typically found at least one essay length variable to dominate. In Page (1994), a large proportion of the variance was always accounted for by the fourth root of the essay length, and in Landauer, et al (1997), a vector length variable was very important. In contrast, our results only found length variables to be prominent when Bayesian classifiers were not included in the regression. In all three data sets, the regression selected *Rootwds*, the fourth root of the essay length in words, as an important variable when only text complexity variables were included. In contrast, when Bayesian classifiers were included in the regression equation, at least two Bayesian classifiers were always selected, and length variables were not consistently selected. A likely explanation is that the Bayesian classifiers and length variable captured the same patterns in the data. An essay that received a high score from a Bayesian classifier would contain a large number of terms with positive weights for that classifier, and would thus have to be long enough to contain that large number of terms.

EXPERIMENT 2

Experiment 2 covered data sets G1 and G2. Grades were assigned by two separate human judges as well as the final grade given to each essay. This permitted a comparison between the level of agreement on the automatic grading and the final grade with the level of agreement found between the two human graders. This comparison makes the absolute levels of performance more interpretable than in Experiment 1. The training procedure was the same as in Experiment 1.

Results

Table 4.5 and Table 4.6 summarize the results on the last two data sets. The results on G2 are completely consistent with Experiment 1. Bayesian classifiers were superior to text-complexity and k-nearest-neighbor methods. The combination of all classifiers was at best only slightly better than the combination of Bayesian classifiers.

On G1, the exception to the pattern was that the text-complexity variables alone performed as well as the Bayesian classifiers. The combination classifier was superior to all the others, particularly in the exact score.

TABLE 4.5
Results on *G1* data set

Variable	Exact	Adjacent	r	Components
Text	.51	.94	.86	Diffwds, Sents,BW6
Knn (220)	.42	.84	.75	
B1 (300)	.36	.82	.69	
B2 (320)	.47	.95	.84	
B3 (300)	.48	.94	.84	
B4 (280)	.47	.92	.83	
B5 (380)	.47	.94	.82	
B6 (600)	.50	.96	.86	
All Bayes	.50	.96	.86	B1, B2, B5, B6
All	.55	.97	.88	B1, B5, B6, BW5, BW6, Sents, Rootwds, Knn

Note. Knn = k-nearest-neighbor classifier; B1 = A binary Bayesian classifier trained to distinguish essays which received a score of 1 from all other scores; B2 = A binary Bayesian classifier trained to distinguish essays which received scores of 2 and above from essays which received scores below 2; B3 = A binary Bayesian classifier trained to distinguish essays which received scores of 3 and above from essays which received scores below 3; B4 = A binary Bayesian classifier trained to distinguish essays which received scores of 4 and above from essays which received scores below 4; B5 = A binary Bayesian classifier trained to distinguish essays which received scores of 5 and above from essays which received scores below 5; B6 = A binary Bayesian classifier trained to distinguish essays which received scores of 6 and above from essays which received scores below 6; All Bayes = Score based on stepwise linear regression of all the Bn's (Bayesian classifiers) above; Diffwds = The number of different words in the document; Sents = The number of sentences in the document; BW6 = Number of words longer than 6 characters ; BW5 = Number of words longer than 5 characters; Rootwds = The fourth root of the number of words in the document.

TABLE 4.6
Results on *G2* data set

Variable	Exact	Adjacent	r	Components
Text	.42	.92	.83	BW5
Knn (180)	.34	.84	.77	
B1 (600)	.36	.86	.77	
B2 (320)	.48	.95	.85	
B3 (300)	.46	.96	.86	
B4 (280)	.52	.95	.85	
B5 (300)	.48	.95	.85	
B6 (680)	.48	.95	.84	
All Bayes	.52	.96	.86	B1, B3, B5
All	.52	.96	.88	B1, B3, B5, BW8, Diffwds, Rootwds

Note. Knn = *k*-nearest-neighbor classifier; B1 = A binary Bayesian classifier trained to distinguish essay which received a score of 1 from all other scores; B2 = A binary Bayesian classifier trained to distinguish essays which received scores of 2 and above from essays which received scores below 2; B3 = A binary Bayesian classifier trained to distinguish essays which received scores of 3 and above from essays which received scores below 3; B4 = A binary Bayesian classifier trained to distinguish essays which received scores of 4 and above from essays which received scores below 4; B5 = A binary Bayesian classifier trained to distinguish essays which received scores of 5 and above from essays which received scores below 5; B6 = A binary Bayesian classifier trained to distinguish essays which received scores of 6 and above from essays which received scores below 6; BW5 = Number of words longer than 5 characters; BW8 = Number of words longer than 8 characters; All Bayes = Score based on stepwise linear regression of all the Bn's (Bayesian classifiers) above; Diffwds = The number of different words in the document; Rootwds = The fourth root of the number of words in the document.

Comparison with Human Graders

Table 4.7 shows the agreement between the final manually assigned grades and the grade automatically assigned by the combination All. For comparison, the agreement between the two human graders also is shown. The numbers are very close.

TABLE 4.7
Comparison with Human Graders

	Exact	Adjacent	r
G1: auto vs. manual(final)	.55	.97	.88
G1: manual A vs. B	.56	.95	.87
G2: auto vs. manual(final)	.52	.96	.86
G2: manual A vs. B	.56	.95	.88

Note.. G1 = A set of essays on one general question; G2 = A set of essays responding to a fairly specific question .

DISCUSSION

Automated essay grading works surprisingly well. Correlations are generally in the high .70s and .80s, depending on essay type and presumably on the quality of the human ratings. These levels are comparable to those attained by Landauer (1997) and Page (1994).

For the *Exact* and *Adjacent* measures, our algorithms found the "correct" grade around 50% to 65% of the time on the four- and six-point rating scales, and were within one point of the "correct" grade 90% to 100% of the time. This is about the same as the agreement between the two human judges on G1 and G2 and is comparable to what other researchers have found.

Previous work, particularly by Page (1994), has had great success with text-complexity variables like those listed in the Text Complexity Features section earlier. We found these variables to be adequate only for one of the five data sets, G1. G1 was the only opinion question in the group. For this type of question, the fluency with which ideas are expressed may be more important than the content of those ideas. However, some of Page's variables were more sophisticated than ours; for example those involving a measure of how successfully a parsing algorithm could parse the essay. It is possible the use of more sophisticated text-complexity measures would have improved the performance.

It was surprising to find that the best Bayesian classifiers contained so many features. The usual guidelines are to have a ratio of 5 to 10 training samples per feature, although others recommend having as many as 50 to 100 (Lewis, 1992a). Our tuning procedure yielded as many as 680 features for some classifiers, which seemed large, and motivated some additional post hoc analyses to see how the test results varied with this parameter. On the training data, variations in number of features yielded quite small changes in the correlations between the binary classifier scores and the grade, except at the extreme low end. These variations produced larger differences in the test data. In fact, the tuning on the training data did choose roughly the best performing classifiers for the test data. It might have made more sense to tune the number of features on a separate set of data, but there were not enough essays in this set to separate the training data into two parts. Given that the large number of features really was improving the classifiers, why would this be so?

Normally a classifier is doing the job of inferring whether a document is about something or relevant to something. One expects the core of a category to be characterized by a few key concepts, and perhaps some larger number of highly associated concepts. The job of feature selection is to find these. In contrast, in essay grading, the classifier is trying to determine whether an essay is a "good" essay about a topic. This kind of judgment depends on the exhaustiveness with which a topic is treated, and it can be treated many different ways, hence a very large number of different features can contribute to the "goodness" of an essay.

This large number of terms in the binary classifiers is a likely explanation of why essay length variables were not found to be as important as in other studies of essay grading. Length variables are summary measures of how many words, or how many different words are used in an essay, and may also reflect the writer's fluency. The scores on our binary classifiers are summary measures that capture how many words are used in the essay which are differentially associated with "good" essays. These scores would be highly correlated with length, but would probably be better than length in cases where a successful essay must cover a specific set of concepts.

Another interesting outcome of the parameter tuning on these data was the high value of k found for the k-nearest-neighbor classifier. In previous studies of k-nearest-neighbor classification for text, values of k on the order of 10 to 30 were found to be optimal (Larkey & Croft, 1996; Masand, et al., 1992; Stanfill & Waltz, 1986; Yang & Chute, 1994). In this context, the high values of k in this experiment were surprising. A reasonable explanation may be the following: In most categorization studies, the k-nearest-neighbor classifier tries to find the small subset of documents in a collection that are in the same class (or classes) as the test document. The essay grading case differs, however, in that all the documents are about the same topic as the test document, so the grade assigned to any similar document has something to contribute to the grade of the test essay.

This work showed the k-nearest-neighbor approach to be distinctly inferior to both the other approaches. Landauer et al. (1997) have applied Latent Semantic Analysis in a k-nearest-neighbor approach to the problem of essay grading. They got very good results, which suggests that the use of more sophisticated features or a different similarity metric may work better.

In conclusion, binary classifiers, which attempted to separate "good" from "bad" essays, produced a successful automated essay grader. The evidence suggests that many different approaches can produce approximately the same level of performance.

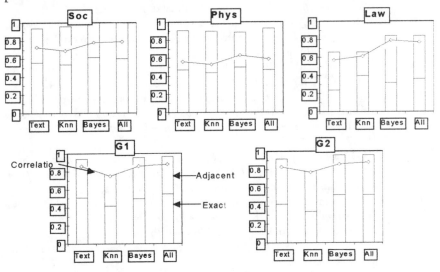

FIG 4.1 Summary results on all five data sets.

ACKNOWLEDGMENTS

This material is based on work supported in part by the National Science Foundation, Library of Congress, and Department of Commerce under cooperative agreement number EEC-9209623. Any opinions, findings, and conclusions or recommendations expressed in this material are the author's and do not necessarily reflect those of the sponsor. We would like to thank Scott Elliot for helping us obtain the data from ETS, and for his many suggestions.

REFERENCES

Bookstein, A., Chiaramella, Y., Salton, G., & Raghavan, V. V. (Eds.) (1991). *Proceedings of the 14th Annual International ACM SIGIR Conference on Research and Development in Information Retrieval.* Chicago, IL: ACM Press.

Belkin, N. J., Ingwersen, P., & Leong, M. K. (Eds.) (2000). *SIGIR 2000: Proceedings of the 23rd Annual International ACM SIGIR Conference on Research and Development in Information Retrieval.* Athens, Greece: ACM Press.

Belkin, N. J., Ingwersen, P., & Pejtersen, A. M. (Eds.) (1992). *Proceedings of the 15th Annual International ACM-SIGIR Conference on Research and Development in Information Retrieval.* Copenhagen, Denmark: ACM Press.

Burstein, J., Kukich, K., Wolff, S., Lu, C., & Chodorow, M. (1998, April). *Computer analysis of essays.* Paper presented at the NCME Symposium on Automated Scoring, San Diego, CA.

Callan, J. P., Croft, W. B., & Broglio, J. (1995). TREC and TIPSTER experiments with INQUERY. *Information Processing and Management, 31,* 327-343.

Cooper, W. S. (1991). Some inconsistencies and misnomers in probabilistic information retrieval. *Proceedings of the Fourteenth Annual International ACM SIGIR Conference on Research and Development in Information Retrieval.* Chicago, IL, 57–61.

Croft, W. B., Harper, D. J., Kraft, D. H., & Zobel, J. (Eds.) (2001). *Proceedings of the 24th Annual International ACM SIGIR Conference on Research and Development in Information Retrieval.* New Orleans, LA: ACM Press.

Croft, W. B., & van Rijsberger, C. J. (Eds.) (1994). *Proceedings of the 17th Annual International ACM-SIGIR Conference on Research and Development in Information Retrieval.* Dublin, Ireland: ACM/Springer Press.

Duda, R. O., & Hart, P. E. (1973). *Pattern classification and scene analysis.* New York: Wiley & Sons.

Fox, E. A., Ingerwersen, P., & Fidel, R. (Eds.) (1995). *Proceedings of the 18th Annual International ACM-SIGIR Conference on Research and Development in Information Retrieval.* Seattle, WA: ACM Press.

Fuhr, N. (1989). Models for retrieval with probabilistic indexing. *Information Processing and Management, 25,* 55-72.

Frei, H. P., Harman, D., Schäble, & Wilkinson, R. (Eds.) (1996). *Proceedings of the 19th Annual International ACM-SIGIR Conference on Research and Development in Information Retrieval.* Zurich, Switzerland: ACM Press.

Korfhage, R., Rasmussen, E. M., & Willett, P. (Eds.) (1993). *Proceedings of the 16ᵗʰ Annual International ACM-SIGIR Conference on Research and Development in Information Retrieval.* Pittsburgh, PA: ACM.

Krovetz, R. (1993). Viewing morphology as an inference process. *Proceedings of the Sixteenth Annual International ACM SIGIR Conference on Research and Development in Information Retrieval*, USA, 191-203.

Landauer, T., Laham, D., Rehder, B., & Schreiner, M. (1997). How well can passage meaning be derived without using word order? A comparison of latent semantic analysis and humans. *Proceedings of the Nineteenth Annual Conference of the Cognitive Science Society* (p. 412–417). Hillside, NJ: Lawrence Erlbaum Associates.

Landauer, T. K., Laham, D., & Foltz, P. W. (2000). The Intelligent Essay Assessor. *IEEE Intelligent Systems, 15*, 27-31.

Larkey, L. S. (1998). Automatic essay grading using text categorization techniques. *Proceedings of the 21st Annual International SIGIR Conference on Research and Development in Information Retrieval,* Melbourne, Australia, 90-95.

Larkey, L. S., & Croft, W. B. (1996). Combining classifiers in text categorization. *Proceedings of the 19th Annual International ACM SIGIR Conference on Research and Development in Information Retrieval,* Zurich, Switzerland, 289-298.

Lewis, D. D. (1992a). An Evaluation of Phrasal and Clustered Representations on a Text Categorization Task, *Proceedings of the Fifteenth Annual International ACM SIGIR Conference on Research and Development in Information Retrieval,* Copenhagen, Denmark (pp. 37-50).

Lewis, D. D. (1992b). *Representation and learning in information retrieval.* Unpublished doctoral dissertation, University of Massachusetts. Amherst.

Lewis, D. D., Shapire, R. E., Callan, J. P., & Papka, R. (1996). Training algorithms for linear text classifiers. *Proceedings of the 19th Annual International ACM SIGIR Conference on Research and Development in Information Retrieval,* Zurich, Switzerland. 298-306.

Maron, M. E. (1961). Automatic indexing: An experimental inquiry. *Journal of the Association for Computing Machinery, 8*, 404-417.

Masand, B., Linoff, G., & Waltz, D. (1992). Classifying news stories using memory based reasoning. *Proceedings of the Fifteenth Annual International ACM SIGIR Conference on Research and Development in Information Retrieval,* Copenhagen, Denmark, 59-65.

McCallum, A., Rosenfeld, R., Mitchell, T. M., & Ng, A. Y. (1998). Improving text classification by shrinkage in a hierarchy of classes. In A. Danyluk (Ed.), *Machine Learning: Proceedings of the Fifteenth International Conference on Machine Learning.* San Francisco, CA: Morgan Kaufmann (pp. 359-367).

Miller, D. R. H., Leek, T., & Schwartz, R. M. (1999). A hidden markov model information retrieval system. *Proceedings of SIGIR '99: 22nd International Conference on Research and Development in Information Retrieval, USA,* 214-221.

Mitchell, T. M. (1997). *Machine learning.* Boston: McGraw-Hill.

Page, E. B. (1994). Computer grading of student prose, using modern concepts and software. *Journal of Experimental Education, 62*(2), 127-142.

Ponte, J. M., & Croft, W. B. (1998). A language modeling approach to information retrieval. *Proceedings of the 21st Annual International ACM SIGIR Conference on*

Research and Development in Information Retrieval, Melbourne, Australia, 275-281.

Robertson, S. E., & Walker, S. (1994). Some simple effective approximations to the 2-Poisson Model for probabilistic weighted retrieval. *Proceedings of the Seventeenth Annual International ACM-SIGIR Conference on Research and Development in Information Retrieval,* Dublin, Ireland, 232-241.

Salton, G. (1989). *Automatic text processing: The transformation, analysis, and retrieval of information by computer.* Reading, MA: Addison-Wesley.

Stanfill, C., & Waltz, D. (1986). Toward memory-based reasoning. *Communications of the ACM, 29*(12), 1213-1228.

Turtle, H., & Croft, W. B. (1991). Evaluation of an inference network-based retrieval model. *ACM Transactions on Information Systems, 9,* 187-222.

van Rijsbergen, C. J. (1979). *Information retrieval.* London: Butterworths.

Yang, Y., & Chute, C. G. (1994). An Example-Based Mapping Method for Text Categorization and Retrieval. *ACM Transactions on Information Systems, 12*(3), 252-277.

5
IntelliMetric™: From Here to Validity

Scott Elliot
Vantage Learning

IntelliMetric™ has been shown to be an effective tool for scoring essay-type, constructed response questions across Kindergarten through 12th grade (K-12), higher education, and professional training environments, as well as within a variety of content areas and for a variety of assessment purposes. This chapter describes IntelliMetric™ and summarizes the research supporting the validity of this automated essay scorer.

OVERVIEW OF INTELLIMETRIC™

IntelliMetric™ is an intelligent scoring system that emulates the process carried out by human scorers and is theoretically grounded in the traditions of cognitive processing, computational linguistics, and classification. The system must be "trained" with a set of previously scored responses containing "known score" marker papers for each score point. These papers are used as a basis for the system to infer the rubric and the pooled judgments of the human scorers. Relying on Vantage Learning's proprietary CogniSearch™ and Quantum Reasoning™ technologies, the IntelliMetric™ system internalizes the characteristics of the responses associated with each score point and applies this intelligence in subsequent scoring (Vantage Learning, 2001d). The approach is consistent with the procedure underlying holistic scoring.

IntelliMetric™ creates a unique solution for each stimulus or prompt. This is conceptually similar to prompt-specific training for human scorers. For this reason, IntelliMetric™ is able to achieve both high correlations with the scores of human readers and matching percentages with scores awarded by humans.

IntelliMetric™ is based on a blend of artificial intelligence (AI), natural language processing and statistical technologies. It is essentially a learning engine that internalizes the characteristics of the score scale through an iterative learning process. In essence, IntelliMetric™ internalizes the pooled wisdom of many expert scorers. It is important to note that AI is widely believed to better handle "noisy" data and develop a more sophisticated internalization of complex relations among features. IntelliMetric™ was first commercially released in January 1998 and was the first AI–based essay-scoring tool made available to educational agencies (Vantage Learning, 2001d).

IntelliMetric™ uses a multistage process to evaluate responses. First, IntelliMetric™ is exposed to a subset of responses with known scores from which it derives knowledge of the characteristics of each score point. Second, the model reflecting the knowledge derived is tested against a smaller set of responses with known scores to validate the model developed and confirm generalizability. Third, once generalizability is confirmed, the model is applied to score novel responses with unknown scores. Using Vantage Learning's proprietary Legitimatch technology, responses that are anomalous either based on the expectations established by the set of essays used in initial training or with respect to expectations for edited American English are identified as part of the process.

IntelliMetric™ has been used to evaluate open-ended, essay-type questions in English, Spanish, Hebrew, and Bahasa. Functionality for the evaluation of text in Dutch, French, Portuguese, German, Italian, Arabic, and Japanese is currently available as well.

IntelliMetric™ can be applied either in "Instructional" or "Standardized Assessment" Modes. When run in Instructional Mode, the IntelliMetric™ engine allows for student revision and editing. The Instructional Mode provides feedback on overall performance and diagnostic feedback on several rhetorical dimensions (e.g., organization) and analytical dimensions (e.g., sentence structure) of writing (Vantage Learning, 2001m) and provides detailed diagnostic sentence-by-sentence feedback on grammar, usage, spelling, and conventions. In Standardized Assessment Mode, IntelliMetric™ is typically configured to provide for a single student submission with an overall score and, if appropriate, feedback on several rhetorical and analytical dimensions of writing

Features

IntelliMetric™ analyzes more than 300 semantic, syntactic and discourse level features. These features fall into five major categories:

- Focus and Unity—Features pointing toward cohesiveness and consistency in purpose and main idea.
- Development and Elaboration—Features of text looking at the breadth of content and the support for concepts advanced.
- Organization and Structure—Features targeted at the logic of discourse including transitional fluidity and relationships among parts of the response.
- Sentence Structure—Features targeted at sentence complexity and variety.
- Mechanics and Conventions—Features examining conformance to conventions of edited American English.

This model is illustrated in Figure 5.1 (Vantage Learning, 2001d).

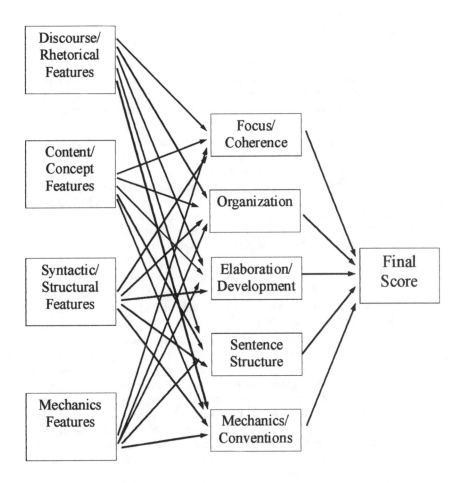

FIG. 5.1. IntelliMetric™ Feature Model.

IntelliMetric™ Research

More than 140 studies have been conducted to explore the validity of IntelliMetric™ (Vantage Learning, 2001d). The summary following is based on approximately 30 of those studies that have been documented.

Research Designs. There are several designs that have been employed in the exploration of the validity of IntelliMetric™. These designs fall into three major categories:

- *IntelliMetric™-Expert Comparison Studies.* The system provides a direct comparison between the scores produced by experts and those produced by IntelliMetric™. Typically, two experts are asked to score a set of papers and IntelliMetric™ is then employed to score those same papers. The expert agreement rates are then compared to the agreement rate between IntelliMetric™ and the average score of the experts or each expert.

- *True Score Studies.* In the case of true score studies, a large number of experts are asked to score a set of papers and the average of those expert scores for each paper serves as a proxy for the true score. Both expert scorers alone or in combination are compared to the true score as are the IntelliMetric™ scores.

- *Construct Validity Studies.* The scores produced by IntelliMetric™ and experts are compared to other external measures to evaluate whether IntelliMetric™ performs in manner consistent with the expectations for the construct. Comparisons may include other measures of the underlying construct being measured or extraneous variables that may inadvertently contribute to the variance in IntelliMetric™ scores.

Statistics. The vast majority of IntelliMetric™ studies have used either measures of agreement or correlations to explore the relationship between IntelliMetric™ and expert scoring.

- *Descriptive Statistics.* The means and standard deviations are typically calculated for both human experts and IntelliMetric™. This allows a comparison of central tendency and spread across human and IntelliMetric™ scoring methods.

- *Agreement.* Agreement statistics generally compare the percentage of scores that agree exactly between two or more experts or between IntelliMetric™ and experts, or adjacent agreement, which refers to the percentage of time experts or IntelliMetric™ and experts agree with each other within one point. These agreement rates may be explored more molecularly by looking at the percentage agreement rates at each individual score point. Agreement is typically higher in the middle of the scale than at the tails- for both human experts and IntelliMetric™.

- *Correlation.* The Correlation between experts or between experts and IntelliMetric™ is calculated in many studies. Typically, the Pearson r statistic is used for this purpose. This statistic is used less often due to problems with restriction of range and oversensitivity to outliers.

A Cautionary Note. The studies reported later were conducted between 1996 and 2001. During that period, IntelliMetric™ (8.0) has gone through seven major versions and many smaller release changes. The latest version of IntelliMetric™ was just released showing an approximately 3% increase in agreement rates—an indication of incremental improvements over time. To evaluate the current accuracy levels of IntelliMetric™ the 2000 and 2001 studies offer the best information.

Validity

Validity is the central concern of any measurement effort (American Educational Research Association, American Psychological Association, National Council on Measurement in Education, 1999). This is particularly true of any innovation in measurement where there is a significant departure from traditional practice. It is incumbent on the user to demonstrate that the scores from any measurement effort are valid.

Over the past 6 years, Vantage Learning, Inc. has conducted more than 140 studies involving the use of IntelliMetric™. Listed later are a series of conclusions we have drawn based on these 6 years of research. Following this listing is a conclusion by conclusion analysis of the evidence: IntelliMetric™.

1. Agrees with expert scoring, often exceeding the performance of expert scorers.
2. Accurately scores open-ended responses across a variety of grade levels, subject areas, and contexts.
3. Shows a strong relation to other measures of the same writing construct.
4. Shows stable results across samples.

IntelliMetric™ seems to perform best under the following conditions:

- Larger number of training papers: 300+ (although models have been constructed with as few as 50 training papers).
- Sufficient papers defining the tails of the distribution: For example, on a 1 to 6 scale it is helpful to have at least 20 papers defining the "1" point and the "6" point.
- Larger number of expert scorers used as a basis for training: Two or more scorers for the training set seem to yield better results than one scorer.
- Six-point or greater scales: The variability offered by six as opposed to three or four point scales appears to improve IntelliMetric™ performance.
- Quality expert scoring used as a basis for training: Although IntelliMetric™ is very good at eliminating "noise" in the data, ultimately, the engine depends on receiving accurate training information.

Under these conditions, IntelliMetric™ will typically outperform human scorers.

The largest body of evidence supporting IntelliMetric™'s performance comes from the numerous studies conducted between 1998 and 2001 comparing IntelliMetric™ scores to expert scores for a common set of responses.

Early Graduate Admissions Study. 1996 and 1997 provide the earliest explorations of IntelliMetric™. Although results are typically much stronger than the results reported here, this provides an early glimpse into IntelliMetric™. Two graduate admissions essays (n = ~300) scored on a scale from 1 to 6 were examined (Vantage Learning, 1999a, 1999b).

For essay 1, IntelliMetric™ correlated about as highly with Scorer 1 and Scorer 2 (.85), as did Scorer 1 and 2 with each other (.87). The observed correlation between the final resolved score and the IntelliMetric™ score was .85. IntelliMetric™ achieved an adjacent agreement rate of 95% compared to Scorer 1 and 94% compared to Scorer 2. The comparable rate for the two human scorers was 95%. Scorer 1 and Scorer 2 achieved an exact agreement rate of 56%, whereas IntelliMetric™ agreed exactly with human scorers about half the time (IntelliMetric™ to scorer 1 = 50%, IntelliMetric™ to scorer 2 = 47%; Vantage Learning, 2001h).

For essay 2, the correlations between IntelliMetric™ and the scores assigned by the human scorers obtained for essay 2 were comparable to those obtained for essay 1.

2002 Repeat of Graduate Admissions Study. A repeat of the graduate admissions study examining essay 1 using the 2002 version of IntelliMetric™ (version 8.0) shows a significant increase in agreement rates. IntelliMetric™ agrees with experts within one point 98% of the time and agrees with experts exactly 60% of the time. This represents a marked improvement in performance over 6 years since the initial research was completed.

True Score Studies. Further evidence—and perhaps stronger evidence—comes from studies conducted using a true score approach to evaluating IntelliMetric™ and expert scoring. Here, expert scores and IntelliMetric™ scores are compared to a proxy for the true score derived from the average score produced by multiple scorers.

IntelliMetric™ scores were compared to the average of 8 to 10 expert scores(true score proxy) for an 11th-grade statewide high stakes assessment. We compared both IntelliMetric™ and individual expert scores to the true score for a narrative, descriptive and persuasive writing prompt. Approximately 600 responses, 200 from each prompt, were drawn from a larger sample of responses collected.

Each response was scored on five dimensions of writing: focus, content, style, organization, and conventions. Each dimension was scored on a scale from 1 to 4 using a rubric approved by writing educators in the state.

The means and standard deviations for the true score and IntelliMetric™ score were comparable. These data are summarized in Table 5.1:

TABLE 5.1
True Score and IntelliMetric™ Descriptive Statistics

Source	N	Mean	Standard Deviation
True Score	594	2.88	.77
IntelliMetric™	594	2.89	.72

Overall True Score Results. IntelliMetric™ was somewhat more accurate than individual experts overall, agreeing with the average of the expert grader scores ("true score") within 1 point 98% to 100% of the time, and exactly with the average of the expert grader scores ("true score") 60% to 82% of the time. Expert graders agreed with the average of the expert grader scores ("true score") within 1 point 97% to 100% of the time, and exactly with the average of the expert grader scores ("true score") 53% to 81% of the time (Vantage Learning, 2001g).

With respect to dimensional scoring, IntelliMetric™ showed somewhat superior performance in scoring "Content," whereas expert scoring showed better performance in scoring the "Conventions" dimension. The remaining three dimensions showed similar performance across the two scoring methods.

Eight scorers were used to establish a proxy for a true score. Although the true score remains unknown, and arguably is more appropriately determined by a panel of writing experts through consensus, this was seen as a reasonable approximation of the likely true score for purposes of evaluating scoring accuracy. More recent studies of this type may explore the relation between expert and IntelliMetric™ scoring in comparison to consensus expert scores.

The eight individual expert scores were compared to the true score proxy. Similarly, the IntelliMetric™ generated score was compared to this value. With eight comparisons versus a single comparison, one could argue that there was a greater chance that one of the eight scorers might disagree with the "true score." Although this point is well taken, this is a fairly accurate representation of what may happen in practice. Any one of these expert scorers participating in the study could affect a student's scoring outcome.

College Entry True Score. This study was aimed at determining how well IntelliMetric™ is able to score entry-level college student responses holistically and analytically with respect to five dimensions of writing: content, creativity, style, mechanics, and organization. The data used as a basis of this research is drawn from a FIPSE (Fund for the Improvement of Postsecondary Education) study of eighteen topics (prompts) administered to entry-level college students to assess writing skill levels.

In this study, 1,202 responses were scored by six expert scorers. Responses were scored on a 1 to 4 scale, both holistically and on five dimensions: content, creativity, style, mechanics, and organization. Again, the average score across the six expert scorers was used as a proxy for the "true score" for the study.

The rate of agreement with the "true score" was computed for both IntelliMetric™ and each of the six expert scorers. For each expert scorer comparison, the individual scorers results were removed from the "true score" computation (yielding a true score based on the five remaining scorers). The results are summarized later for all of the prompts with at least 25 responses.

For virtually all prompts and scoring dimensions, IntelliMetric™ showed greater accuracy in scoring than the expert scorers. This is illustrated in Table 5.2 (Vantage Learning, 2001e).

TABLE 5.2
College Entry Level True Score Results

Scoring Category	Expert Exact Agreement	Expert Adjacent Agreement	IntelliMetric™ Exact Agreement	IntelliMetric™ Adjacent Agreement
Overall	67%–100%	12–64%	98%–100%	57%–72%
Content	76%–100%	14–69%	99%–100%	57%–76%
Creativity	62%–97%	18–72%	99%–100%	55%–74%
Style	65%–99%	9–66%	99%–100%	52%–71%
Organization	68%%–98%	17–64%	97%–100%	57%–72%
Mechanics	66–98%	17–56%	98%–100%	57%–77%

IntelliMetric™ accurately scores open-ended responses across a variety of grade levels, subject areas and contexts.

Secondary School Admissions Tests. As one requirement for admission to private, secondary schools, students must complete a creative thinking essay offered by the Secondary School Admissions Testing Board. Students are provided with a famous "saying" and are asked to provide an analysis. We examined one such prompt, comparing IntelliMetric™ scoring to the scores produced by expert scorers.

Three hundred and six student responses were scored first by experts and then by IntelliMetric™ on a scale ranging from 1 to 6. The correlation between IntelliMetric™ and the scores assigned by expert graders was .78. IntelliMetric™ agreed with the expert graders within one point 100% of the time, and exactly with human scorers 74% of the time. These figures meet or exceed the levels typically obtained by expert graders (Vantage Learning, 2000).

International Student. Similar results were found for international secondary students. A single narrative-style question was administered to approximately 500 secondary school students in the UK. The prompt asked students to produce a narrative essay based on introductory story material provided. Each response was scored on a scale ranging from 1 to 7.

The correlation between IntelliMetric™ and the scores assigned by expert graders was .90. IntelliMetric™ agreed with the expert graders within one point 100% of the time, and exactly with human scorers 62% of the time. This compares with an expert to expert correlation of .89, adjacent agreement of 99%, and exact agreement of 64% (Vantage Learning, 2001).

College Placement Essay. Students entering colleges are often called on to respond to a prompt in writing to determine the proper placement into entry-level English courses. We examined one such assessment administered as part of the College Board's WritePlacer Program. Four hundred and sixty-four responses were used in this study. Each response was scored on a scale ranging from 1 to 4.

The rate of agreement for both IntelliMetric™ and expert graders was compared. IntelliMetric™ agreed with the expert graders within 1 point 100% of the time, exactly with scorer one 76% of the time, and exactly with scorer 2 80% of the time. These figures compare favorably with the expert scorer to expert scorer agreement of 100% (adjacent) and 78% exact (Vantage Learning, 2001i).

Secondary Literary Analysis. Some high stakes testing programs at the secondary level include an assessment of English literature knowledge and skills. We examined two questions administered to secondary school students as part of one such statewide high stakes English assessment. Prompt 1 asked students to analyze examples of vivid and descriptive language in a passage provided. Prompt 2 asked students to compare and contrast two poems on the basis of subject matter and theme.

Approximately 347 responses were provided for questions 1 and 381 responses to question 2. Each response was scored on a scale ranging from 1 to 4.

For question 1, the correlation between IntelliMetric™ and the scores assigned by expert graders was .89. For question 2, the correlation was .88. For both questions, IntelliMetric™ agreed with the expert graders within one point 100% of the time. IntelliMetric™ agreed exactly with human scorers 72% of the time for question 1 and 74% of the time for question 2. This is comparable to the results typical of expert scoring (Vantage Learning, 2000).

Grade eleven dimensional scoring. In Pennsylvania, 11th grade students are required to take a high stakes assessment including a measure of writing skills. We examined three prompts for this program: one narrative, one persuasive and one descriptive, administered to students in 11th grade in the Fall of 1999 to assess writing skill levels statewide (Vantage Learning, 2001h).

Responses were scored on five dimensions: focus, content, organization, style, and conventions.

Each dimension was scored on a scale ranging from 1 to 4 using a rubric developed by Pennsylvania educators. Exactly 477 responses (excluding off topic essays) were available for the persuasive prompt, 477 for the descriptive prompt and 479 for the narrative prompt.

The rate of agreement and correlation between scores was computed for the three comparisons of interest: Expert 1-Expert 2, Expert 1-IntelliMetric™ and Expert 2-IntelliMetric™. The results are summarized below for each of the three styles of prompts.

Persuasive Prompt. Across all five dimensions, the two experts agreed with each other within 1 point about 99% to 100% of the time. Similarly, IntelliMetric™ agreed with the experts within 1 point about 99% to 100% of the time. IntelliMetric™ performed somewhat better when looking at exact match for the four of the five dimensions, while the experts had a somewhat higher agreement rate for the fifth conventions dimension.

Descriptive Prompt. Across all five dimensions, the two experts agreed with each other within 1 point about 99% to 100% of the time. Similarly, IntelliMetric™ agreed with the experts within 1 point about 99% to 100% of the time. The experts performed somewhat better when looking at exact match for the five dimensions, with exact match rates about 4% higher on average.

Narrative Prompt. Across all five dimensions, the two experts agreed with each other within 1 point about 99% to 100% of the time. Similarly, IntelliMetric™ agreed with the experts within one point about 99% to 100% of the time. IntelliMetric™ performed somewhat better when looking at exact match for the five dimensions, with exact match rates about 5% higher on average (Vantage Learning, 2001m).

Grade 9 National Norm Referenced Testing. Most of the major national standardized assessments offer a direct writing assessment. Historically, these writing assessments are administered to students and then returned to the provider for expert scoring. We compared the accuracy of the scores provided by experts to those produced by IntelliMetric™ for a single question administered as part of a 1999 standardized writing assessment for ninth graders. The prompt was a persuasive writing task asking examinees to write a letter to the editor.

Exactly 612 responses were scored on a scale ranging from 1 to 6. IntelliMetric™(tm) agreed with the expert graders within 1 point 99% to 100% of the time, and exactly with human scorers 64% of the time. IntelliMetric™ scores correlated with the average of two expert grader scores at .85 (Vantage Learning, 2001c).

Medical Performance Assessment. The data used as a basis of this research is drawn from two medical case-based performance assessments. Each response was scored by a single scorer on a scale from 1-5 using a rubric.

Because of the small data set, training was repeated three times. Three separate "splits" of the data were undertaken as a vehicle for determining the stability of the predictions.

Case 1. IntelliMetric™ agreed with the expert grader scores within 1 point 95% to 100% of the time, and exactly with the expert grader scores 60% to 70% of the time. Only one discrepancy was found across the three models. While the agreement rates are impressive, it is likely that larger sample sizes would show even stronger performance see Table 5.3).

TABLE 5.3
Case 1 Agreement Rates (Vantage Learning, 2001h)

Model	Exact	Adjacent	Discrepant
Model 1	12 (60%)	8 (40%)	0 (0%)
Model 2	12 (60%)	7 (35%)	1 (5%)
Model 3	14 (70%)	6 (30%)	0 (0%)

Case 2. IntelliMetric™ agreed with the expert grader scores within 1 point 95% to 100% of the time, and exactly with the expert grader scores ("true score") 55% to 65% of the time. Only one discrepancy was found across the three models. This is illustrated in Table 5.4. Although the agreement rates are impressive, it is likely that larger sample sizes would show even stronger performance (Vantage Learning, 2001n).

TABLE 5.4
Case 2 Agreement Rates (Vantage Learning, 2001f)

Model	Exact	Adjacent	Discrepant
Model 1	12 (60%)	8 (40%)	0(0%)
Model 2	11 (55%)	8 (40%)	1 (5%)
Model 3	13 (65%)	7 (25)%	0 (0%)

IntelliMetric™ shows a strong relationship to other measures of the same writing construct.

An important source of validity evidence is the exploration of IntelliMetric™ in relation to expectations for performance with other measures.

International Construct Validity Study. An international study of student writing for students ages 7, 11, and 14 served as the backdrop for the exploration of the construct validity of IntelliMetric™. Approximately 300 students completed a creative writing piece centering on the completion of a story with the first line provided by assessors. Each response was scored by two trained expert scorers. In addition, each student's teacher provided an overall judgment of the student's writing skill. Students also completed a multiple-choice measure of writing ability.

IntelliMetric™ Relationship to Multiple Choice Measures of Writing.. IntelliMetric™ scores correlated with multiple choice measures of writing about as well ($r = .78$) as the scores produced by expert scorers correlated with the multiple choice measures (scorer 1 $r = .77$; scorer 2 $r = .78$). In fact, at the 7 year old level, IntelliMetric™ actually showed a stronger correlation with multiple choice measures of writing (.56) than did the scores produced by expert scorers (scorer 1 $r = .46$; scorer 2 $r = .45$); (Vantage Learning, 2001).

IntelliMetric™ Relationship to Teacher Judgments of Student Writing Skill.. IntelliMetric™ correlated with teacher judgments of overall writing skill ($r = .84$) about as well as expert scorers correlated with teacher judgments (scorer 1 $r = .81$; scorer 2 $r = .85$). In fact at the seven year old level, IntelliMetric™ actually showed a stronger correlation with teacher ratings of writing skill (.46) than did the scores produced by expert scorers (scorer 1 $r = .30$; scorer 2 $r = .41$); (Vantage Learning, 2001l).

Richland College Construct Validity Study. A study of entry level college students was conducted at Richland College in Texas in 2001. 445 students took WritePlacer Plus and also indicated the writing course they took the previous semester (course placement; Vantage Learning, 2001i).

Courses follow a progression from lower level writing skill to higher level writing skill. The average (Mean) score for students in each of the courses was computed. The means for each course in the skill hierarchy were compared as a measure of construct validity. If WritePlacer Plus performed as expected, one would expect students in lower level courses to achieve lower WritePlacer Plus scores. The results confirm this assumption and clearly provide construct validity evidence in support of WritePlacer Plus. Students in the lowest level writing course achieved a mean score of 3.62, while students in the most advanced course achieved a mean score of 4.94.

Effect of Typing Skill on Writing Performance. The Richland College study described above also examined the impact of self reports of typing ability. Four hundred forty five students took WritePlacer Plus and also indicated their judgment of their own writing ability on a three point scale.

The results show a significant correlation of .174 ($p < .05$) between student self judgments of typing ability and the score they received from IntelliMetric™ on their writing. This reflects only 3% of the variance providing support to the notion that scores are not substantially due to typing ability. IntelliMetric™ shows stable results across samples (Vantage Learning, 2001i).

A critical issue in examining the validity of IntelliMetric™ surrounds the ability of IntelliMetric™ to produce stable results regardless of the sample of papers used for training. Obviously idiosynchratic results offer little benefit for operational scoring.

Eighth Grade Integrated Science Assessment Cross Validation Study. One of the earliest studies of IntelliMetric™ explored the stability of IntelliMetric™ scoring across sub samples of a set of approximately 300 responses to a large-scale testing program targeted at eighth-grade science.

We examined the stability of IntelliMetric™ with a single question administered as part of a 1998 statewide eighth grade assessment. The prompt was an integrated science and writing task asking examinees to write a letter to a government official to persuade them to reintroduce an endangered species into the national forests.

Approximately 300 responses scored on a scale ranging from 1 to 6 were used to train and evaluate IntelliMetric™. IntelliMetric™ was trained using approximately 250 responses and then used to score the remaining 50 "unknown" responses. This procedure was repeated with ten random samples from the set to assess the stability of IntelliMetric™ (Vantage Learning, 2000).

Correlations and agreement rates between IntelliMetric™ and the expert graders were consistently high. Most importantly for this study, the results showed consistency across the 10 samples suggesting that IntelliMetric™ is relatively stable. These results are presented in the Table 5.5.

K-12 Norm Referenced Test Cross Validation Study. A similar cross-validation study was conducted using a a single persuasive prompt drawn from a 1998 administration of a national K–12 norm-referenced test.

In this case, cross validation refers to the process where a dataset is separated into a number of groups of approximately the same size and prevalence, and then these groups are each tested versus a model trained using the remainder of the dataset. In this way, a fair representation of the predictive power of the general model may be seen, while never testing on a data element used for training.

TABLE 5.5
IntelliMetric™(tm)–Expert Grader Agreement Rates
and Correlations (Vantage Learning, 2001g)

Sample Number	Percentage Agreement (IntelliMetric™ to Human)	Percentage Discrepant (IntelliMetric™ to Human)	Pearson R Correlation (IntelliMetric™ to Human)
1	98%	2%	.89
2	98%	2%	.90
3	92%	8%	.85
4	94%	6%	.88
5	96%	4%	.90
6	98%	2%	.85
7	96%	4%	.89
8	94%	6%	.88
9	94%	6%	.90
10	90%	10%	.89

Approximately 612 responses were selected for use in this study. Each response was scored on a scale ranging from 1 to 6.

The 612 responses were randomly split into six sets of 102 responses to be used as validation sets. For each of the randomly selected 102 to 103 response validation sets, the remaining 510 responses were used to train the IntelliMetric™ scoring engine. In other words, the set of 102 validation responses in each case was treated as unknown, while the second set of 510 remaining responses was used as a basis for "training" the IntelliMetric™ system. IntelliMetric™ predictions were made "blind;" that is, without any knowledge of the actual scores.

The correlations and agreement rates between IntelliMetric™ and the scores assigned by expert graders were consistently high. These results are presented in Table 5.6 (Vantage Learning, 2001k).

In addition to supporting the claim of stability, the results confirm our earlier findings that IntelliMetric™ accurately scores written responses to essay-type questions. IntelliMetric™ showed an average adjacency level (within 1 point) of 99% and an average exact agreement rate of 61%. Moreover, the correlation between expert scores and IntelliMetric™ scores ranged from .78 to .85 (Vantage Learning, 2001k).

TABLE 5.6
IntelliMetric™(tm)-Expert Grader Agreement Rates and Correlations

Sample Number	Percentage Agreement (Exact Match IntelliMetric™ to Human)	Percentage Adjacent (Within 1 point (IntelliMetric™ to Human)	Percentage Discrepant (IntelliMetric™ to Human)	Pearson R Correlation (IntelliMetric™ to Human)
1	56%	99%	1%	.78
2	59%	99%	1%	.80
3	64%	99%	1%	.85
4	62%	100%	0%	.84
5	66%	99%	1%	.83
6	59%	99%	1%	.81

This compares favorably with the expert Scorer 1 to expert Scorer 2 comparisons. The two expert scores showed a 68% exact agreement rate and a 97% adjacency rate with a correlation of about .84 (Vantage Learning, 2001k). IntelliMetric™ produced consistent results regardless of which randomly drawn set of essays were used for training or testing.

The data set used was somewhat concentrated in the middle of the distribution of scores with few "1"s and few "6"s. This deficiency tends to lead to somewhat lower IntelliMetric™ performance. From past studies, the addition of more responses at the tails would likely yield even stronger results. Even with this limitation, IntelliMetric™ was able to achieve levels of performance comparable with expert graders.

Degradation Study. One source of unwanted variation stems from the size of the training set, that is, the number of papers used as a basis for training IntelliMetric™. To explore this, 400 responses obtained from graduate admissions test were analyzed. For this set of experiments, the size of the training set varies from 10 to 350. New training sets are selected randomly for 10 individual training sessions at each of nine levels of training set size (Vantage Learning, 1999b).

TABLE 5.7
Summary Results for Degradation Experiments

N of Training Cases	Pearson R Correlation	Average Agreement %	Average Discrepant %	N of Discrepant Standard Deviation
350	0.87	94.8	5.20	1.71
300	0.89	94.6	5.40	1.83
250	0.88	94.8	5.20	1.51
200	0.89	97.4	2.60	1.34
150	0.86	94.2	5.80	1.45
100	0.87	94.2	5.80	1.73
50	0.85	92.4	7.60	1.40
25	0.74	83.4	16.60	4.72
10	0.79	88.0	12.00	4.11

As can be seen from the data in Table 5.7, IntelliMetric™ showed strong stability with training sets as low as 50 papers.

How Many Graders/Papers are Enough?. Vantage Learning, Inc. studied the impact of numbers of scorers and number of training papers using data obtained from a statewide student assessment. In each case, a set of Persuasive Grade 8 essays were scored on a scale from 1 to 4 by experts.

The impact of graders and training papers was examined and is summarized in Table 5.8 and 5.9 below. Four levels of graders were examined: 1, 2, 4, and 8; at each level three separate runs were executed. Three levels of training papers were assessed: 150, 100, 50. Again, three runs were executed at each level (Vantage Learning, 2001n).

TABLE 5.8
Impact of Number of Graders (Three Cross Validations)

Number of Graders	Exact Agreement	Adjacent Agreement	Pearson R	N of Index of Agreement (Mean Pearson R)
8	68,70,76	100,100,100	.72,.75,.79	(.75)
4	70,72,72	100,100,100	.75,.76,.76	(.76)
2	70,70,72	100,100,100	.73,.74,.76	(.74)
1	64,64,70	100,100,100	.67,.68,.76	(.70)

TABLE 5.9
Impact of Number of Training Papers (Three Cross Validations; Vantage Learning, 2001)

Number of Training Papers	Exact Agreement	Adjacent Agreement	Pearson R	Index of Agreement (Mean Pearson R)
150	72,72,74	100,100,100	.76,.78,.78	(.77)
100	64,68,70	100,100,100	.67,.72,.74	(.71)
50	64,66,70	100,100,100	.67,.69,.73	(.70)

The results clearly show the importance of raters and training papers in the training of IntelliMetric™. Interestingly however, there is less gain than might be expected when going beyond two raters.

IntelliMetric and Other Automated Essay Scoring Engines. One important source of validity evidence derives from an examination of the relationship between a measure and other measures of the construct. Towards this end, we report the relationship between IntelliMetric scoring and other scoring engines from several studies conducted by test publishers and other testing agencies. IntelliMetric and other automated essay scorers were compared. In 2000, in a study of the writing component of an eighth and third grade standardized assessment from a major K-12 test publisher, IntelliMetric and two other major automated scoring engines showed relatively consistent results with, IntelliMetric showing somewhat greater scoring accuracy than the other two major scoring engines examined. IntelliMetric showed significantly greater exact match rates and smaller adjacent match advantages. A similar study conducted by another major test publisher examining an eighth grade national standardized writing assessment confirmed these results finding relative consistency among scoring engines with IntelliMetric again producing greater exact and adjacent match rates than the other major scoring engine it was compared to.

CONCLUSION

IntelliMetric™ has established a substantial base of validity evidence in support of its use. Continued research in this area will continue to explore validity issues.

Most notably, studies are underway examining the impact of extraneous "unwanted" sources of variance.

REFERENCES

American Educational Research Association (AERA), American Psychological Association (APA), National Council on Measurement in Education (NCME; 1999). *The Standards for Educational and Psychological Testing.* Washington, DC: American Educational Research Association.

Vantage Learning. (1999a). *RB 304 – UK study.* Yardley, PA: Author.

Vantage Learning. (1999b). *RB 302 – Degradation study.* Yardley, PA: Author.

Vantage Learning. (2000). *RB 386 – Secondary literary analysis.* Yardley, PA: Author.

Vantage Learning. (2001c). *RB 586 – Third grade NRT simulation.* Yardley, PA: Author.

Vantage Learning. (2001d). *RB 504 – From here to validity.* Yardley, PA: Author

Vantage Learning. (2001e). *RB 539 – Entry college level essays.* Yardley, PA: Author.

Vantage Learning. (2001f). *RB 508 – Phase II PA 2001 study.* Yardley, PA: Author

Vantage Learning. (2001g). *RB 397 – True score study.* Yardley, PA: Author

Vantage Learning. (2001h). *RB 507 – Phase I PA 2001 study.* Yardley, PA: Author.

Vantage Learning. (2001i). *RB 612 – WritePlacer research summary.* Yardley, PA: Author.

Vantage Learning. (2001k). *RB 540 – Third grade NRT cross validation.* Yardley, PA: Author.

Vantage Learning. (2001l). *RB 323A – Construct validity.* Yardley, PA: Author.

Vantage Learning. (2001m). *RB 594 – Analytic scoring of entry essays.* Yardley, PA. Author.

Vantage Learning. (2001n). *RB 516 – MCAT study.* Yardley, PA: Author.

6

Automated Scoring and Annotation of Essays with the Intelligent Essay Assessor™

Thomas K Landauer
University of Colorado and Knowledge Analysis Technologies
Darrell Laham
Knowledge Analysis Technologies
Peter W. Foltz
New Mexico State University and Knowledge Analysis Technologies

The Intelligent Essay Assessor (IEA) is a set of software tools for scoring the quality of the conceptual content of essays based on Latent Semantic Analysis (LSA). Student essays are cast as LSA representations of the meaning of their contained words and compared with essays of known quality on degree of conceptual relevance and amount of relevant content. An advantage of using LSA is that it permits scoring of content–based essays as well as creative narratives. This makes the analyses performed by the IEA suitable for providing directed content–based feedback to students or instructors. In addition, because the content is derived from training material, directed feedback can be linked to the training material. In addition to using LSA, the IEA incorporates a number of other natural language processing methods to provide an overall approach to scoring essays and providing feedback.

This chapter provides an overview of LSA and its application to automated essay scoring, a psychometric analysis of results of experiments testing the IEA for scoring, and finally, a discussion of the implications for scoring and training.

LATENT SEMANTIC ANALYSIS

In contrast to other approaches, the methods to be described here concentrate primarily on the conceptual content, the knowledge conveyed in an essay, rather than its grammar, style, or mechanics. We would not expect evaluation of knowledge content to be clearly separable from stylistic qualities, or even from sheer length in words, but we believe that making knowledge content primary has much more favorable consequences; it will have greater face validity, be harder to counterfeit, more amenable to use in diagnosis and advice, and be more likely to encourage valuable study and thinking activities.

The fundamental engine employed for this purpose in the IEA is LSA. LSA is a machine learning method that acquires a mathematical representation of the meaning relations among words and passages by statistical computations applied to a large corpus of text. The underlying idea is that the aggregate of all the word contexts in which a given word does and does not appear provides a set of mutual constraints that largely determines the similarity of meaning of words and sets of words to each other. Simulations of psycholinguistic phenomena show that LSA similarity measures are highly correlated with human meaning similarities among words and naturally produced texts. For example, when the system itself, after training, is used to select the right answers on multiple-choice tests, its scores overlap those of humans on standard vocabulary and subject matter tests. It also closely mimics human word sorting and category judgments, simulates word–word and passage–word lexical priming data and can be used to accurately estimate the learning value of passages for individual students (Landauer, Foltz, and Laham, 1998; Wolfe et al., 1998). LSA is used in Knowledge Analysis Technologies' IEA to assess the goodness of conceptual semantic content of essays, to analyze essays for the components of content that are and are not well covered, and to identify sections of textbooks and other sources that can provide needed knowledge.

Before proceeding with a description of how LSA is integrated into automatic essay evaluation and tutorial feedback systems, and reports of various reliability and validity studies, we present a brief introduction to how LSA works. The basic assumption is that the meaning of a passage is contained in its words, and that all its words contribute to a passage's meaning. If even one word of a passage is changed, its meaning may change. On the other hand, two passages containing quite different words may have nearly the same meaning. All of these properties are obtained by assuming that the meaning of a passage is the sum of the meanings of its words.

We can rewrite the assumption as follows:

meaning of word$_1$ + meaning of word$_2$ + ... + meaning of word$_n$ = meaning of passage.

Given this way of representing verbal meaning, how does a learning machine go about using data on how words are used in passages to infer what words and their combinations mean? Consider the following abstract mini–passages, which are represented as equations:

ecks + wye + wye = eight
ecks + wye + three = eight.

They imply that *ecks* has a different meaning from *wye* (like *two* and *three* in English), although they always appear in the same passages. Now consider:

ecks + wye + aye = bea
ecks + wye + wye = bea
ecks + wye + cee = dee
ecks + wye + ecks = dee

Although this set of passage equations does not specify an absolute value (meaning) for any of the variables (words), it significantly constrains the relations among them. We know that *aye* and *wye* are synonyms, as are *cee* and *ecks*, despite the fact that they never appeared in the same passage. Finally, consider the following two passages:

ecks + aye = gee
cee + wye = eff

To be consistent with the previous passages, these two passages must have the same meaning: (*eff = gee*) although they have no words in common.

The next step formalizes and generalizes this idea. We treat every passage in a large corpus of text, one representing the language experience of a person writing an essay to a given prompt, as an equation of this kind. The computational method for accomplishing this is called Singular Value Decomposition (SVD)[1]. SVD is a matrix algebraic technique for reducing the equations in a linear system to sums of multidimensional vectors. A good introduction to the mathematics may be found in Berry (1992) and its use in language modeling in Deerwester et al (1990) Landauer and Dumais (1997), and Landauer, Foltz, and Laham (1998).

This is by no means a complete model of linguistic meaning. However, for practical purposes the question is the sufficiency with which it simulates human judgments and behavior, and the proof is in the utility of systems built on it. Empirically, LSA meets this test quite well. Some readers may want more explanation and proof before accepting the plausibility of LSA as reflection of knowledge content. Landauer and Dumais (1994) and Landauer, Foltz and Laham (1998) provided an in–depth introduction to the model and summary of related empirical findings.

THE INTELLIGENT ESSAY ASSESSOR

The IEA, although based on LSA for its content analyses, also takes advantage of other style and mechanics measures for scoring, for validation of the student essay as appropriate English prose, and as the basis for some tutorial feedback. The high level IEA architecture is shown in Figure 6.1. The functionality will be described below within the context of experiments using the IEA.

Essay Scoring Experiments

A number of experiments have been done using LSA measures of essay content derived in a variety of ways and calibrating them against several different types of standards to arrive at quality scores. An overall description of the primary method is presented first along with summaries of the accuracy of the method as compared to expert human readers. Then, individual experiments are described in more detail.

---

[1] Singular Value Decomposition is a form of eignevector or eigenvalue decomposition. The basis of factor analysis, principal components analysis, and correspondence analysis, it is also closely related to metric multidimensional scaling, and is a member of the class of mathematical methods sometimes called spectral analysis that also includes Fourier analysis.

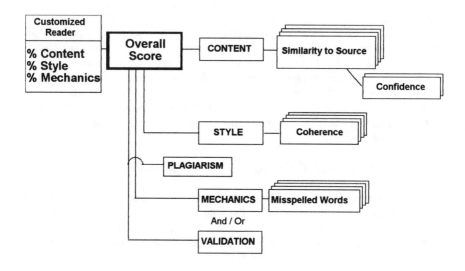

FIG. 6.1 The Intelligent Essay Assessor architecture

   To understand the application of LSA to essay scoring and other educational
and information applications, it is sufficient to understand that it represents the
semantic content of an essay as a vector (which can also be thought of equivalently
as a point in hyper–space, or a set of factor loadings) that is computed from the set
of words that it contains. Each of these points can be compared to every other
through a similarity comparison, the cosine measure. Each point in the space also
has a length, called the vector length, which is the distance from the origin to the
point.
   LSA has been applied to evaluate the quality and quantity of knowledge
conveyed by an essay using three different methods. The methods vary in the
source of comparison materials for the assessment of essay semantic content; a)
pre–scored essays of other students; b) expert model essays and knowledge source
materials; c) internal comparison of an unscored set of essays. These measures
provide indicators of the degree to which a student's essay has content of the same
meaning as that of the comparison texts. This may be considered a semantic
direction or quality measure.
   The primary method detailed in this chapter, Holistic, involves comparison of
an essay of unknown quality to a set of prescored essays which span the range of
representative answer quality. The second and third methods are briefly described
in this chapter in Experiment 1.

Description of the Holistic Method

In LSA, vectors are used to produce two independent scores, one for the semantic quality of the content, the other for the amount of such content expressed. The quality score is computed by first giving a large sample (e.g., 50 or more) of the student essays to one or more human experts to score. Each of the to–be–scored essays is then compared with all of the humanly scored ones. Some number, typically 10, of the pre-scored essays that are most similar to the one in question are selected, and the target essay is given the weighted—by cosine—average human score of those in the similar set. Fig. 6.2 illustrates the process geometrically.

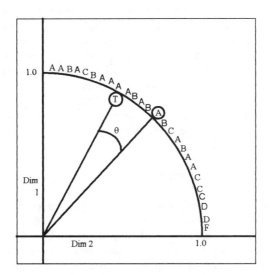

FIG. 6.2. Scored essays represented in two–dimensional space.

Each essay in the space is represented by a letter corresponding to the score for the essay (A, B, C, D, F). This representation shows how essays might be distributed in the semantic space, as seen by the cosine measure, on the surface of a unitized hyper–sphere. The to–be–scored target essay is represented by the circled–"T." The target in this figure is being compared to the circled–"A" essay. Theta is the angle between these two essays from the origin point. The to–be–scored essay is compared to every essay in the pre–scored representative set of essays. From these comparisons, the ten prescored essays with the highest cosine to the target are selected. The scores for these ten essays are averaged, weighted by their cosine with the target, and this average is assigned as the target's quality score.

The vector representation of an essay has both a direction in high dimensional space, whose angle with a comparison model is the basis of the quality measure just described, and a length. The length summarizes how much domain relevant content, that is, knowledge represented in the semantic space as derived by LSA from the training corpus, is contained in the essay independent of its similarity to the quality standard. Because of the transformation and weighting of terms in LSA, and the way in which vector length is computed, for an essay's vector to be long, the essay must tap many of the important underlying dimensions of the knowledge expressed in the corpus from which the semantic space was derived. The vector length algebraically is the sum of its squared values on each of the (typically 100–400) LSA dimensions or axes (in factor–analytic terminology, the sum of squares of its factor loadings.) The content score is the weighted sum of the two components after normalization and regression analysis.

Another application of LSA-derived measures is to produce indexes of the coherence of a student essay. Typically, a vector is constructed for each sentence in the student's answer, then an average similarity between; for example, each sentence and the next within every paragraph, or the similarity of each sentence to the vector for the whole of each paragraph, or the whole of the essay, is computed. Such measures reflect the degree to which each sentence follows conceptually from the last, how much the discussion stays focused on the central topic, and the like (Foltz, Kintsch, & Landauer, 1998). As assessed by correlation with human expert judgments, it turns out that coherence measures are positively correlated with essay quality in some cases but not in others. Our interpretation is that the correlation is positive where correctly conveying technical content requires such consistency, but negatively related when a desired property of the essay is that it discussed a number of disparate examples. The coherence measures are included in the Style index of the IEA.

Meta–Analysis of Experiments

This chapter reports on application of this method to ten different essay questions written by a variety of students on a variety of topics and scored by a variety of different kinds of expert judges. The topics and students were:

Experiment 1: Heart Essays. This involved a question on the anatomy and function of the heart and circulatory system which was administered to 94 undergraduates at the University of Colorado before and after an instructional session (N = 188) and scored by two professional readers from Educational Testing Service (ETS).

Experiment 2: Standardized Essay Tests. Two questions from the Graduate Management Admissions (GMAT) administered and scored by ETS on the state of tolerance to diversity (N = 403) and on the likely effects of an advertising program (N = 383) and a narrative essay question for grade-school children (N = 900).

Experiment 3: Classroom Essay Tests. This involved three essay questions answered by students in general psychology classes at the University of Colorado, which were on operant conditioning (N = 109), attachment in children (N =55), and aphasia (N = 109), an 11th-grade essay question from U.S. history, on the era of the depression (N= 237), and two questions from an undergraduate level clinical psychology course from the University of South Africa, on Sigmund Freud (N = 239) and on Carl Rogers (N = 96).

Total sample size for all essays examined is 3,396, with 2,263 in standardized tests and 1,033 in classroom tests (Experiment 1 being considered more like a classroom test). For all essays, there were at least two independent readers. In all cases, the human readers were ignorant of each other's scores. In all cases, the LSA system was trained using the resolved score of the readers, which in most cases was a simple average of the two reader scores, but could also include resolution of scores by a third reader when the first two disagreed by more than 1 point (GMAT essays), or adjustment of scores to eliminate calibration bias (CU psychology).

Inter–rater Reliability Analyses. The best indicator that the LSA scoring system is accurately predicting the scores is by comparison of LSA scores to single reader scores. By obtaining results for a full set of essays for both the automated system and at least two human readers, one can observe the levels of agreement of the assessment through the correlation of scores. Fig. 6.3 portrays the levels of agreement between the IEA scores and single readers and between single readers with each other. For all standardized essays, the data were received in distinct training and testing collections. The system was trained on the former, with reliabilities calculated using a modified jackknife method, wherein each essay was removed from the training set when it was being scored, and left in the training set for all other essays. The test sets did not include any of the essays from the training set. For the classroom tests, the same modified jack–knife method was employed, thus allowing for the maximum amount of data for training without skewing the resulting reliability estimates.

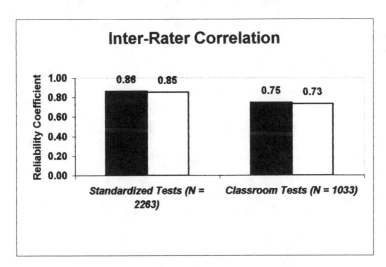

FIG. 6.3 Inter–rater correlations for standardized and classroom tests

Across all examinations, the IEA score agreed with single readers as well as single readers agreed with each other. The differences in reliability coefficients is not significant as tested by the z–test for two correlation coefficients.

The LSA system was trained using the resolved scores of the readers, which should be considered the best estimate of the true score of the essay. In Classical Test theory, the average of several equivalent measures better approximates the true score than does a single measure (Shavelson & Webb, 1991). Fig. 6.4 extends the results shown in Fig. 6.3 to include the reliability between the IEA and the resolved score. Note that although the IEA to Single Reader correlations are slightly, but not significantly, lower than the Reader 1 to Reader 2 correlations, the

IEA to Resolved Score reliabilities are slightly, but not significantly, higher than are those for Reader to Reader.

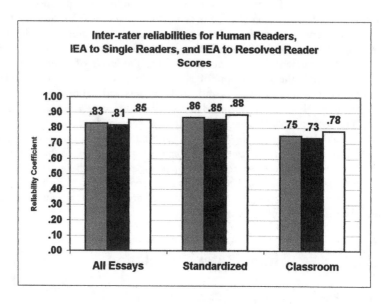

FIG. 6.4 Interrater reliabilities for resolved reader scores

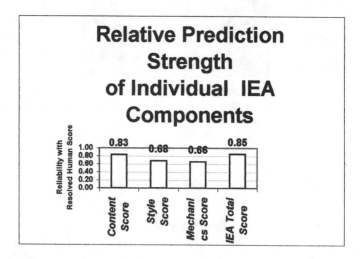

Fig. 6.5 Relative prediction strength of individual IEA components

Relative Prediction Strengths for LSA and other measures. In all of the examination sets, the LSA content measure was found to be the most significant predictor, far surpassing the indices of Style and Mechanics. Fig. 6.5 gives the reliability of the individual scoring components with the criterion human assigned scores.

While Style and mechanics indices do have strong predictive capacity on their own as indicated in Fig. 6.5, their capacity is overshadowed by the content measure. When combined into a single index, the IEA total score, the content measure accounts for the most variance. The relative percentage contribution to prediction of essay scores, as determined by an analysis of standardized correlation coefficients, ranges from 70% to 80% for the content measure, from 10% to 20% for the style measure, and approximately 11% for the mechanics measure (see Fig. 6.6).

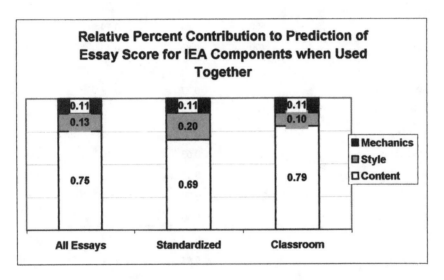

FIG 6.6 Relative percent contribution for IEA components

The following Tables 6.1, 6.2, and 6.3 provide a synopsis of the overall and component reliabilities for each independent data set. Table 6.1 has the reliabilities between human assigned scores and both of the LSA measures independently and combined into a total score. Table 6.2 breaks out the reliabilities for the IEA scoring components of content style and mechanics. Table 6.3 compares the Reader to Reader reliability with the IEA to Single Reader reliability. In all three tables, the differences for all essays, standardized, and classroom was not significant using z test for differences in Reliability Coefficients; Critical Z at alpha (.05) = 1.96Z (ALL) = .153; Z (STANDARD) = 1.53, Z (CLASSROOM) =.70

TABLE 6.1
Reliability scores by individual data sets for LSA measures

Standardized		N	LSA Quality	LSA Quantity	Total LSA Score
gm1.train		403	0.81	0.77	0.88
gm1.test		292	0.75	0.76	0.85
gm2.train		383	0.81	0.75	0.87
gm2.test		285	0.78	0.77	0.86
narrative.train		500	0.84	0.79	0.86
narrative.test		400	0.85	0.80	0.88
Classroom					
great depression		237	0.77	0.78	0.84
heart		188	0.78	0.70	0.80
aphasia		109	0.36	0.62	0.62
attachment		55	0.63	0.49	0.64
operant		109	0.56	0.52	0.66
freud		239	0.79	0.48	0.79
rogers		96	0.60	0.56	0.69
All Essays		3296	0.77	0.73	0.83
Standardized		2263	0.81	0.78	0.87
	Classroom	1033	0.69	0.62	0.76

TABLE 6.2
Reliability scores by individual data sets for IEA components

Standardized	N	IEA content	IEA Style	IEA Mechanics	IEA Score
gm1.train	403	0.88	0.84	0.68	0.90
gm1.test	292	0.85	0.80	0.59	0.87
gm2.train	383	0.87	0.70	0.63	0.87
gm2.test	285	0.86	0.67	0.64	0.87
narrative.train	500	0.86	0.73	0.79	0.89
narrative.test	400	0.88	0.74	0.81	0.90
Classroom					
Great depression	237	0.84	0.65	0.72	0.84
Heart	188	0.80	0.56	0.57	0.80
Aphasia	109	0.62	0.45	0.62	0.70
Attachment	55	0.64	0.36	0.57	0.70
Operant	109	0.66	0.57	0.49	0.73
Freud	239	0.79	0.55	0.53	0.80
Rogers	96	0.69	0.38	0.38	0.70
All Essays	3296	0.83	0.68	0.66	0.85
Standardized	2263	0.87	0.75	0.70	0.88
Classroom	1033	0.76	0.54	0.57	0.78

Note. gm1 – GMAT Question 1; gm2 – GMAT Question 2; narrative – stories; train refersto results on prescored training essays, test to scores on held-out test essays

TABLE 6.3
Reliability scores by individual data sets for single readers

Standardized	N	Reader 1 to Reader 2	IEA–Single Reader
gm1.train	403	0.87	0.88
gm1.test	292	0.86	0.84
gm2.train	383	0.85	0.83
gm2.test	285	0.88	0.85
narrative.train	500	0.87	0.86
narrative.test	400	0.86	0.87
Classroom			
Great depression	237	0.65	0.77
Heart	188	0.83	0.77
Aphasia	109	0.75	0.66
Attachment	55	0.19	0.54
Operant	109	0.67	0.69
Freud	239	0.89	0.78
Rogers	96	0.88	0.68
All Essays	*3296*	*0.83*	*0.81*
Standardized	*2263*	*0.86*	*0.85*
Classroom	*1033*	*0.75*	*0.73*

Note. IEA – Intelligent Essay Assessor; gm1 = GMAT question 1; gm2 = GMAT question 2

This meta–analyses has covered the most important results from the research. A review of some additional modeling experiments performed on some of the unique datasets is presented next.

Experiment 1: Heart Studies

Ninety-four undergraduates fulfilling introductory psychology course requirements volunteered to write approximately 250-word essays on the structure, function and biological purpose of the heart. They wrote one such essay at the beginning of the experiment, then read a short article on the same topic chosen from one of four sources: an elementary school biology text, a high school text, a college text, or a professional cardiology journal. They then wrote another essay on the same topic. In addition, both before and after reading the students were given a short answer test that was scored on a 40-point scale. The essays were scored for content, that is, the quality and quantity of knowledge about the anatomy and function of the heart—without intentional credit for mechanics or style— independently by two professional readers employed by ETS. The short answer tests were scored independently by two graduate students who were serving as research assistants in the project.

The LSA semantic space was constructed by analysis of all 94 paragraphs in a set of 26 articles on the heart taken from an electronic version of Grolier's Academic American Encyclopedia. This was a somewhat smaller source text corpus than has usually been used, but it gave good results and attempts to expand it by the addition of more general text did not improve results.

First each essay was represented as an LSA vector. The sets of before– after– reading essays were analyzed separately. Each target essay was compared with all the others; the 10 most similar by cosine measure were found, and the essay in question given the cosine weighted average of the human assigned scores.

Alternative methods of analysis. In another explored method, instead of comparing a student essay with other student essays, the comparison is with one or more texts authored by experts in the subject. For example, the standard might be the text that the students have read to acquire the knowledge needed, or a union of several texts representative of the domain, or one or more model answers to the essay question written by the instructor. In this approach, it is assumed that a score reflects how close the student essay is to a putative near–ideal answer, a "gold standard."

For this experiment, instead of comparing each essay with other essays, each was compared with the high-school level biology text section on the heart. An advantage of this method as applied here, of course, is that the score is derived without the necessity of human readers providing the comparison set, but it does require the selection or construction of an appropriate model.

In a third method, the scoring scale is derived solely from comparisons among the student essays themselves rather than from their relation to human scores or model text. The technique rests on the assumption that in a set of essays intended to tap the amount of knowledge conveyed, the principal dimension along which the essays will vary will be the amount of knowledge conveyed by each essay: that is, because students will try to do what they are asked, the task is difficult, and the students vary in ability, the principal difference between student products will be in how well they have succeeded. The LSA–based analysis consists of computing a matrix of cosines between all essays in a large collection. These similarities are converted into distances (1–cosine), then subjected to a single dimensional scaling (also known as an unfolding; Coombs, 1964). Each essay then has a numerical position along the single dimension that best captures the similarities among all of the essays; by assumption, this dimension runs from poor quality to good. The analysis does not tell which end of the dimension is high and which low, but this can be trivially ascertained by examining a few essays. The unfolding method, when tested on the heart essays, yielded an average correlation of .62 with the scores given by ETS readers. This can be compared with correlations of .78 for the holistic quality score, .70 for the holistic quantity score and .65 when source texts are used in the comparison. All methods gave reliabilities that are close to those achieved by the human readers, and well within the usual range of well–scored essay examinations.

Validity Studies Using Objective Tests. Because the essay scoring in Experiment 1 was part of a larger study with more analysis, some accessory investigations that throw additional light on the validity of the method were possible. First, we asked whether LSA was doing more than measuring the number of technical terms used by students. To explore this, the words in the essays were classified as either topically relevant content words or topically neutral words, including common function words and general purpose adjectives, that might be found in an essay on any subject. This division was done by one of the research assistants with intimate knowledge of the materials. The correlation with the average human score was best when both kinds of words were included, but was, remarkably, statistically significant even when only the neutral words were used. However, as to be expected, relevant content words alone gave much better results than the neutral words alone.

The administration of the essay test before and after reading in Experiment 1 provides additional indicants of validity. First, the LSA relation between the before–essay and the text selection that a student read yielded substantial predictions in accordance with the zone of optimal learning hypothesis for how much would be learned; had students been assigned their individually optimal text as predicted by the relation between it and their before–reading essay, they would, on average, have learned a significant 40% more than if all students were given the one overall best text. The same effects were reflected in LSA after–reading essay scores and short–answer tests. These results make it clear that the measure of knowledge obtained with LSA is not superficial; it does a good job of reflecting the influence of learning experiences and predicting the expected effects of variations in instruction.

A final result from this experiment is of special interest. This is the relation between the LSA score and the more objective short answer test. The correlation between LSA scores and short-answer tests was .76. The correlation between the Reader 1's essay score and the short answer test was .72.; for Reader 2 it was .81, for an average of .77. This lack of a difference indicates that the LSA score had an external criterion validity that was at least as high as that for combined expert human judgments.

Experiment 2: Standardized Tests

This experiment used a large sample of essays taken from the ETS GMAT exam used for selection of candidates for graduate business administration programs. There were two topics: The essays on both topics were split by ETS into training and test sets. An interesting feature of these essays is that they have much less consistency either in what students wrote or what might be considered a good answer. There was opportunity for a wide variety of different good and bad answers, including different discussions of different examples reaching different conclusions and using fairly disjoint vocabularies, and at least an apparent opportunity for novel and creative answers to have received appropriate scores from the human judges. Although it was therefore thought that the Holistic approach might be of limited value, the method was nevertheless applied. To our surprise, it worked quite well. As described in Table 6.1 the reliabilities for the IEA matched the reliabilities for the well–trained readers.

A third set of grade school student essays, require narrative writing from an open–ended prompt (e.g., "Usually they went to school, but on that day things were different... "). The examination question allowed for infinite variability in writer response. Almost any situation could have followed this prompt, yet the LSA content measure was actually slightly stronger for this case than for any other tested (See Table 6.1).

An explanation of this finding could be the following: over the fairly large number of essays scored by LSA, almost all of the possible ways to write a good, bad or indifferent answer, and almost all kinds of examples that would contribute to a favorable or unfavorable impression on the part of the human readers, were represented in at least a few student essays. Thus, by finding the 10 most similar to a particular essay, LSA was still able to establish a comparison that yielded a valid score. The results are still far enough from perfect to allow the presence of a few unusual answers not validly scored, although the human readers apparently did not, on average, agree with each other in such cases any more than they did with LSA.

Experiment 3: Classroom Studies

An additional 845 essays from six exams from three educational institutions were also scored using the holistic method. In general, the inter–rater reliability for these exams is lower than for standardized tests, but is still quite respectable. The reliability results for all of these sets are also detailed in Tables 1–3.

Auxiliary Findings. In addition to the reliability and validity studies, the research examined a variety of other aspects of scoring the essays. These explorations are detailed in this section.

Count Variables and Vector Length. Previous attempts to develop computational techniques for scoring essays have focused primarily on measures of style and mechanics. Indices of content have remained secondary, indirect, and superficial. For example, in the extensive work of Page and his colleagues (Page, 1966, 1994) over the last 30 years, a growing battery of computer programs for analysis of grammar, syntax, and other nonsemantic characteristics has been used. Combined by multiple regression, these variables accurately predict scores assigned by human experts to essays intended primarily to measure writing competence. By far the most important of these measures, accounting for well over half the predicted variance, is the sheer number of words in the student essay.

Although this might seem to be a spurious predictor, and certainly one easily counterfeited by a test-taker who knew the scoring procedure, it seems likely that it is, in fact, a reasonably good indicator variable under ordinary circumstances. The rationale is that most students, at least when expecting their writing to be judged by a human, will not intentionally write nonsense. Those who know much about the topic at hand, those who have control of large vocabularies and are fluent and skillful in producing discourse, will write, on average, longer essays than those lacking these characteristics. Thus, it is not a great surprise that a measure of length, especially when coupled with a battery of measures of syntax and grammar that would penalize gibberish, does a good job of separating students who can write well from those who can't, and those who know much from those who don't. The major deficiencies in this approach are that its face validity is extremely low, that it appears easy to fake and coach, and that its reflection of knowledge and good thinking on the part of the student arise, if at all, only out of indirect correlations over individual differences.

It is important to note that while vector length in most cases is highly correlated with the sheer number of words used in an essay, or to the number of content–specific words, it need not be that way. For example, unlike ordinary word count methods, an essay on the heart consisting solely of the words "the heart" repeated hundreds of times would generate a low LSA quantity measure, that is, a short vector.

In many of our experiments, the vector length has been highly correlated with the number of words, as used in the Page (1996) measures, and collinear with it in predicting human scores, but in others it has been largely independent of length in number of words, but nevertheless, strongly predictive of human judgments. The standardized essays resemble more closely those studied by Page and others in which word count and measures of stylistic and syntactic qualities together were sufficient to produce good predictions of human scores. Analyses of the relative contributions of the quality and quantity measures and their correlations with length in words for two contrasting cases are shown in Fig. 6.7. It should be mentioned that count variables have been expressly *excluded* from any of the IEA component measures.

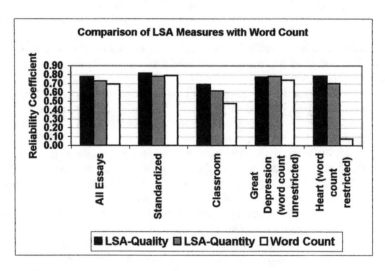

Fig. 6.7 Comparison of Latent Semantic Analysis measures with word count.

One reader training compared with resolved score training. As stated previously, all essay sets had at least two readers, and the LSA models were trained on the resolved score of the readers. In an interesting set of side experiments, on the GMAT issue prompt and on the heart prompt, new analyses were conducted wherein the LSA training used only one or the other of the independent reader scores, rather than the resolved score. This situation would parallel many cases of practical application where the expense of two readers for the calibration set would be too high. In all three cases, where the training used the Resolved scores, the Reader 1 scores, or the

Reader 2 scores, the LSA Quality measure predicts the Resolved scores at a slightly higher level of reliability than it predicts the individual reader scores. The resolved score is the best estimate of the true score of the essay, a better estimate than either individual reader all things being equal. This method, even when using single reader scores, better approximates the true score than does the single reader alone. The results are shown in Fig. 6.8 for the GMAT issue essays, and in Fig. 6.9 for the Heart essays.

An implication of this is that a single reader could use LSA scoring after hand scoring a set of essays, to act as if he or she were two readers, and thereby arrive at a more reliable estimate of the true scores for the entire set of essays. This application would tend to alert one to or smooth out any glaring inconsistencies in scoring by considering each of the semantically-near essays as though they were alternative forms.

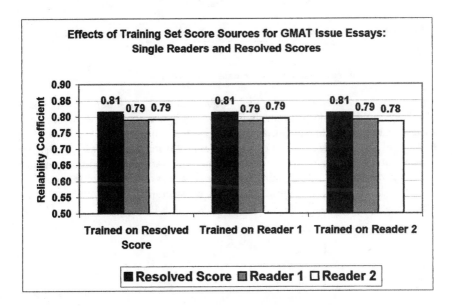

Fig. 6.8. Effects of training set score source for GMAT issue essays

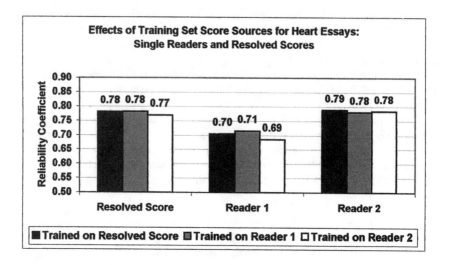

FIG 6.9 Effects of training set score source for heart essays.

Confidence measures for LSA Quality Score. The LSA technique itself makes possible several ways to measure the degree to which a particular essay has been scored reliably. One such measure is to look at the cosines between the essay being scored and the set of k to which it is most similar. If the essays in the comparison set have unusually low cosines with the essay in question (based on the norms of the essays developed in the training stage), or if their assigned grades are unusually variable (also assessed by considering the training norms), it is unlikely that an accurate score can be assigned (See also Fig. 6.10 & 6.11).

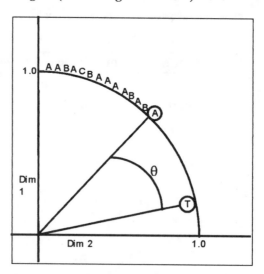

FIG 6.10 Confidence Measure 1: The nearest neighbor has too low of a cosine.

Such a situation could indicate that the essay is incoherent with the content domain. It could also reflect an essentially good or bad answer phrased in a novel way, or, even one that is superbly creative and unique. Again, if the essay in question is quite similar to several others, but they are quite different from each other (which can happen in high–dimensional spaces), the essay in question is also likely to be unusual.

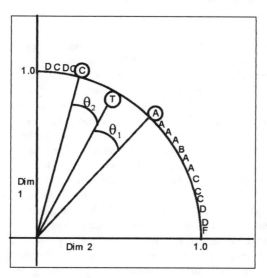

FIG 6.11 Confidence Measure 2. The near neighbor grades are too variable.

On the other hand, if an essay has an unexpectedly high cosine with some other it would be suspected of being a copy. In all these cases, one would want to flag the essay for additional human evaluation. Of course, the application of such measures will usually require that they be renormed for each new topic, but this is easily accomplished by including the necessary statistical analyses in the IEA software system that computes LSA measures.

Validation Measures for the Essay. Computer-based style analyzers offer the possibility of giving the student or teacher information about grammatical and stylistic problems encountered in the student's writing, for example data on the distribution of sentence lengths, use of passives, disagreements in number and gender, and so forth. This kind of facility, like spelling checkers, has become common in text editing and word processing systems. Unfortunately, we know too little about their validity relative to comments and corrections made by human experts, or of their value as instructional devices for students. These methods also offer no route to delivering feedback about the conceptual content of an essay or emulating the criticism or advice that might be given by a teacher with regard to such content.

In addition to the LSA–based measures, the IEA calculates several other sensibility checks. It can compute the number and degree of clustering of word–type repetitions within an essay, the type--token ratio or other parameters of its word frequency distribution, or of the distribution of its word–entropies as computed by the first step in LSA. Comparing several of these measures across the set of essays would allow the detection of any essay constructed by means other than normal composition. For example, forgery schemes based on picking rare words specific to a topic and using them repeatedly, which can modestly increase LSA measures, are caught. Yet another set of validity checks rests on use of available automatic grammar, syntax, and spelling checkers. These also detect many kinds of deviant essays that would get either too high or too low LSA scores for the wrong reasons.

Finally, the IEA includes a method that determines the syntactic cohesiveness of an essay by computing the degree to which the order of words in its sentences reflect the sequential dependencies of the same words as used in printed corpora of the kinds read by students (the primary statistics used in automatic speech recognition "language models"). Gross deviations from normative statistics would indicate abnormally generated text; those with good grammar and syntax will be near the norms. Other validity checks which might be added in future implementations include comparisons with archives of previous essays on the same and similar topics either collected locally or over networks. On one hand, LSA's relative insensitivity to paraphrasing and component reordering would provide enhanced plagiarism detection, on the other, comparisons with a larger pool of comparable essays could be used to improve LSA scoring accuracy.

The Required Size for the Set of Comparison Essays. A general rule of thumb used in acquiring the comparison sets is that the more pre-scored essays that are available, all else being equal, the more accurate the scores determined by the LSA Quality measure (the only measure affected by pre-scoring), especially on essay questions that have a variety of good or correct answers.

To help understand the increase in reliability as comparison set size grows, the GMAT Issue test set was scored based on comparison sets which ranged in size from six essays (one randomly selected at each score point) to 403 (the full training set). As can be seen in Fig. 6.12, even the six-essay comparison set did a reasonable job in prediction. The highest levels of reliability began at around 100 essays and continued through 400 essays. When the six–essay measure was supplemented by the other IEA components, the six–essay and the 400–essay models had equal reliability coefficients of .87.

Plagiarism detection. Another useful property with which LSA imbues IEA is a robust ability to detect copying. As an extension of the normal process of IEA scoring, every essay is compared with every other in a set. If two essays are unusually similar to each other, they are flagged for examination. With LSA, two essays will be very similar despite substitution of synonyms, paraphrasing, restatement, or rearrangement of sentences. In one case, for example, one student had copied another's essay, but had changed most of the content words to synonyms. The professor had read the two essays minutes apart without noticing their similarity.

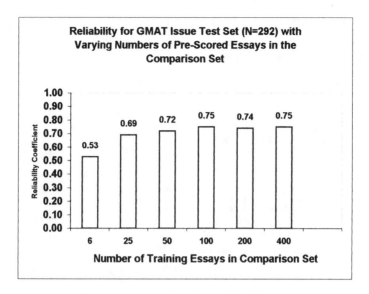

FIG 6.12. Reliability for GMAT essays with varying size of comparison set.

CONCLUSIONS

The IEA provides a rich set of tools for scoring essays and providing feedback. Through its use of LSA, the IEA is able to score content–based essays as well as to pinpoint missing content within the essays. In addition to content–based essays, the IEA can score creative narratives equally well. Because LSA is initially trained on a large amount of background domain text, the IEA does not require many essays in its training set. As described earlier, 100 essays appear to be sufficient for training. Indeed, a new method under development permits scoring of essays with no training set.

An example of the application of the IEA for scoring and providing feedback is provided in Fig. 6.13. The figure shows the feedback given in a web–based interface for training U.S. Army soldiers who are practicing writing memos. Along with an overall holistic score, the interface provides trait scores for content, style and mechanics. In addition, the writer receives feedback as to whether the reading level of the memo is appropriate for its audience, problems with formatting of the memo, and componential feedback on each section of the memo.   This componential feedback describes which sections of the memo are adequately covered and which are in need of revision. Thus, while the IEA can provide overall assessment, the feedback from the IEA can be used to help writers improve their writing skills.

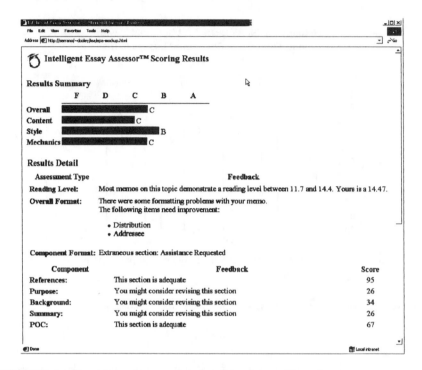

FIG. 6.13 Intelligent Essay Assessor interface for training writing of memos.

On the Limits of LSA Essay Scoring

What does the LSA method fail to capture? First of all, it is obvious LSA does not reflect all discernible and potentially important differences in essay content. In particular, LSA alone does not directly analyze syntax, grammar, literary style, logic, or mechanics (e.g., spelling and punctuation). However, this does not necessarily— or empirically often—cause it to give scores that differ from those assigned by expert readers and, as shown in Fig. 6.5, these measures add little prediction value to the LSA-only model. The overall reliability statistics shown in Fig. 6.3 demonstrate that this must be the case for a wide variety of students and essay topics. Indeed, the correspondence between LSA's word–order independent measures and human judgments is so close that it forces one to consider the possibility that something closely related to word combination alone is the fundamental basis of meaning representation, with syntax usually serving primarily to ease the burden of transmitting word–combination information between agents with limited processing capacity (Landauer, Laham and Foltz, 1998). It should be noted, though, that although LSA does not consider word order, other measures incorporated into the IEA do take these factors into account, permitting more robust scoring and more focused feedback.

In addition to its lack of syntactic information and perceptual grounding, LSA obviously cannot reflect perfectly the knowledge that any one human or group thereof possesses. LSA training always falls far short of the background knowledge that humans bring to any task, experience based on more and different text, and, importantly, on interaction with the world, other people, and spoken language. In addition, on both a sentence and a larger discourse level, it fails to measure directly such qualities as rhyme, sound symbolism, alliteration, cadence, and other aspects of the beauty and elegance of literary expression. It is clear, for example, that the method would be insufficient for evaluating poetry or important separate aspects of creative writing. However, it is possible that stylistic qualities restrict word choice so as to make beautiful essays resemble other beautiful essays to some extent even for LSA.

Nonetheless, some of the esthetics of good writing undoubtedly go unrecognized. It is thus surprising that the LSA measures correlate so closely with the judgments of humans who might have been expected to be sensitive to these matters either intentionally or unintentionally. However, it bears noting that in the pragmatic business of assessing a large number of content–oriented essays, human readers may also be insensitive to, largely ignore, or use these aspects unreliably. Indeed, studies of text comprehension, have found that careful readers often fail to notice even direct contradictions (van Dijk & Kintsch, 1983). And, of course, judgments of aesthetic qualities, as reflected, for example, in the opinion of critics of both fiction and nonfiction, are notoriously unreliable and subject to variation from time to time and purpose to purpose.

Appropriate Purposes for Automatic Scoring

There are some important issues regarding the uses to which LSA scoring is put. These differ depending on whether the method is primarily aimed at assessment or at tutorial evaluation and feedback. We start with assessment: There are several ways of thinking about the object of essay scoring. One is to view assessment as determining whether certain people with special social roles or expertise, (e.g., teachers, critics, admissions officers, potential employers, parents, politicians, or taxpayers) will find the test–taker's writing admirable. Obviously, the degree to which an LSA score will predict such criteria will depend in part on how many of what kind of readers are used as the calibration criterion.

One can also view the goal of an essay exam to be accurate measurement of how much knowledge the student has about a subject. In this case correlation with human experts is simply a matter of expedience; even experts are less than perfectly reliable and valid, thus their use can be considered only an approximation. Other criteria, such as other tests and measures, correlations with amounts or kind of previous learning, or long-term accomplishments—for example, course grades, vocational advancement, professional recognition, or earnings—would be superior ways to calibrate scores.

Theoretical Implications of Automated Scoring

Every successful application of the LSA methodology in information processing, whether in strictly applied roles or in psychological simulations, adds evidence in support of the claim that LSA must, in some way, be capturing the performance characteristics of its human counterparts. LSA scores have repeatedly been found to correlate with a human reader's score as well as one human score correlates with another. Given that humans surely have more knowledge and can use aspects of writing, such as syntax, that are unavailable to LSA, how can this be? There are several possibilities. The first is very strong correlation in different writing skills across students. In general, it has long been known that there is a high correlation over students between quality of performance on different tasks and between different kinds of excellence on the same and similar tasks. It is not necessary to ask the origin of these correlations to recognize that they exist. The issue that this raises for automatic testing is that almost anything that can be detected by a machine that is a legitimate quality of an essay is likely to correlate well with any human judgment based on almost any other quality. So, for example, measures of the number of incorrect spellings, missing or incorrect punctuation marks, or the number of rare words is likely to correlate fairly well with human judgments of quality of arguments or of the goodness and completeness of knowledge. As an example, the LSA scores for the Grade School Narrative essays correlated with the Handwriting scores of the same essays at .76 even though the LSA system had no access to the handwritten essays themselves.

However, no matter how well correlated, we would be uncomfortable in using superficial, intrinsically unimportant properties as the only or main basis of student evaluation, and for good reasons. The most important reason is that by so doing we would tend to encourage students to study and teachers to teach the wrong things; inevitably, the more valuable skills and attitudes would decline and the correlations would disappear. Instead, we want to assess most directly the properties of performance we think most important so as to reward and shape the best study, pedagogical, and curricular techniques and the best public policies.

Where do the automated methods, then, come in? First, they can greatly reduce the expert human effort involved in using essay exams. Even if used only as a "second opinion" as suggested, they would reduce the effort needed to attain better reliability and validity. Second, they offer a much more objective measure.

However, what about the properties of the student that are being measured? Are they the ones that we truly want to measure? Does measuring and rewarding their achievement best motivate and guide a society of learners and teachers? This is not entirely clear. Surely students who study more "deeply," who understand and express knowledge more accurately and completely will tend to receive higher LSA based scores. On the other hand, LSA scores do not capture all and exactly the performances we wish to encourage. Nonetheless, the availability of accurate machine scoring should shift the balance of testing away from multiple–choice and short-answer toward essays, and therefore towards greater concentration on deep comprehension of sources and discursive expression of knowledge.

CHALLENGES AND FUTURE EFFORTS

Although IEA has been developed primarily for assessment and tutorial feedback with regard to the knowledge content of expository essays, it has also been applied successfully to evaluation of creative narratives. There is therefore interest in expanding its detailed componential analyses to such writing qualities as organization, voice, and audience focus, and syntactic, grammatical, and mechanical aspects. Traditional writing instruction and assessment has often focused primarily on these matters rather than knowledge content. Current IEA assesses related but more global characteristics such as word choice, variety, flow, coherence, and readability. It also can assess organization at the paragraph or section level when a predetermined order of exposition is specified, as, for example, in standard format military or medical communications and records. However, IEA does not yet attempt to provide the detail that composition teachers and editors do in their red and blue marks and marginal notes, and in their classroom and one–on–one critiques and scaffolding guidance. In our opinion, doing most of that sufficiently well to be pedagogically valuable is beyond current scientific understanding and technological capabilities. Nonetheless, some lower–level skill components, such as spelling and capitalization errors, can be detected by machine, and others, such as possible errors in agreement, tense, and number, can be noted.

For assessment purposes, at least for students beyond the earliest stages of writing, both the success of IEA, and our exploratory research using human scoring for lower skills show that the various qualities of writing are so closely linked that their separate scoring as individual difference measures is of little additional value. Existing natural language technology for analyses at the level of syntax, grammar, argument, and discourse structure, relies heavily on the detection and counting of literal word types and patterns. Compared to content, these proxies are very easily coached and counterfeited. We fear that their widespread use, especially in high–stakes assessment programs, would encourage teaching–to–the–test of counterproductive skills. Therefore, we favor moving in this direction with caution awaiting a deeper and more general understanding and technological foundation. Our own research in this direction, unsurprisingly, is focused on improvements in LSA and related machine–learning approaches.

REFERENCES

Berry, M. W. (1992). Large scale singular value computations. *International Journal of Supercomputer Applications, 6*,13–49.

Coombs, C. (1964). *A theory of data.* New York: John Wiley

Deerwester, S., Dumais, S. T., Furnas, G. W., Landauer, T. K., & Harshman, R. (1990). Indexing by latent semantic analysis. *Journal of the American Society For Information Science, 41*, 391–407.

Foltz, P. W. (1996) Latent semantic analysis for text–based research. *Behavior Research Methods, Instruments and Computers. 28*, 197–202.

Foltz, P. W., Kintsch, W., & Landauer, T. K. (1998). Analysis of text coherence using latent semantic analysis. *Discourse Processes, 25*, 2&3, 285–307.

Landauer, T. K., & Dumais, S. T. (1997). A solution to Plato's problem: The latent semantic analysis theory of the acquisition, induction, and representation of knowledge. *Psychological Review, 104*, 211–240.

Landauer, T. K, Foltz, P. W. & Laham, D. (1998) An introduction to latent semantic analysis. *Discourse Processes, 25*, 259–284.

Landauer, T. K., Laham, D., & Foltz, P. W., (1998). Learning human–like knowledge by singular value decomposition: A progress report. In M. I. Jordan, M. J. Kearns & S. A. Solla (Eds.), Advances in neural information processing systems (pp. 45–51). Cambridge, MA: MIT Press.

Page, E. B. (1966). The imminence of grading essays by computer. *Phi Delta Kappan,* *48,* 238–243.

Page, E.B. (1994). Computer grading of student prose, using modern concepts, and software. *Journal of Experimental Education, 62,* 127–142.

Shavelson, R. J., & Webb, N. M. (1991). *Generalizability theory: A primer.* Newbury Park, CA: Sage.

van Dijk, T. A., & Kintsch, W. (1983). Strategies of Discourse Comprehension. New York: Academic.

Wolfe, M. B., Schreiner, M. E., Rehder, B., Laham, D., Foltz, P. W., Kintsch, W., & Landauer, T. K. (1998). Learning from text: Matching readers and text by latent semantic analysis. *Discourse Processes, 25,* 309–336.

7

The *E-rater*® Scoring Engine:
Automated Essay Scoring With Natural Language Processing

Jill Burstein
ETS Technologies, Inc.

Educational Testing Service (ETS) has been doing research in writing assessment since its founding in 1947. ETS administered the Naval Academy English Examination and the Foreign Service Examination as early as 1948 (Educational Testing Service, 1949-1950), and the Advanced Placement (AP) essay exam was administered in the spring of 1956. Some of the earliest research in writing assessment laid the foundation for holistic scoring—a scoring methodology used currently by ETS for large-scale writing assessments (see Coward, 1950 and Huddleston, 1952).

There has been a strong interest from the assessment community to introduce increasingly more writing components onto standardized tests. Due to this interest, several large-scale assessment programs now contain a writing measure. These programs include the Graduate Management Admissions Test (GMAT), the Test of English as a Foreign Language (TOEFL), the Graduate Record Examination (GRE), Professional Assessments for Beginning Teachers (Praxis), the College Board's Scholastic Assessment Test II Writing Test and Advanced Placement (AP) exam, and the College-Level Examination Program (CLEP) English and writing tests. Some of these tests have moved to computer-based delivery, including the GMAT, TOEFL, GRE, and Praxis. Computer-based delivery allows for the possibility of automated scoring capabilities.

In February 1999, ETS began to use *"e-rater*®" for operational scoring of the GMAT Analytical Writing Assessment (AWA) (see Burstein et al., 1998, and Kukich, 2000). The GMAT AWA has two test question types (prompts): the issue prompt and the argument prompts. The issue prompt asks examinees to give their opinion in response to a general essay question, and use personal experiences and observations to support their point of view. To respond to the argument prompt, examinees are presented with an argument. The examinee is asked to evaluate and give his or her opinion about the argument. Examinees can use examples from personal observations and experiences to support their evaluation.

Prior to the use of *e-rater*®, both the paper-and-pencil, and initial computer-based versions of the GMAT AWA were scored by two human readers on a 6-point holistic scale. A final score was assigned to an essay response based on the original two reader scores if these two scores differed by no more than 1 score point. If the two readers were discrepant by more than 1 point, a third reader score was introduced to resolve the final score. Only in rare cases was a fourth reader asked to read an essay, if the initial three readers all disagreed by more than 1 point —for instance, if the original three reader scores were "1," "3," and "5."

Since February 1999, test-taker essays have been assigned an *e-rater*® score and one human reader score. Using the GMAT score resolution procedures for two human readers, if the *e-rater*® and human reader scores differ by more than one point, a second human reader is used to resolve the discrepancy. Otherwise, if the *e-rater*® and human reader scores agree within 1 point, these two scores are used to compute the final score for the essay.

Since *e-rater*® was made operational for GMAT AWA scoring, it has scored approximately 360,000 essays per year. The reported discrepancy rate between *e-rater*® and one human reader score has been less than 3% percent. So, only in 3% percent of cases does a second human reader intervene to resolve discrepancies between an *e-rater*® and a human reader score. What this means is that *e-rater*® and a human score differ by no more than a single point 97% of the time which is comparable to the discrepancy rate between two human readers.

The ability to use automated essay scoring in operational environments reduces the time and costs associated with having multiple human readers score essay responses. As stated earlier, agreement between two human readers, and between *e-rater*® and one human reader, has been noted to be comparable (Burstein et al., 1998). Therefore, automated essay scoring would appear to be a favorable solution toward the introduction of more writing assessments on high-stakes standardized tests, and in a lower-stakes environment—for practice assessments and classroom instruction.

E-rater® DESIGN AND HOLISTIC SCORING

Holistic essay scoring departs from the traditional, analytical system of teaching and evaluating writing. In the holistic scoring approach, readers are told to read quickly for a total impression and to take into account all aspects of writing as specified in the scoring guide. The final score is based on the reader's total impression (Conlan, 1980). Since e-*rater*'s® inception, a goal of the system's developers has been to implement features (used in *e-rater*® scoring) that are related to the holistic scoring guide features. Generally speaking, the scoring guide indicates that an essay that stays on the topic of the question has a strong, coherent, and well-organized argument structure, and displays a variety of word use, and syntactic structure will receive a score at the higher end of the 6-point scale (5 or 6); *e-rater*® features include discourse structure, syntactic structure, and analysis of vocabulary usage (topical analysis) described in following sections. The set of *e-rater*® features does not include direct measures of length, such as word count in essays, or transformations of word count.

NATURAL LANGUAGE PROCESSING (NLP)?

Natural Language Processing (NLP) is the application of computational methods to analyze characteristics of electronic files of text or speech. Because *e-rater®* is a text-based application, this section discusses a few NLP-based applications related to the analysis of text.

Statistical- and linguistic-based methods are used to develop a variety of NLP-based tools, designed to carry out various types of language analyses. Examples of these tools follow: part-of-speech taggers, assignment of part-of-speech labels to words in a text (Brill, 1999); syntactic parsers, analysis of the syntactic structures in a text (Abney, 1996); discourse parsers, analysis of the discourse structure of a text (Marcu, 2000); and lexical similarity measures, analysis of word use in a text (Salton, 1989).

One of the earliest research efforts in NLP was for machine translation. This application involves using computational analyses to translate a text from one language to another. For machine translation, computing techniques are used to find close associations between words, terms, and syntactic forms of one language and the target translation language. A well-known research effort in machine translation took place during the Cold War era, when the United States was trying to build programs to translate Russian into English. Although research continues in machine translation to further develop this capability, off-the-shelf machine translation software is available. An overview of some approaches to machine translation can be found in Knight, 1997. Another NLP application that has been researched since the 1950s is automatic summarization tasks. Summarization techniques are used to automatically extract the most relevant text from a document (Jing & McKeown, 2000; Marcu, 2000; and Teufel and Moens, 1999, 2000). Summarized texts can be used, for example, to automatically generate abstracts. A practical application of automatic abstracting, for instance, is the generation of abstracts from legal documents (Moens, et al., 1999). Search engines for Internet browsers may also use NLP. When we enter a search phrase, or query into a browser's search engine, automated analysis must be done to evaluate the content of the query. An analysis of the vocabulary in the original query is performed that enables the browser's search engine to return the most relevant responses (Salton, 1989).

E-rater® and NLP

e-rater® uses a corpus-based approach to model building. In this approach, actual essay data are used to analyze the features in a sample of essay responses. A corpus-based approach is in contrast to a theoretical approach in which feature analysis and linguistic rules might be hypothesized a priori based on the kinds of characteristics one might expect to find in the data sample (in this case, a corpus of first-draft, student essay responses.)

When using a corpus-based approach to build NLP-based tools for text analysis, researchers and developers typically use copyedited text sources. The corpora often include text from newspapers, such as *The Wall Street Journal*, or the Brown corpus, which contains 1 million words of text across genres (e.g., newspapers, magazines, excerpts from novels, and technical reports). For instance, an NLP tool known as a part of speech tagger (Brill, 1999) is designed to label each word in a text with its correct part of speech (e.g., noun, verb, preposition). Text that has been automatically tagged (labeled) with part-of-speech identifiers can be used to develop other tools, such as syntactic parsers, in which the part-of-speech tagged text is used to generate whole syntactic constituents. These constituents detail how words are connected into larger syntactic units, such as noun phrases, verb phrases, and complete sentences. The rules that are used in part-of-speech taggers to determine how to label a word are developed from copyedited text sources such as those mentioned earlier. By contrast, *e-rater*® feature analysis and model building (described below) are based on unedited text corpora representing the specific genre of first-draft essay writing.

E-rater Details: Essay Feature Analysis and Scoring

E-rater® is designed to identify features in the text that reflect writing qualities specified in human reader scoring criteria. The application contains several independent modules. The system includes three NLP-based modules for identifying scoring guide relevant features from the following categories: syntax, discourse, and topic. Each of the feature recognition modules described later identifies features that correspond to scoring guide criteria features. These features, namely, syntactic variety, organization of ideas, and vocabulary usage, correlate to essay scores assigned by human readers. *E-rater*® uses a model building module to select and weight predictive features for essay scoring. The model building module reconfigures the feature selections and associated regression weightings given a sample of human reader scored essays for a particular test question. Another module is used for final score assignment.

Syntactic Module

E-rater's® current syntactic analyzer (parser) works in the following way to identify syntactic features constructions in essay text.[1] A part-of-speech tagger (Ratnaparkhi, 1996) is used to assign part-of-speech labels to all words in an essay. Then, the syntactic "chunker" (Abney, 1996) finds phrases (based on the part-of-speech labels in the essay) and assembles the phrases into trees based on subcategorization information for verbs (Grishman, MacLeod, & Meyers, 1994). This e-*rater*® parser identifies various clauses, including infinitive, complement, and subordinate clauses. The ability to identify such clause types allows *e-rater*® to

---

[1] The parser used in *E-rater* was designed and implemented by Claudia Leacock, Tom Morton and Hoa Dang Trang.

capture syntactic variety in an essay. As part of the process of continual *e-rater*® development, research is currently being done to refine the current parser. More accurate parses might improve *e-rater's*® overall performance.

Discourse Module

E-rater® identifies discourse cue words, terms, and syntactic structures. These discourse identifiers are used to annotate each essay according to a discourse classification schema (Quirk, Leech & Svartik, 1985). Generally, *e-rater's*™ discourse annotations denote the beginnings of arguments (the main points of discussion), or argument development within a text, as well as the classification of discourse relations associated with the argument type (e.g., the "parallel relation" is associated with terms including, "first," "second," and "finally"). Some syntactic structures in the text of an essay can function as discourse cues. For instance, syntactic structures such as complement clauses are used to identify the beginning of a new argument, based on their position within a sentence, and within a paragraph. *E-rater's*® discourse features can be associated with the scoring guide concept, organization of ideas.

E-rater® uses the discourse annotations to partition essays into separate arguments. These argument partitioned versions of essays are used by the topical analysis module to evaluate the content of individual arguments (Burstein & Chodorow, 1999; Burstein, et al, 1998). *E-rater's*® discourse analysis produces a flat, linear sequence of units. For instance, in the essay text *e-rater's*® discourse annotation indicates that a contrast relations exists, based on discourse cue words, such as *however*. Hierarchical discourse-based relations showing intersentential relationships are not specified. Other discourse analysis programs do identify such relationships (Marcu, 2000).

Topical Analysis Module

Vocabulary usage is another criterion listed in human reader scoring guides. To capture use of vocabulary, or identification of topic, *e-rater*® uses a topical analysis module. The procedures in this module are based on the vector-space model, commonly found in information retrieval applications (Salton, 1989). These analyses are done at the level of the essay (big bag of words) and the argument.

For both levels of analysis, training essays are converted into vectors of word frequencies, and the frequencies are then transformed into word weights. These weight vectors populate the training space. To score a test essay, it is converted into a weight vector, and a search is conducted to find the training vectors most similar to it, as measured by the cosine between the test and training vectors. The closest matches among the training set are used to assign a score to the test essay.

As already mentioned, *e-rater*® uses two different forms of the general procedure sketched earlier. For looking at topical analysis at the essay level, each of the training essays (also used for training *e-rater*®) is represented by a separate vector in the training space. The score assigned to the test essay is a weighted mean of the scores for the six training essays whose vectors are closest to the vector of the test essay.

In the method used to analyze topical analysis at the argument level, all of the training essays are combined for each score category to populate the training space with just six "supervectors." one each for scores 1 to 6. The argument-partitioned version of the essays generated from the discourse module were used in the set of test essays. Each test essay is evaluated one argument at a time. Each argument is converted into a vector of word weights and compared to the six vectors in the training space. The closest vector is found and its score is assigned to the argument. This process continues until all the arguments have been assigned a score. The overall score for the test essay is based on a mean of the scores for all arguments (see Burstein & Marcu, 2000, for details).

Model Building and Scoring

The syntactic, discourse, and topical analysis feature modules each yield numerical outputs that are used for model building and essay scoring. Specifically, counts of identified syntactic and discourse features are computed. The counts of features in each essay are stored in vectors for each essay. Similarly, for each essay, the scores from the topical analysis by-essay and topical analysis by-argument procedures are stored in vectors. The values in the vectors for each feature category are then used to build scoring models for each test question as described later

As mentioned earlier, a corpus-based linguistics approach is used for *e-rater®* model building. To build models, a training set of human-scored sample essays that is representative of the range of scores is randomly selected. Essays are generally scored on a 6-point scale, where a "6" indicates the score assigned to the most competent writer, and a score of "1" indicates the score assigned to the least competent writer. Optimal training set samples contain 265 essays that have been scored by two human readers. The data sample is distributed in the following way with respect to score points: 15 "1"s, and 50 in each of the score points "2" through "6."

The model building module is a program that runs a forward-entry stepwise linear regression. Feature values stored in the syntactic, discourse, and topical analysis vector files are the input to the regression program. This regression program automatically selects the features that are predictive for a given set of training data (from one test question). The program outputs the predictive features and their associated regression weightings. This output composes the model that is then used for scoring.

In an independent scoring module, a linear equation is used to compute the final essay score. To compute the final score for each essay, the sum of the product of each regression weighting and its associated feature integer is calculated.

CRITERION[SM]

On-line essay evaluation: E-*rater®* for different writing levels

E-*rater®* is currently embedded in *Criterion*[SM], an on line essay evaluation product of ETS Technologies, Inc., a for-profit wholly-owned subsidiary of ETS. The version of *e-rater®* in *Criterion*[SM] is web-based. This essay evaluation system is being used by institutions for high- and low-stakes writing assessment, as well as for classroom instruction. Using a web-based, real-time version of the system, instructors and students can see the *e-rater®* score, and score-relevant feedback within seconds.

This research in automated essay scoring has indicated that *e-rater®* performs comparably to human readers at different grade levels. *e-rater®* models exist for prompts based on data samples from grades 4 through 12 using national standards prompts; for undergraduates, using English Proficiency Test and PRAXIS prompts; and for non native English speakers, using TOEFL prompts. ETS programs, including GMAT, TOEFL, and GRE are currently using *e-rater®* with Criterion[SM] for low-stakes, practice tests.

E-*rater®* Targeted Advisories

Since one of *Criterion's*[SM] primary functions is to serve as an instructional tool, a central research effort is the development of evaluative feedback capabilities. The initial feedback component in use with *Criterion*[SM] is referred to as the *advisory component*.[2] The component generates advisories based on statistical measures that evaluate word usage in essay responses in relation to the stimuli, and a sample of essay responses to a test question. The advisories provide additional feedback about qualities of writing related to topic and fluency, but are generated independently from the *e-rater®* score. It is important to note that these advisories are not used to compute the *e-rater®* score, but provide a supplement to the score.

The advisory component includes feedback to indicate the following qualities of an essay response: (a) the text is too brief to be a complete essay (suggesting that the student write more), (b) the essay text does not resemble other essays written about the topic (implying that perhaps the essay is off-topic), and (c) the essay response is overly repetitive (suggesting that the student use more synonyms).

---

[2] This advisory component was designed and implemented by Martin Chodorow and Chi Lu. The advisory also is intended to flag misuses of the system, that is, where users try to 'torpedo' the system inputting essays not written in good faith. Users often attempt to trick the system by typing in erroneous texts (see Herrington and Moran, 2001). Of course, this is not the intended use of automated essay scoring technology. The intention is to provide an environment for serious use the system that that their writing can be assessed, or so that they can practice and get a reasonable assessment of their work.

Discussion

Since the *e-rater®* scoring engine was introduced into high stakes assessment for the GMAT AWA in 1999, its application has become more varied and widespread through its use with Criterion[SM]. *E-rater®* is currently being used not only for high-stakes assessment, but for practice assessments and classroom instruction. Additionally, our research has indicated that *e-rater®* can be used across many populations, specifically, across different grade levels from elementary school through graduate school, and with both native and non-native English populations. Testing programs representing all of these populations are using *e-rater®* with Criterion[SM].

The version of *e-rater®* described in this chapter scores essays based on a prompt-specific model. More recent research focuses on the development of generic *e-rater®* scoring models. For instance, a model might be built on several prompts for one population, such as sixth-grade persuasive writing. The idea is that this model may be used to score any number of new topics, given the same population, and same genre of the persuasive essay. In addition, work is being pursued to provide meaningful scores to specific essay traits, related to grammaticality, usage, and style.

The research to enrich the *E-rater®* scoring engine is on-going, and the development of the system continues to be informed by the writing community.

REFERENCES

Abney, S. (1996). Par of Speech Tagging and Partial Parsing. In Church, Young, and Bloothooft (Eds.), *Corpus-based methods in language and speech.* Dordrecht: Kluwer.

Brill, E. (1999). Unsupervised learning of disambiguation rules for part of speech tagging, natural language processing using very large corpora. Dordrecht, The Netherlands: Kluwer.

Burstein, J. and Marcu, D. (2000). Towards using text summarization for essay-based feedback. *Le 7e Conference Annuelle sur Le Traitement Automatique des Langues Naturelles TALN'2000*, Switzerland *Automated*, 51–59.

Burstein, J., and Chodorow, M. (1999). Essay Scoring for nonnative English speakers. Proceedings of a workshop on computer-mediated language assessment and evaluation in natural language processing. Joint symposium of the Association of Computational Linguistics and the International Association of Language Learning Technology. College Park, MD, 68-75.

Burstein, J., Kukich, K. Wolff, S. Lu, C., Chodorow, M., Braden-Harder, L., et al. (1998). Automated scoring using a hybrid feature identification technique. Proceedings of the 36th Annual Meeting of the Association of Computational Linguistics, Montreal, Canada, 206-210.

Conlan, G. (1980). *Comparison of analytic and holistic scoring.* Unpublished.

Coward, A. F. (1950). The method of reading the Foreign Service Examination in English composition (ETS RB–50–57). Princeton, NJ: Educational Testing Service.

Educational Testing Service. (1949-1950). *Educational Testing Service Annual Report.* Princeton, NJ: Author.

Grishman, R., MacLeod, C., & Meyers, A. (1994). *"COMLEX syntax: Building a computational lexicon" proceedings of Coling, Kyoto, Japan.* Retrieved May 9, 2002 from http://cs.nyu.edu/cs/projects/proteus/comlex/

Herrington, A., & Moran, C. (2001). What happens when machines read our student writing? *College English, 61*(4), 480–499.

Huddleston, E. M. (1952). *Measurement of writing ability at the college-entrance level: Objective vs. subjective testing techniques* (ETS RB–52–57). Princeton, NJ: Educational Testing Service.

Jing, H., & McKeown, K. (2000). Cut and paste text summarization. *Proceedings of the frist meeting of the North American chapter of the Association for Computational Linguistics, Seattle, Washington,* 178–185.

Knight, K. (1997). Automating Knowledge Acquisition for Machine Translation. *AI Magazine, 18*(4).

Kukich, K. (2000). Beyond automated essay scoring. *IEEE Intelligent System, September-October,* 22–27.

Marcu, D. (2000). *The theory and practice of discourse parsing and summarization.* MIT Press.

Meons, M. F., Vyttendael, C., Dumartier, J. (1999). Abstracting of Legal Cases: The potential of clustering based on the selection of represent399ative objects. *Journal of the American Society for Information Science, 50*(2), 151-161.

Quirk, R., Greenbau, S., Leech, S., & Svartik, J. (1985). *A comprehensive grammar of the English language.* New York: Longman.

Ratnaparkhi, A. (1996). A maximum entropy part-of-speech tagger. *Proceedings of the Empirical Methods in Natural Language Processing Conference, USA, 19,* 1133-1141.

Salton, G. (1989). *Automatic text processing: The transformation, analysis, and retrieval of information by computer. Reading, MA: Addison-Wesley.*

Teufel, S., & Moens, M. (1999). Argumentative classification of extracted sentences as a first step towards flexible abstracting. In Mani & Maybury (Eds.), *Advances in automatic text summarization* (pp. 155-175). Cambridge, MA: MIT Press.

IV. Psychometric Issues in Automated Essay Scoring

8

The Concept of Reliability in the Context of Automated Essay Scoring

Gregory J. Cizek
Bethany A. Page
University of North Carolina at Chapel Hill

As demonstrated by the authors of other chapters in this volume, automated scoring of extended responses to test items or prompts is a *fait accompli*. Many changes and circumstances of the present age have facilitated this capability. Among these are the persistence of testing for licensure, certification, and selection in business and the professions; a proliferation of testing for measuring pupil proficiency in American schools; a renewed emphasis on constructed–response test formats; advances in computing power and software sophistication; and the permeation of technology into nearly all aspects of modern life. It is worth noting the rapid pace and short time span in which these changes have taken place.

Some essential testing concepts and practices have remained the same, however. In the arenas of educational and psychological testing, validity of test score interpretations remains the reigning deity (Ebel, 1961), and the potence of validity remains undergirded by reliability. The newest version of the *Standards for Educational and Psychological Testing* (American Educational Research Association AERA, American Psychological Association, APA, National Council on Measurement in Education, NCME, 1999) testifies to the continuing primacy of validity and reliability by locating these topics as the first and second chapters, respectively, in that volume. These placements have not changed over previous editions of the *Standards* published in 1966 and 1985.

The potential for users of tests to make accurate inferences about persons via their test scores—that is, validity—is the ultimate criterion by which tests are judged. However, it is still widely regarded in traditional psychometric parlance that the penultimate criterion of reliability "is a necessary but not sufficient condition for validity" (Cherry & Meyer, 1993, p. 110). As such, it can be said that reliability enables validity to assume the throne; more colloquially, it might be said that validity and reliability have a codependent relationship.

In the following sections of this chapter, we further explore some basic concepts involving reliability and distinguish it from other, related, psychometric concepts. We probe the common and unique meanings of reliability in the context of automated scoring; we review some mechanics for expressing reliability in the context of automated scoring; and, we conclude with limitations, cautions, and suggestions for the future.

THE CONCEPT OF RELIABILITY AND RELATED NOTIONS

Some confusion persists about the definition of *reliability*. Informally, reliability refers to the consistency, dependability, or reproducibility of scores yielded by some measurement procedure. Even in this non-technical definition, there is need to reiterate the caveat that reliability refers to a characteristic of scores or data. Reliability is not a characteristic of a test. The same test administered to different populations of test–takers would almost certainly yield different estimates of reliability. Furthermore, as is apparent in the previous statement, we note that it is also more accurate to speak of reliability estimates. The "true" reliability coefficient is a parameter. As such, according to statistical theory, it is a conceivable but essentially unknowable description of a characteristic of a population that must be estimated from sample data. Thus, all reported reliability coefficients are only estimates of that characteristic, not established with certitude.

According to classical test theory (CTT; Gulliksen, 1950; Spearman, 1904), reliability is more formally presented as the correlation $\rho_{xx'}$, between two sets of scores yielded by the administration of parallel test forms. Reliability may also be expressed as ρ_x^2, which is the symbolic way of representing the ratio of true variation in a set of scores to the observed variation in the set of scores (i.e., σ_T^2 / σ_X^2). Though masked in the preceding definitions, the noble obsession of classical measurement specialists (and others) is that of quantifying, estimating, and controlling error variation. As Traub has summarized: "Classical test theory is founded on the proposition that measurement error, a random, latent variable, is a component of the observed score random variable" (1997, p. 8).

According to CTT, errors of measurement come in two flavors: systematic and random. The impact of systematic errors can be illustrated with reference to the physical measurement of the height. If a group of persons were to have their heights measured while standing on a 12–inch platform, the measurement of each person's height would be systematically "off" by approximately 12 inches. These systematic errors may not be practically important, however, at least in the sense the person who is truly the tallest will be judged to be the tallest, despite the inaccuracy introduced by the use of the platform. Likewise, if all persons are measured on the same platform, conclusions about who is the second tallest person, who is the shortest person, and so on, will still be accurate. As the *Standards for Educational and Psychological Testing* indicate, "…individual systematic errors are not generally regarded as an element that contributes to unreliability. Rather, they constitute a source of construct–irrelevant variance and thus may detract from validity" (AERA, APA, NCME, 1999, p. 26)

By extending the analogy involving the measurement of height, it is possible to illustrate the distinction in nature and effect of systematic and random errors. The systematic errors described earlier posed comparatively benign consequences; they did not degrade inferences about which person is tallest, next tallest, and so on.

On the other hand, random errors of measurement would pose serious threats to accurate interpretations of the measurements. Random errors of measurement might be introduced if the measurement of each person's height was performed with a different yardstick. Now, in addition to the systematic errors attributable to the platform, there are other errors introduced that are more serendipitous—attributable to whatever yardstick happens to be selected for the measurement of a certain individual. These random errors have the potential to result in misinformation about heights of the individuals. For example, if the yardsticks are seriously discrepant, a taller person could have a measured height that is less than a person who is, in truth, shorter. Although both systematic and random sources of error are of concern to measurement specialists, estimation of the variability of random errors is a paramount concern in CTT because of its comparatively more serious consequences for accurate interpretations of scores. This focus on random errors is, in a more or less salient way, the object of scrutiny in other measurement paradigms such as generalizability theory (GT) and item response theory (IRT).

A notion related to reliability is that of *agreement*. Although the tools of CTT can yield coefficients representing perfect reliability (i.e., $r_{xx'} = 1.0$) between two sets of scores, those coefficients can attain values as high as 1.0 even when each of the measurements in one set differs from its counterpart in the second set of measurements. For example, consider the ratings, on a 1 to 5 scale, assigned by two scorers to essays produced by 10 students. Suppose that Scorer A rated the 10 essays as follows [5, 5, 5, 4, 4, 4, 4, 3, 3, 2], whereas Scorer B's ratings were [4, 4, 4, 3, 3, 3, 3, 2, 2, 1]. The reliability (correlation) of these scores would be 1.0, although the scorers did not agree on the rating for even one of the students.

To address this aspect of score dependability, statistical methods have been developed for estimating agreement. The simplest approach involves calculation of the percentage of cases in which the raters generated identical scores. Alternatively, one can calculate an agreement coefficient, p_o (by dividing the number of cases for which the two raters produced identical scores by the total number of cases), or an agreement index (see, for example, Burry–Stock, Shaw, Laurie, & Chissom, 1996). Because two raters could, by chance alone, agree (e.g., two raters could assign the same scores to a student essay, without even having read the essay), additional procedures have been developed to correct for spuriously high agreement indices (see Livingston & Lewis, 1995; Subkoviak, 1976).

When calculating and reporting agreement indices, it is important to distinguish between exact agreement and what is called adjacent agreement. *Exact agreement* considers agreement to occur only when two raters assign precisely the same value to an essay. The term *adjacent agreement* is used when raters assign ratings within one scale point of each other. For example, suppose an essay were scored on a 1 to 5-point scale. Two raters who scored the essay as a 4 and a 5, respectively, could be considered in adjacent agreement. These raters would, however, be considered as not in agreement if exact agreement were used. Consequently, if exact agreement is the criterion employed when calculating an agreement index, the resulting value will tend to be less than that which would result if adjacent agreement were used.

It is not clear that choice of exact agreement for such calculations is more or less appropriate than the choice to use adjacent agreement. What is clear is that those who report agreement indices should carefully specify which method has been utilized. Further, we recommend that consumers of agreement information consider the relative inflation in agreement index that is the consequence of choosing to use an adjacent agreement criterion.

RELIABILITY IN THE CONTEXT OF AUTOMATED SCORING

As noted previously, classical and modern test theories focus particularly on random errors. Methods of expressing reliability, such as the standard error of measurement (SEM) are, by definition, estimates of the variability in random errors of measurement. These errors occur, for example, when a student responds to a series of multiple–choice items, or when multiple scorers rate students' essays. However, when scores on those essays are the result of automated scoring, traditional methods of estimating reliability are, in some cases, inappropriate or uninformative. Would it make sense to estimate interrater agreement by comparing the results generated by two computers using the same software and rating the same set of essays? Obviously not. What about having a single computer generate test–retest coefficients by producing two sets of ratings for the same group of essays? Silly.

Unlike the context of human scoring, random errors in the computer scoring process are essentially eliminated. As Stanley (1998) observed, automated scoring eliminates reliability threats such as sequence and contrast effects. Computers don't see halos, succumb to fatigue, or experience "drift" in the application of a scoring protocol. Nonetheless, certain types of random errors of measurement still exist, of course, and the estimation of their magnitude remains of interest.

The following sections of this chapter examine three general areas of concern relating to reliability of scores. The first section reviews basic sources of unreliability that should be considered regardless of the scoring procedure (i.e., traditional or automated). The second section presents some issues related to reliability of scores that are unique to the context of automated scoring. The third section extends the discussion of reliability of scores to the specific measurement context in which it is not the total score, but a classification based on the total score that is of greatest concern. The chapter ends with conclusions and recommendations for the future.

OMNIPRESENT RELIABILITY CONCERNS

Although automated scoring virtually eliminates random errors of measurement introduced by a scoring process, it cannot address many sources of error inherent in any social science measurement. Sources of unreliability that persist regardless of the procedure used for scoring include those resulting from a) personal characteristics of examinees; b) characteristics of the essay prompt or item stimulus; and c) characteristics of the condition under which the test is administered.

Student performance on an essay is certain to vary to some degree from administration to administration. The personal characteristics of an examinee can contribute to this fluctuation in performance or, in other words, to the error variation. For example, a student who is fatigued on one occasion may have difficulty concentrating, causing him or her to make careless grammatical errors or depressing his or her capability to effectively express ideas. The score assigned to this essay is not a reliable estimate of this student's true score or ability, given that the same student, when less fatigued, would likely produce a different essay response and receive a different essay score. This "inconsistency of student performance lessens our ability to rely on a single writing sample to make judgments about a student's writing ability" (Cherry & Meyer, 1993, p. 112). Other related characteristics that might lead to atypical student performance include illness, mood, motivation, efficacy, and anxiety, to name a few such examinee characteristics that would be expected to differ across testing occasions.

As Cherry and Meyer (1993) suggested, a test is only a sample of a student's performance and, consequently, the student's performance is bound to differ at least somewhat on successive administrations of the same test or a parallel form. It is important, however, to investigate how error attributable to variation in student characteristics can be minimized. Several familiar and often–utilized strategies exist for conducting such investigations. For example, it is common for many large–scale assessment programs to send a letter, prior to test administration, to students parents, or guardians, advising them of the upcoming test and providing recommendations for student preparation. The letter might express the need for a good night's rest, an adequate meal, and so forth. Assuming the student's parents or guardians implement the suggested strategies, the probability of examinees being uniformly prepared physically and emotionally is enhanced and variability attributable to some construct–irrelevant sources of variation is lessened.

Characteristics of the essay prompt can also contribute to the unreliability of essay scores. Prompts used to evaluate students' writing ability represent only a sample from a universe of possible prompts. Clearly, this is problematic because "the decision maker is almost never interested in the response given to the particular stimulus objects or questions;" rather, "the ideal datum on which to base the decision would be something like the person's mean score over all acceptable observations" (Cronbach, Gleser, Nanda, & Rajaratnam, 1972, p. 15). If the difficulty of the essay prompts differ, a student's score will depend on the prompt used to assess his or her ability. For example, a prompt requiring a student to compose a narrative may prove more difficult than an essay requiring him or her to produce a persuasive essay. As a result, the student's score will likely be lower for the narrative than for the persuasive essay, indicating that the scores are not dependable or generalizable beyond the prompts used to obtain them. Even two prompts that each require the production of a narrative essay are likely to vary in difficulty, and evoke similar issues involving score dependability.

Another potential threat to reliability involves the conditions and procedures under which the test is administered. If the room is noisy, for instance, students might be distracted and perform atypically. Poor lighting or temperature control might also contribute to uncharacteristic student performance. Similarly, if administration procedures (e.g., instructions) are not uniform, students' performances are apt to vary across successive administrations. Adequately preparing and selecting the testing area as well as providing a standard set of instructions for administering the test can help minimize these effects.

Finally, inconsistencies in performance are also present in responses to the same prompt administered on different occasions. A student's answer to a question about the Civil War will differ to some degree from one occasion to the next. The general idea underlying the text may be the same, but the organization of those ideas, the sentence structure, grammar, word usage, and so forth will likely vary. To the extent that this disparity in response produces different essay scores, the dependability or reliability of those scores will vary. When automated scoring is used (or when more traditional scoring methods are used), it is important that these sources of variation in students' performances be evaluated.

INVESTIGATING SCORE DEPENDABILITY

Fortunately, there are methods available to estimate the extent to which total score variation can be attributed to components or facets of the measurement process such as the essay prompt or testing occasion. One such method is found in generalizability theory, or G–theory (see Brennan, 1983; Cronbach, et al, 1972).

> G–theory "...enables the decision maker to determine how many occasions, test forms, and administrations are needed to obtain dependable scores. In the process, G–theory provides a summary coefficient reflecting the level of dependability, a generalizability coefficient that is analogous to classical test theory's reliability coefficient" (Shavelson & Webb, 1991, p. 2).

G–theory also permits quantification and estimation of the relative sources of variation, or facets, such as occasions, prompts, or raters. The estimates are obtained via a *G-study*, in which analysis of variance methods are used to derive *variance components*. The variance components can be used in subsequent *d-studies* which allow an operational measurement procedure to be configured in such a way as to minimize undesirable sources of variation.

For example, imagine a situation in which 25 students in a social studies class have completed an essay test by responding to two prompts pertaining to the Civil War. All students respond to both prompts, and each essay is scored by the students' teacher and one other social studies teacher. The teachers, or raters, score each essay on a scale from 1 *(lowest)* to 4 *(highest)* according to preestablished criteria.

The dependability of the teachers' ratings could be assessed using G–theory. The design described earlier would, in G–theory terms, be considered a crossed, two–facet random–effects design. Students are the objects of measurement in this case, and we are interested in the sources of variation in their scores on the essays. The two facets in this situation are raters (*r*) and prompt (*p*). Because all students respond to both prompts and each rater scores all responses to both prompts, this

G-study design is said to be "fully crossed." Further, because the specific prompts used for the essays and the specific teachers who rated the essays could be considered to be samples from a population of possible prompts and raters, the design is also called a "random effects" design.

According to Shavelson and Webb (1991),

> Samples are considered random when the size of the sample is much smaller than the size of the universe, and the sample either is drawn randomly or is considered to be exchangeable with any other sample of the same size drawn from the universe. (Shavelson & Webb, 1991, p. 11).

When the conditions of the facet represent all possible conditions in the universe, then it is fixed and not random. For instance, achievement tests usually include subtests covering content from mathematics and English. In this case, the items for each subtest would be random facets and the subjects (i.e., mathematics and English) would be fixed facets.

Other G–study designs are possible and, in some cases, may be preferable to the fully crossed design described previously. For example, had raters scored responses to different prompts (e.g., Rater one scores-responses to prompt 1 and Rater two score's responses to prompt 2), the design would be called "partially nested." (It is not fully nested because students are still responding to both prompts and receiving scores from both raters.)

Again, prompts and raters are the two facets, or sources of error variation, in the design described previously. The essay prompts will likely vary in difficulty. Similarly, a rater may score the essays for the first prompt more stringently than for the second, or score the essays for some students more leniently than for others. These sources of variation reduce the ability to generalize beyond the sample of prompts and raters used in this study to the universe of all possible equivalent prompts and raters.

For the hypothetical social studies example, a G–study was conducted to estimate the variance components associated with the object of measurement (students), the two facets (prompts and raters), and their interactions. Table 8.1 shows the relevant variance components formulas for this crossed, two–facet, random–effects design. In all, seven variance components were estimated:

- students ($\hat{\sigma}_s^2$): Universe–score variance. Indicates the amount of variability in students' scores that can be attributed to differences in their knowledge about the Civil War and writing ability.

- prompts ($\hat{\sigma}_p^2$): Main effect for prompts. Indicates the amount of variability in scores attributable to some prompts being more difficult or easier than others.

- raters ($\hat{\sigma}_r^2$): Main effect for raters. Indicates the amount of variability in scores attributable to some raters being more lenient or stringent than others.

- sp ($\hat{\sigma}^2_{sp}$): Student by prompt interaction. Indicates the amount of variability attributable to inconsistencies in student performance from one prompt to another.

- sr ($\hat{\sigma}^2_{sr}$): Student by rater interaction. Indicates the amount of variability attributable to inconsistencies in raters from one student to another.

- pr ($\hat{\sigma}^2_{pr}$): Prompt by rater interaction. Indicates the amount of variability attributable to inconsistencies in raters from one prompt to another.

- spr,e ($\hat{\sigma}^2_{spr,e}$): Students by prompt by rater interaction. Indicates the amount of variability attributable to the three–way interaction spr plus residual (unmeasured, unattributable) variation e.

Generalizability analyses use traditional analysis of variance (ANOVA) methods to obtain the sums of squares and mean squares associated with each variance component. In our example, to calculate the mean square for students, the sums of squares for students was divided by its respective degrees of freedom (df), using the data presented in Table 8.2:

$$MS_s = \frac{52.32}{24} = 2.18$$

All of the relevant calculations can be performed by hand: The equation for the residual (spr,e) should be solved first, followed by the interactions, and the main effects. (The reason for this is the equations for interaction components include the estimated variance component of the residual, and the equations for the main effects include the estimated variance components of the interactions.) However, computer programs exist that are specifically developed to generate G–theory analyses (see, e.g., Crick & Brennan, 1984).

The sample estimate for the residual variance component is equal to the residual's mean square

$$(\hat{\sigma}^2_{spr,e} = MS_{spr,e})$$

The variance components for the interactions are estimated by subtracting the residual variance component from the mean square for the interaction and then dividing by the total n for the effect not included in the interaction, for example, the student-by-rater interaction variance component would be solved in the following manner, using the data found in Table 8.2:

$$\hat{\sigma}^2_{sr} = \frac{\left(MS_{sr} - \hat{\sigma}^2_{spr,e}\right)}{n_p} = \frac{(.5058 - .0308)}{2} = .2375$$

Variance components for each main effect are obtained by subtracting the residual variance component and each interaction variance component containing

TABLE 8.1

ANOVA Table for a Crossed, Two-Facet Random–Effects Design

Source of Variation	Sums of Squares	df	Mean Squares	Estimated Variance Component	Percentage of Total Variance
Students (s)	SS_s	n_s-1	$MS_s = SS_s/df_s$	$\hat{\sigma}_s^2 = \left(MS_s - n_r\hat{\sigma}_{sp}^2 - n_p\hat{\sigma}_{sr}^2 - \hat{\sigma}_{spr,e}^2\right)/n_p n_r$	$\hat{\sigma}_s^2 / \hat{\sigma}_{total}^2$
Prompts (p)	SS_p	n_p-1	$MS_p = SS_p/df_p$	$\hat{\sigma}_p^2 = \left(MS_p - n_r\hat{\sigma}_{sp}^2 - n_s\hat{\sigma}_{pr}^2 - \hat{\sigma}_{spr,e}^2\right)/n_s n_r$	$\hat{\sigma}_p^2 / \hat{\sigma}_{total}^2$
Raters (r)	SS_r	n_r-1	$MS_r = SS_r/df_r$	$\hat{\sigma}_r^2 = \left(MS_r - n_p\hat{\sigma}_{sr}^2 - n_s\hat{\sigma}_{pr}^2 - \hat{\sigma}_{spr,e}^2\right)/n_p n_s$	$\hat{\sigma}_r^2 / \hat{\sigma}_{total}^2$
sp	SS_{sp}	$(n_s-1)(n_p-1)$	$MS_{sp}=SS_{sp}/df_{sp}$	$\hat{\sigma}_{sp}^2=\left(MS_{sp}-\hat{\sigma}_{spr,e}^2\right)/n_r$	$\hat{\sigma}_{sp}^2 / \hat{\sigma}_{total}^2$
sr	SS_{sr}	$(n_s-1)(n_r-1)$	$MS_{sr}=SS_{sr}/df_{sr}$	$\hat{\sigma}_{sr}^2=\left(MS_{sr}-\hat{\sigma}_{spr,e}^2\right)/n_p$	$\hat{\sigma}_{sr}^2 / \hat{\sigma}_{total}^2$
pr	SS_{pr}	$(n_p-1)(n_r-1)$	$MS_{pr}=SS_{pr}/df_{pr}$	$\hat{\sigma}_{pr}^2=\left(MS_{pr}-\hat{\sigma}_{spr,e}^2\right)/n_s$	$\hat{\sigma}_{pr}^2 / \hat{\sigma}_{total}^2$
spr,e	$SS_{spr,e}$	$(n_s-1)(n_p-1)(n_r-1)$	$MS_{spr,e}=SS_{spr,e}/df_{spr,e}$	$\hat{\sigma}_{spr,e}^2=MS_{spr,e}$	$\hat{\sigma}_{spr,e}^2 / \hat{\sigma}_{total}^2$

the main effect (multiply by the total n of the effect not in the interaction before subtracting) from the mean square of the main effect and dividing by the product of the total n for the other main effects. The following provides an illustration for calculating the main effect for students using the data in Table 8.2.

$$\hat{\sigma}_s^2 = \frac{\left(MS_s - n_r\hat{\sigma}_{sp}^2 - n_p\hat{\sigma}_{sr}^2 - \hat{\sigma}_{spr,e}^2\right)}{n_p n_r} = \frac{(2.1800 - (2\times.0000) - (2\times.2375) - .0308)}{(2)(2)} = \frac{1.6742}{4} = .4186$$

The estimated variance components are shown in Table 8.2. As evident in the table, the variance component for students is relatively large (48% of the total variation), suggesting that a substantial amount of the variation in students' scores on the prompts is attributable to real differences in their knowledge about the Civil War and writing ability. The variance component for raters also accounted for a sizable amount of variation (21% of total variation), suggesting that a good deal of variation in students' scores can also be attributed to the fact that raters generally differed in the stringency and leniency with which they scored the essays. The student x rater interaction variance component (27% of total variation) indicates that the relative standing of students differed across raters; in other words, particular raters scored particular students more stringently or leniently than others.

TABLE 8.2
Estimated Variance Components for Social Studies Example

Source of Variation	Sums of Squares	df	Mean Squares	Estimated Variance Component	Percentage of Total Variance
Students (s)	52.32	24	2.18	0.42	48%
Prompts (p)	0.01	1	0.01	0.01	1%
Raters (r)	9.61	1	9.61	0.18	21%
sp	0.74	24	0.03	0.00	0%
sr	12.14	24	0.51	0.24	27%
pr	0.03	1	0.03	0.00	0%
spr,e	0.74	24	0.03	0.03	4%

Based on G–study results, a decision study, or d–study, can be configured. D–studies enable calculation of the optimal number of conditions for each facet (e.g., number of raters or prompts) necessary to obtain a desired level of reliability or generalizability, and consideration of a wide variety of alternative data collection designs (such as fully–crossed, partially–nested, fully–nested, random–effects, mixed–effects, and so on).

G–theory provides reliability–like indices that distinguish between decisions based on the relative standing or ranking of individuals and decisions based on the absolute level of individuals' scores. For example, college admissions offices may use the relative standing of applicants based on their test scores to make admissions decisions, with only the top–performing students being admitted to the school. In contrast, decisions for licensure are usually based on absolute level of performance on a test, with only those who obtain a specified score on the examination being awarded a license to practice in the profession. For relative decisions, all variance components that include the object of measurement contribute to error variation ($\hat{\sigma}^2_{Rel}$). For absolute decisions, all variance components except for the object of measurement contribute to error ($\hat{\sigma}^2_{Abs}$). The reliability or generalizability coefficient for relative decisions is

$$\hat{\rho}^2 = \frac{\sigma^2_s}{\left(\sigma^2_s + \sigma^2_{Rel}\right)}$$

and the phi coefficient for absolute decisions is

$$\hat{\phi} = \frac{\sigma^2_s}{\left(\sigma^2_s + \sigma^2_{Abs}\right)}.$$

Table 8.3 provides the results of three d–studies based on the G–study results provided previously. The d–studies were designed to determine the optimal number of raters (because the largest source of error variation was for raters) and compare the relative reliability advantages of a fully–crossed design to a partially nested design. The study provides reliability estimates for instances of two raters and two prompts, three raters and two prompts, and four raters and two prompts, for a fully crossed design (s x p x r) and for a partially nested design in which raters are nested within prompt (i.e., different raters score responses for each prompt). A fully–crossed G–study design is usually preferable for estimating variance components because the fully–crossed design allows the calculation of all estimable effects and enables a wider variety of options for potential d–study designs.

In this d–study, the raters–nested–within–prompts ($r{:}p$) effect is the sum of the variance components for raters (r) and the prompts x raters interaction (pr). Variance components for the different combinations of raters and prompts are calculated by dividing the affected variance component estimates from the G–study by the desired number of raters and/or prompts. For example, in the crossed design the variance estimate for the student-by-rater interaction was .2375. The variance estimate for this effect when four raters and two prompts are used is:

$$\frac{.2375}{4} = .0594$$

TABLE 8.3

Comparison of Two-Facet, Crossed s x p x r and Two-Facet,
Partially-Nested s x (r:p) d-Study Random-Effects Designs

Crossed Design: s x p x r

Source of Variation	$\hat{\sigma}^2$	$n'_r=1$, $n'_p=1$	$n'_r=2$, $n'_p=2$	$n'_r=3$, $n'_p=2$	$n'_r=4$, $n'_p=2$
Students (s)	$\hat{\sigma}^2_s$	.4185	.4185	.4185	.4185
Prompts (p)	$\hat{\sigma}^2_p$	.0102	.0051	.0051	.0051
Raters (r)	$\hat{\sigma}^2_r$	.1821	.0911	.0607	.0455
sp	$\hat{\sigma}^2_{sp}$	.0000	.0000	.0000	.0000
sr	$\hat{\sigma}^2_{sr}$	.2375	.1188	.0792	.0594
pr	$\hat{\sigma}^2_{pr}$	.0000	.0000	.0000	.0000
spr,e	$\hat{\sigma}^2_{spr,e}$	.0308	.0077	.0051	.0039
	$\hat{\sigma}^2_{Rel}$	.2683	.1265	.0843	.0632
	$\hat{\sigma}^2_{Abs}$	.4606	.2226	.1501	.1139
	$\hat{\rho}^2$	.6	.77	.83	.87
	$\hat{\phi}$	.48	.65	.74	.79

Partially Nested Design: s x (r:p)

Source of Variation	$\hat{\sigma}^2$	$n'_r=1$, $n'_p=1$	$n'_r=2$, $n'_p=2$	$n'_r=3$, $n'_p=2$	$n'_r=4$, $n'_p=2$
Students (s)	$\hat{\sigma}^2_s$	.4185	.4185	.4185	.4185
Prompts (p)	$\hat{\sigma}^2_p$	.0102	.0051	.0051	.0051
Raters: (r:p) Prompts	$\hat{\sigma}^2_{r,pr}$	.1821	.0911	.0607	.0455
sp	$\hat{\sigma}^2_{sp}$	.0000	.0000	.0000	.0000
sr,spr,e	$\hat{\sigma}^2_{sr,spr,e}$	.2683	.0671	.0447	.0335
	$\hat{\sigma}^2_{Rel}$	.2683	.0671	.0447	.0335
	$\hat{\sigma}^2_{Abs}$	.4606	.1633	.1105	.0841
	$\hat{\rho}^2$	.61	.86	.90	.93
	$\hat{\phi}$	.48	.72	.79	.83

As evident from Table 8.3, if only one rater and one prompt were used, the generalizability and phi coefficients would be .61 and .48 for both the crossed and partially nested design. However, once the number of raters and prompts increases, the coefficients are greater for the partially–nested than for the crossed– design. The largest increase for either design occurs in the first d–study containing two raters and two prompts. Based on this information, it appears the partially– nested design with two raters and two prompts is sufficient for relative decisions ($\hat{\rho}^2 = .86$) and the partially–nested design with four raters and two prompts is more desirable for absolute decisions ($\hat{\phi} = .83$).

DECISION CONSISTENCY

As has been described in previous sections, automated scoring addresses only one threat to obtaining reliable information: that posed by random errors introduced in the scoring process. Random errors of measurement still occur, and estimates of score variation attributable to errors of measurement are still expressed in traditional terms; for example, as reliability coefficients, standard errors of measurement, generalizablity coefficients(G-coefficients), and so on.

In many (perhaps most) educational measurement contexts, it is not nearly as important to estimate the degree of confidence in the precision of a score as it is to express the confidence in any categorical grouping, label, or judgment based on the score. For example, suppose that a test consisting of 100 dichotomously–scored, multiple–choice items were administered for the purpose of identifying appropriate placements for students into introductory, intermediate, or advanced levels of foreign language instruction on entry to college. Further, suppose that cut scores were established in some defensible manner (see Cizek, 2001) to create 3 points along the 0 to 100 scale. Finally, suppose that performance below 35 established a student's placement at the introductory level, performance between 35 and 78 determined placement in an intermediate course, and a score of 79 or above indicated placement in an advanced course.

In this situation, it would not be nearly as helpful to know the precision with which a student's score of, say 84, were estimated, as it would be to know the degree of confidence that could be associated with placement in an advanced course. Situations similar to the language placement example arise quite frequently. Even more common, perhaps, is the case in which only two categories are possible, as is the case when a test is used as part of the process to promote or retain a student in a grade, award or withhold a diploma, grant or deny a license or certification, accept or reject an applicant, or other pass or fail classifications in business, industry, and the professions. In such cases, the type of reliability information that is most salient is referred to as decision consistency.

The *Standards for Educational and Psychological Testing* (AERA, APA, NCME, 1999) indicate that information concerning decision consistency is highly desirable. According to the *Standards*:

> When a test or combination of measures is used to make categorical decisions, estimates should be provided of the percentage of examinees who would be classified in the same way on two applications of the procedure, using the same form or alternate forms of the instrument. (p. 35)

Estimates of decision consistency, such as represented by the statistics $\hat{\rho}_o$ or $\hat{\kappa}$, are easily obtained using procedures outlined by Subkoviak (1976). The procedures described by Subkoviak are useful for situations involving dichotomously–scored items and a single cut–score resulting in two classification categories, or via the procedures described by Livingston and Lewis (1995) for situations in which a combination of item scoring schemes (e.g., dichotomous scoring and polytomous scoring) is used.

CONDITIONAL STANDARD ERRORS OF MEASUREMENT

It is common practice to report an overall standard error of measurement (SEM) for a test administration. The procedure for calculating an overall SEM is a familiar equation to most testing specialists:

$$\text{SEM} = S_x \sqrt{1 - r_{xx'}}$$

where S_x is the standard deviation in the set of scores and; $r_{xx'}$ is the reliability estimate for the set of scores.

However, in addition to overall SEMs, many authors (see, e.g., Cizek, 1996) recommend that conditional standard errors of measurement (CSEMs) be reported in situations in which cut scores are used to distinguish between categories or levels of performance on the test. Conditional standard errors are estimates of the error variance at specified points along the score scale for a test. The reporting of CSEMs is also recommended by the *Standards for Educational and Psychological Testing* (AERA, APA, NCME, 1999). According to the *Standards*:

> Conditional standard errors of measurement should be reported at several score levels if constancy cannot be assumed. Where cut scores are specified for selection or classification, the standard errors of measurement should be reported in the vicinity of each cut score. (p. 35)

Reporting CSEMs at important score levels is desirable for many reasons, one of which being that overall SEMs are likely to over–estimate or underestimate the actual error variance at any given point along the score scale. The nature of this over–estimation or underestimation has been explained by Kolen, Hanson, and Brennan:

For the purposes of facilitating score interpretation, raw scores typically are transformed to scale scores. If raw–to–scale score transformations were linear, then the scale score reliability would be the same as the raw score reliability. Also the conditional standard errors of measurement for scale scores would be a multiple of the raw score conditional standard errors of measurement. However, raw scores are often transformed to scale scores using nonlinear methods to facilitate score interpretation. Some examples include transforming the raw scores so that the scale scores are approximately normally distributed, truncating the scale scores to be within prescribed limits, and using a considerably smaller number of scale score points than raw score points. [These] nonlinear transformations can alter reliability and affect the relative magnitude of conditional standard errors of measurement along the score scale. (1992, pp. 285–286)

Thus, CSEMs should be reported at each of the cut scores used to establish performance categories. Conditional standard errors of measurement may be reported in terms of the raw score scale, although reporting on the scaled score metric is preferred when scaled scores are used to report on examinee performance, and a number of sources exist for information on how to calculate CSEMs. The specific approach to calculation of CSEMs depends on a number of factors, including: the psychometric model used (e.g., classical test theory or item response theory); the type of item scoring (dichotomous or polytomous); the scale in which test scores will be reported (i.e., raw score or scaled score units); and the data collection design (e.g., whether alternate forms of the test are given to the same group of examinees or whether CSEMs must be estimated from one administration of a single test form).

It is assumed that, in most cases, CSEMs must be estimated based on information (i.e., examinee responses) gathered on a single occasion using a single test form. An alternative introduced by Lord (1984, p. 241) provides the simplest method of deriving the conditional SEM associated with a given raw score, x:

$$SEM_x = \sqrt{\frac{x(n-x)}{(n-1)}}$$

where: x is the desired observed raw score level and n is the number of items in the test.

Another classical test theory procedure was suggested by Keats (1957):

$$\hat{\sigma}^2_{E\bullet X_p} = \frac{(n - X_p)(X_p)(1 - \hat{\rho}_{xx'})}{(n-1)(1 -_{21}\hat{\rho}_{xx'})}$$

where: $\hat{\sigma}^2_{E\bullet X_p}$ is the square of the conditional standard error of measurement, n is the number of dichotomously scored items in the test;

X_p is a given score level,

$\hat{\rho}_{xx'}$ is a reliability estimate obtained in a parallel forms or coefficient alpha, and

$_{21}\hat{\rho}_{xx'}$ is the KR21 estimate of reliability.

According to Feldt and Brennan, "perhaps the Keats approach can be recommended. It requires the least computational effort, relying as it does only on the values of KR21 and the most defensible, practical estimate of $\hat{\rho}_{xx'}$." (1989, p. 124).

A thorough, and more recent, overview of the classical test theory procedures for estimating CSEMs in raw score units is provided by Feldt and Brennan (1989, pp. 123–124) and five such procedures are compared in work by Feldt, Steffen, and Gupta (1985). Kolen, et al. (1992) provided a classical test theory extension for estimating CSEMs for scaled scores.

The introduction of IRT facilitated many useful applications to practical testing problems, among them, the estimation of CSEMs (Lord, 1980). Using an IRT test model, the CSEM at a given value of ability ($\square$) is found by taking the reciprocal of the information function at the desired ability level:

$$SE\ (\theta) = \frac{1}{\sqrt{I(\theta)}}$$

where: $I\ (\theta)$ is the value of the test information function at θ (see Hambleton, Swaminathan, & Rogers, 1991, Chap. 6)

Although the preceding formula 4 provides a straightforward estimate of the CSEM at a given level, the score metric is the ability (i.e., θ) scale, which is not usually the metric of choice for actually reporting scores. Alternative IRT approaches for reporting scale score CSEMs have been developed. One such approach, for dichotomously–scored items, has been outlined by Kolen, Zeng, and Hanson (1996) and subsequently generalized to polytomously–scored items (Wang, Kolen, & Harris, 2000).

Finally, a generalizability approach to estimating CSEMs has been suggested by Brennan (1998). This method can be applied to combinations of dichotomously– or polytomously–scored items, provided that an examinee's raw score is simply the sum of the item scores. Brennan's approach yields raw score metric CSEMs; Feldt and Qualls (1998) have developed a companion approach for estimating scale score CSEMs.

SPECIAL RELIABILITY CONCERNS IN THE CONTEXT OF AUTOMATED SCORING

In automated scoring, once the scoring algorithms are established, it is almost certain that the computer–generated scores for a particular essay will be identical no matter how many times it is scored. Similarly, the scoring process will be uniform across all essays because the computers scoring the essays adhere precisely to the scoring standards stipulated by the algorithm. Thus, traditional reliability concepts such as intrascorer and interscorer agreement are not especially germane in the context of automated scoring. However, scoring variation can still exist and should be examined.

Automated scoring must concern itself with "interalgorithm" reliability or the generalizability of the scores beyond the particular scoring algorithms used to generate them.

> "Clearly, the universe of generalization for a test scored using a computerized scoring system is no more intended to be limited to the specific algorithm than a test scored by raters is intended to be limited to the specific sample of raters participating in the scoring" (Clauser, Harik, & Clyman, 2000, p. 246).

The issue, then, is the extent to which variability in scoring algorithms created by different but equally qualified groups is a source of variation in essay scores. To our knowledge, only one study to date has examined this potential source of error variance.

According to the study conducted by Clauser, et al. (2000), the potential exists for introducing a substantial degree of random (error) variability attributable to differences in the particular expert–group selected to develop the scoring algorithm. Fortunately, the authors also note that the effect is relatively easily attenuated via algorithm–development strategies that are practical for most testing situations.

The Clauser, et al. (2000) study involved a computer simulation program used to evaluate a physicians' patient management skills. In each simulated case, examinees receive a patient scenario and respond to the case with free–text entry that contains their decisions regarding how to proceed with the patient's care (e.g., orders tests, orders treatments, admits to the hospital, etc.). Summaries of the physicians' decisions (called "transaction lists") are scored using a regression–based computerized scoring procedure.

Algorithms for the scoring procedure were developed by groups of content experts who review a case and designate an examinee's actions as beneficial or risky to its management. The experts then review and rate a sample of examinee transaction lists. The average of these ratings serves as the dependent variable in a regression equation. The independent variables for the regression equation include six variables representing the number of examinee's actions in specified "beneficial" and "risk" categories associated with the case and one variable representing the timeliness of the examinee's diagnosis and treatment.

Algorithms were developed for each task with the average examinee rating of each group serving as the dependent measure. Algorithms were also developed based on each expert's ratings. Generalizability theory was used to estimate variance components for a design in which examinees were crossed with task (four tasks) and scoring group (three groups) and a design in which examinees were crossed with task and expert (four experts) nested within scoring group. This design permitted a specific answer to the question of the degree of variability in scoring attributable to the particular group of experts who produced the algorithm.

Results reported by Clauser, et al. (2000) showed expected, moderately large variance components associated with task (t) and person by task (pt) interaction; in other words, some variability in examinees' universe score estimates was attributable to the particular task an examinee responded to, and to the particular combination of task and rater who rated the examinee's performance on the task. The relative magnitudes of the p and pt variance components was similar across the three randomly–equivalent expert scoring groups. A moderately large variance component associated with expert group (g) was observed when group was included as a facet. This finding indicates that a non–trivial degree of variability in examinees scores can be attributable to the particular expert group selected to develop the scoring algorithm.

In a subsequent d–study to determine the optimal number of tasks and groups, Clauser, et al. (2000) found that relative error variance was minimized when 15 or more tasks were used, but that the number of expert scoring groups used in the development of the scoring algorithm made essentially no difference. In contrast, absolute error variance was substantially impacted by the number of groups used in the development of a scoring algorithm. Absolute error variance was minimized when groups were nested within task; that is, when groups developed algorithms for a single task, as opposed to for all tasks on which examinees are scored. Such a nesting procedure makes logical and practical sense from a test development perspective, to the extent that content experts would seem to be most appropriately selected to develop scoring algorithms only for those tasks or areas in which they have special expertise.

CONCLUSIONS AND RECOMMENDATIONS

The increasing availability and acceptance of automated scoring for student writing samples has prompted greater attention to psychometric concerns such as, reliability and validity. Concerning reliability, much of the existing writing in the context of automated scoring has focused on demonstrations of the level of agreement between computer–generated ratings of essays and ratings generated by varying numbers of human scorers. A safe—and fairly clear—conclusion from this research is that automated essay scoring can produce ratings that are more highly correlated with individual human raters than human raters' judgments correlate with each other, correlate very strongly with the mean ratings of up to five or more human raters; and can be obtained at a cost that is less than if human raters were used exclusively (see, e.g., Page & Petersen, 1995).

In this chapter, we outlined other reliability concerns that should be attended to in any testing situation and those additional reliability issues that arise in the specific case of automated scoring. For example, the development and application of a specific automated scoring algorithm can be seen as analogous to the development and application of a specific standard–setting procedure. In the standard setting case, we hope for convergent results when differing procedures are applied by equally qualified panels of judges, and that the classification of examinees into categories such as pass or fail or basic, proficient, or advanced does not vary markedly simply as a function of which standard setting method is used. By extension, we would hope that different automated scoring algorithms developed by equally qualified programmers would yield consistent scoring results.

We also note that simple correlational results provide insufficient information about reliability when automated scoring is used in practice. The provision of decision consistency indices and conditional standard errors of measurement are *de rigueur* as far as relevant professional guidelines are concerned and are, in most cases where test scores are used to categorize examinees, the more relevant type of reliability information.

Finally, although the focus of this chapter has been on reliability of automated scoring, we would be amiss not to refer back to our earlier observations about the relationship between reliability and validity. We must conclude that concerns about reliability, although essential, must yield to concerns about validity. While we have confidence in the progress toward increased reliability marked by ever more complex scoring algorithms and identification of other important elements in writing samples, the degree of use and acceptance of automated scoring will not hinge on attainment of breathtakingly high reliability coefficients.

We think validity is important. The future of automated scoring cannot focus on reliability without consideration of the meaning that can be inferred from examinees' scores—however generated—and the extent to which the manner of scoring selected interacts, influences, or impedes measurement of the construct that is under study. We believe that the attention focused on validity will ultimately portend the fate of automated scoring; we urge readers to become familiar with the key validity concerns (see Keith, Chapter 9, this volume). For example, we note that only certain kinds of writing can be scored via computer. At the present stage of development, a student's response that contains any elements not readily amenable to being read as a straight text file is not suitable for automated scoring. How should a student's response that contains outlining, a graph, chart, schematic, and so forth be scored? It is reasonable to suspect that such responses will not likely be encouraged, taught, or practiced. We wonder about the effect this might have in terms of narrowing the range of skills that are valued based on what can be scored via computer. Ultimately, the future of automated scoring will be marked by the progress already witnessed in obtaining highly reliable results in conjunction with progress along the path of ensuring that the process stimulates valid interpretations and defensible instructional practices as well.

ACKNOWLEDGEMENTS

The authors are grateful for informal advice and insights for this chapter provided by Professor Ronald K. Hambleton of the University of Massachusetts—Amherst, and Professor Michael Kolen of the University of Iowa. We also acknowledge the helpful corrections and suggestions provided by the editors of this volume.

REFERENCES

American Educational Research Association, American Psychological Association, National Council on Measurement in Education. (1999). *Standards for educational and psychological testing.* Washington, DC: American Educational Research Association.

Brennan, R. L. (1983). *Elements of generalizability theory.* Iowa City, IA: American College Testing.

Brennan, R. L. (1998). Raw–score conditional standard errors of measurement in generalizability theory. *Applied Psychological Measurement, 22,* 307–331.

Burry–Stock, J. A., Shaw, D. G., Laurie, C., & Chissom, B. S. (1996). Rater agreement indexes for performance assessment. *Educational and Psychological Measurement, 56,* 251–262.

Cherry, R. D., & Meyer, P. R. (1993). Reliability issues in holistic assessment. In M. W. Williamson & B. A. Huot (Eds.), *Validating holistic scoring for writing assessment: Theoretical and empirical foundations* (pp. 109–141). Cresskill, NJ: Hampton.

Cizek, G. J. (1996). Standard–setting guidelines. *Educational Measurement: Issues and Practice, 15*(1), 13–21.

Cizek, G. J. (2001). *Setting performance standards: Concepts, methods, and perspectives.* Mahwah, NJ: Lawrence Erlbaum Associates, Inc.

Clauser, B. E., Harik, P., & Clyman, S. G. (2000). The generalizability of scores for a performance assessment scored with a computer–automated scoring system. *Journal of Educational Measurement, 37,* 245–261.

Crick, J. E., & Brennan, R. L. (1984). GENOVA: *A general purpose analysis of variance system* [Computer software]. Iowa City, IA: American College Testing.

Cronbach, L. J., Gleser, G. C., Nanda, H., & Rajaratnam, N. (1972). *The dependability of behavioral measurements: Theory of generalizability for scores and profiles.* New York: Wiley.

Ebel, R. L. (1961). Must all tests be valid? *American Psychologist, 16,* 640-647.

Feldt, L. S., & Brennan, R. L. (1989). Reliability. In R. L. Linn (Ed.), *Educational measurement, third edition* (pp. 105–146). New York: Macmillan.

Feldt, L. S., Steffen, M., & Gupta, N. C. (1985). A comparison of five methods for estimating the standard error of measurement at specific score levels. *Applied Psychological Measurement, 9,* 351–361.

Feldt, L. S., & Qualls, A. L. (1998). Approximating scale score standard error of measurement from the raw score standard error. *Applied Measurement in Education, 11,* 159–177.

Gulliksen, H. (1950). *Theory of mental tests.* New York: Wiley.

Hambleton, R. K., Swaminathan, H., & Rogers, H. J. (1991). *Fundamentals of item response theory.* Newbury Park, CA: Sage.

Keats, J. A. (1957). Estimation of error variances of test scores. *Psychometrika, 22,* 29–41.

Kolen, M. J., Hanson, B. A., & Brennan, R. L. (1992). Conditional standard errors of measurement for scale scores. *Journal of Educational Measurement, 29,* 285–307.

Kolen, M. J., Zeng, L., & Hanson, B. A. (1996). Conditional standard errors of measurement for scale scores using IRT. *Journal of Educational Measurement, 33,* 129–140.

Livingston, S. A., & Lewis, C. (1995). Estimating the consistency and accuracy of classifications based on test scores. *Journal of Educational Measurement, 32,* 179–197.

Lord, F. M. (1980). *Applications of item response theory to practical testing problems.* Hillsdale, NJ: Lawrence Erlbaum Associates, Inc.

Lord, F. M. (1984). Standard errors of measurement at different ability levels. *Journal of Educational Measurement, 21,* 239–243.

Page, E. B., & Petersen, N. S. (1995). The computer moves into essay grading. *Phi Delta Kappan, 76*, 561–565.

Shavelson, R. J., & Webb, N. M. (1991). *Generalizability theory: A primer.* Newbury Park, CA: Sage.

Spearman, C. (1904). The proof and measurement of association between two things. *Journal of Psychology, 15*, 72–101.

Stanley, J. C. (1998, April). In Ellis B. Page (chair), *Qualitative and quantitative essay grading by computer.* Symposium conducted at the annual meeting of the American Educational Research Association. San Diego, CA.

Subkoviak, M. J. (1976). Estimating reliability from a single administration of a criterion-referenced test. *Journal of Educational Measurement, 13*, 265–276.

Traub, R. E. (1997). Classical test theory in historical perspective. *Educational Measurement: Issues and Practice, 16*, 8-14.

Wang, T., Kolen, M. J., & Harris, D. J. (2000). Psychometric properties of scale scores and performance levels for performance assessments using polytomous IRT. *Journal of Educational Measurement, 37*, 141–162.

9
Validity of Automated Essay Scoring Systems

Timothy Z. Keith
The University of Texas—Austin

Do automated essay scoring (AES) systems produce valid estimates of writing skill? How can researchers establish the validity of AES systems; what kind of evidence should be considered? Given the nontraditional nature of AES, it is tempting to think that such new methods require new forms of validity evidence. It is argued that traditional methods of demonstrating validity will work equally well in demonstrating the validity of AES. This chapter reviews the types of validity evidence that should be relevant for AES; reviews the existing validity evidence for specific AES systems; and discusses the types of additional studies that need to be conducted to demonstrate the validity of AES programs.

TYPES OF VALIDITY EVIDENCE

According to contemporary standards, validity is "an integrated evaluative judgment of the degree to which empirical evidence and theoretical rationales support the adequacy and appropriateness of inferences and actions based on test scores" (Messick, 1989, p. 13). "The process of validation involves accumulating evidence to provide a sound scientific basis for the proposed score interpretations" (American Educational Research Association, American Psychological Association, National Council on Measurement in Education, 1999, p. 9). Several general types of evidence are relevant, including evidence based on test content (content validity), internal structure (internal validity), relations to other variables (external validity), and the consequences of testing (AERA et al., 1999). "A sound validity argument integrates various strands of evidence into a coherent account of the degree to which existing evidence and theory support the intended interpretation of test scores for specific uses" (AERA et al., 1999, p. 17). These types of evidence roughly correspond to traditional definitions of content validity, construct validity, criterion-related validity, and perhaps, treatment validity. Although AES systems have just scratched the surface of demonstrating such evidence, these standards and traditional definitions of validity provide a categorization for validity evidence that has been gathered and a blueprint for future studies. The traditional divisions of content, criterion-related, and construct validity are discussed in the following sections.

Content Evidence

AES systems represent scoring systems rather than tests. The content of essays is independent of the method of scoring; those essays could be (and often are) scored by human raters as well as by AES systems. Thus, content validity evidence applies to the essays themselves, rather than to the scoring method. Content validity evidence, then, is not particularly relevant for AES systems.

Construct Validity

The central question for AES systems—and the nexus of questions from skeptics of AES—is whether the scores derived by AES in fact reflect writing skill or some other characteristic. Certainly these programs produce scores of some type, but do those scores reflect the test takers' skill in writing about a topic, or do they reflect some other characteristic, such as general cognitive ability, or content vocabulary knowledge, or simply the ability to produce a large amount of text in a limited time? Or do the results reflect simple fantasy, with the scores having no real meaning?

Most AES programs have implicitly or explicitly assumed that human raters are indeed able to score prose for general writing skill or content-specific writing skill with some degree of validity. From this orientation, with the assumption that scores from human raters lead to valid inferences of writing skill, then simple correlations of AES programs' scores with those of human judges provide evidence that the AES system also measures the construct of writing. Such correlations may also legitimately be considered evidence of reliability and criterion-related validity.

Exploratory and confirmatory factor analysis of AES scores with other measures of writing are another method of establishing whether methods of scoring measure the same or divergent constructs, and, via inspection of factor loadings, should provide a measure of the relative validity of AES and other scoring methods. AES programs increasingly score components of writing (e.g., Content, Mechanics, etc.); factor analysis of such component scores will also help demonstrate the constructs being measured. When conducted on component scores by themselves, a single factor should provide evidence that the components are all measuring facets of the general construct of writing. When analyzed in conjunction with human ratings of these same components, and using a confirmatory or quasi-confirmatory approach, factors reflecting the different components of writing will provide evidence of whether these components are in fact separable and the relative power of AES—compared to other methods—to measure them.

Such component studies overlap with convergent and discriminant validity research. Additionally, studies should correlate AES scores with other test scores that should, conceptually, run the gamut from closely to distantly related to writing. So, for example, a study might correlate AES scores with student scores on a standardized achievement test. For such a study, we would expect valid AES scores to correlate more highly with writing and reading scores, but at a lower level with mathematics or science achievement test scores.

Criterion-Related Validity

There are many potential criteria with which scores derived from AES systems should correlate. When used with school-age children, AES scores should correlate to various degrees with achievement test scores. When used as a part of a high stakes exam for selection—such as the Graduate Record Examination (GRE)—AES scores should be predictive of subsequent performance in the program for which the exam is used in selection. When used as a part of a writing exam for a class, AES scores should predict the overall, subsequent performance in the class. When used to score essays for other classes (e.g., a psychology paper or book report), AES scores should predict other evaluations in the same classes, such as exams.

ISSUES IN AES VALIDATION RESEARCH

There are a number of issues that need to be considered when evaluating or conducting AES research including, issues that likely affect the outcome of AES studies.

Calibration or Validation?

For most applications, AES programs are first "trained" on a sample of essays that have been scored or rated by human raters. Statistically, this "training" generally uses multiple regression and involves choosing a set of predictor variables and optimal regression weights for predicting the ratings of a human judge or the averaged ratings of more than one judge. The training program may then be used to score another, larger pool of essays that have not been scored by human judges (Elliot, Chapter 5, this volume). A common variation of this procedure is to have multiple judges involved in training, but only the AES system and a single human judge are used in subsequent scoring (cf. Burstein, Kukich, Wolff, Lu, & Chodorow, 1998).

Correlations between AES programs and human judges will vary depending on whether the training, or calibration, sample is used to calculate correlations, or if another validation (or cross-validation) sample is used. If validation research is only conducted with the training sample, the estimates of correlations between the AES programs will be inflated. If a single (training or calibration) sample is used to both create the scoring equation and compare the resulting scores with human judges (who were used to create the scores), the resulting correlations will be a function of the construct measured in common, but also of sample-specific capitalization on chance. Again, such correlations will be inflated estimates of validity (indeed, the correlations will equal the multiple correlation from the original multiple regression).

One alternative is to remove each essay, in turn, from the training step, so each essay is not used in the generation of a score for itself. The advantage of this "jackknife" (Powers, Burstein, Chodorow, Fowles, & Kukich, 2000) method is that any subsequent correlations do not violate the assumption of independence of observations; the disadvantage is that each score is based on a slightly different formula. It is likely, also, that the correlations will still be inflated due to sampling idiosyncrasies.

A preferable approach is to use, separate calibration and validation samples. The AES is trained on the calibration essays. The scoring formula from this training, is used to score a separate group of validation essays, essays that are also scored by human judges. Correlations between the AES scores and human judges are computed using the validation sample, so that one set of essays is not used to both create and validate the scoring rules. The calibration and validation samples may be one sample split in two, or, more conservatively, two entirely different samples. The method used may not be well-described in any one report of AES research, but the distinctions are important. The calibration-validation approach likely produces the most trustworthy estimates of such correlations.

Correlations Among Judges

When multiple judges are used, the reliability and validity of AES scores depend on the correlations among the judges used in training, and validity coefficients will vary depending on the correlations among judges during validation. Other things being equal, validity will increase as the correlations among judges increase, but in a curvilinear fashion. This makes sense; it is well–known that the reliability of a variable places an upper limit on the correlation of that variable with any other. The correlation between human judges can be used to estimate (interrater) reliability. A lower correlation between judges may affect the reliability and validity of AES scores at the calibration or training step by providing a less reliable criterion and limiting the ultimate multiple correlation from the regression. Likewise, when single judges are used, the reliability of that judge's ratings will affect validity. A lower correlation among judges during validation will reduce any obtained validity coefficient. The likely effect on the magnitude of correlation is shown in Figure 9.1.

The X axis shows the reliability of the human judges, as measured by their intercorrelation; the Y axis shows the maximum resulting correlation between an AES system and those human judges (validity). For this graph, a reliability of .95 for the AES system and a "true" correlation between AES and judges of .95 was assumed, both very optimistic assumptions. As these values get lower, the graph would flatten more quickly. Raising the correlation among judges will have a bigger pay-off for lower levels of correlation than for higher levels. Of course, the standard method of increasing human judge reliability is to train the judges in how to score the essays. As this chapter reviews validity studies, the effect of judge reliability becomes obvious.

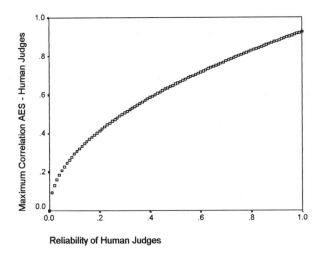

Fig. 9.1. Likely effect of the correlation between human judges on the correlation of AES scores with those judges. It is assumed that the correlation between human judges is a reflection of their scores.

It seems likely that there is a point at which increased correlation between judges may be detrimental. For any given set of essays, there is likely some maximum correlation among judges, unless those judges begin to focus on some irrelevant, but easily scored, aspect of the essays. Under this scenario, measurement would suffer not because of a low correlation between judges, but because that correlation reflected irrelevant variance rather than valid variation (see Loevinger, 1954).

Perhaps more troubling is the use of multiple judges in which, for example, two judges correlate considerably more highly with one another than the average judge correlation. Such an anomaly may suggest a lack of independence across judges.

Number of Judges

Other things being equal, the more judges used in training, the more accurate and valid the AES scores. This makes sense from the standpoint of reliability in that multiple judges serve the same purpose as longer instruments; the more judges the more reliable the instrument. Indeed, it is possible to estimate reliabilities for a different number of judges using the Spearman-Brown formula (Page, 1994). Fig. 9.2, for example, shows the reliabilities for different numbers of judges for different levels of correlation (from .4 to .9) between two judges. From the standpoint of validity, multiple judges should more closely approximate the "true score" for an essay. The more reliable and valid the criterion used in training (average judges' scores), the more valid and reliable the resulting AES scores. Because the number of judges affects the reliability and validity of the criterion, more judges will produce higher validity estimates at the validation step, as well. The effect is curvilinear, with each added judge improving accuracy to a smaller degree. Note that for higher levels of judge correlation, the biggest increase in reliabilities comes from moving from one to two judges. In addition, multiple judges are likely more important when there are lower average correlations among those judges, and less necessary when the judges correlate highly with each other. Several researchers have presented evidence related to the number of judges used in calibration (e.g., Elliot, Chapter 5, this volume; Page, 1994).

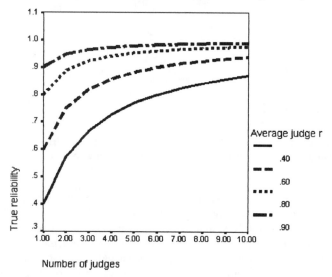

Fig. 9.2. Increasing the number of judges can compensate for low inter-judge correlations by increasing the reliability of composite judge socres.

Averaged Correlations?

Another distinction that is important when reading AES validity research is how averaged correlations were obtained. Very often such research will use several human judges, with the possibility to report several correlations between AES scores and those judges, as well as averaged correlations. It makes a difference whether those averages are averages of individual correlations, or correlations with an average of the multiple judges. For reasons discussed earlier, correlations with average judges will likely produce higher estimates than will averages of correlations with single judges (cf. Landauer, Laham, & Foltz, Chapter 6, this volume; Shermis, Koch, Page, Keith, & Harrington, 2002).

Correlations and Accuracy

Correlations between AES scores and those of human judges are sometimes augmented, or replaced, by percentage agreement between AES scores and human judge scores. The most common method is to report the percentage of agreement within one point (e.g., if the human judge gives an essay a score of 3 versus an AES score of 2). Such statistics are less useful than are correlations. First, although they may pertain to reliability, they have little applicability to validity. Second, such accuracy scores may provide an inflated estimate of the quality of scoring. For example, Elliot (Chapter 5, this volume) reported a study in which Intellimetric™ agreed (within 1 point) with human judges 100% of the time, but for which the correlation between AES and human scores was .78. Landauer, Latham, and Foltz (in press) presented additional objections.

The effect of the number of levels of scores is covered in depth elsewhere in this volume (Shermis & Daniels, Chapter 10, this volume). Interestingly, the coarseness of the scoring system should have different effects on correlations and accuracy estimates. Presumably, if a too-coarse scoring system is used in the calibration stage, the reliability and validity of AES scores should be reduced (Cohen, 1983), and thus validity estimates and other correlations should suffer. At the validation stage, a coarse scoring system may also reduce the correlation of AES scores with various outcomes. A coarse scoring system may increase accuracy estimates, however. Obviously, it is easier to have within-one-point agreement between two 4-point scales than between two 10-point scales

RELATIVE VALIDITY OF AES PROGRAMS

Given this outline of validity evidence needed for AES systems, how much of the work that needs to be done to establish validity has been done? Is there evidence to support the validity of AES systems in general? Do AES systems measure writing skill? Are various AES programs equally valid, or is one program "better" than others? This section reviews the relative validity evidence for each program. This discussion of the validity information pertaining to each program leads into a discussion of the similarities and differences across programs, as well as remarks concerning the validity of AES program in general.

Project Essay Grade

Project Essay Grade, or PEG, was the first AES system. PEG grew out of research of Ellis Page and colleagues in Connecticut in the 1960s and 1970's, and was resurrected in the 1990's by Page when he realized that there was virtually no follow-up on his earlier research. Just as the PEG project in many ways defined the direction of AES programs, so did it virtually define the research agenda for demonstrating the reliability and validity of AES systems. For a description of how PEG works, (see Page 1994; Chapter 3, this volume; Page & Peterson, 1995). Of the AES systems, I am most familiar with PEG, and I have conducted validity research on PEG. For these reasons, I first describe the validity evidence for PEG followed by other AES programs.

Correlations with Human Judges. Even in the 1960s, with computers in their infancy, PEG holistic essay scores correlated .50, on average, with scores of individual judges, about the same level of correlation of those judges with each other (Page, 1966). Even in this early stage, PEG was able to score content in classroom essays (Ajay, Tillett, & Page, 1973). In 1994, using National Assessment of Educational Progress (NAEP) exams, PEG reported averaged correlations between PEG scores and single judges of .659 (later improved to .712, and compared to .545 among human judges), and up to .876 for average correlations between PEG and groups of eight human judges (Page, 1994, Chapter 3, this volume). Cross-validating across separate samples, PEG equations generated using the 1988 NAEP data produced scores that correlated .828 with average scores (six judges) when used with 1990 data. More recent validation studies, using the Educational Testing Service (ETS) Praxis exam and the GRE, are summarized in Table 9.1. Validity coefficients in the .80s are common. Table 9.1 also shows average correlations between single human judges, where available.

TABLE 9.1

Averaged Correlations of AES scores from Project Essay Grade with Groups of Human Judges. All Correlations are from Validation Samples.

Study	One Judge	Two Judges*	Three Judges*	Six Judges*	Average Judge Correlation
NAEP (Page, 1994; Page et al., 1996)	.712	.747	.801	.859	.564
Praxis (Page & Peterson, 1995	.742	.816	.846		.646
GRE (Page, 1997)		.826			
IUPUI (Shermis et al., in press)		.760		.838	.58 (.742 for pairs)
Write America (Page, this volume)	.611	.691			.481

*Scores averaged across judges

Write America (described in Page, Chapter 3, this volume) is also worth mentioning. Write America involved over 60 classrooms across the United States, with each essay scored by the classroom teacher and an independent reader; neither reader was trained, unlike in many large testing programs. PEG was trained on the second reader, and then validated on the teachers with a correlation of .611 (compared to a correlation of .481 between human judges). When trained on a subset of pairs of readers and then validated on the other subset of readers, a correlation of .691 was achieved. Although impressive, especially considering the scope of the project, these correlations are lower than typically found with large testing programs. It is unclear whether the difference is due only to the low reliability of the readers, whether classroom essays are more difficult to score, or some other variables.

All correlations reported earlier were based on validation samples, rather than calibration samples. Correlations within calibration samples, as noted earlier, would be higher (and, in fact, equal to the $\underline{R}$ from the multiple regression equation). For example, for the 1994 NAEP study, the correlation of PEG and human judges in the calibration sample was .877 (average of six judges).

It is also noteworthy that several of the PEG validation studies used "blind tests." For example, for the Praxis study, ETS judges scored 600 essays, but PEG only received judges' scores for the calibration or training essays. After training, PEG was used to score the 300 validation essays, with those scores sent back to ETS; ETS then computed the correlations between PEG scores and human judges for the validation sample (for more detail, see Page & Petersen, 1995). To my knowledge, no other AES program has allowed such external validation.

Trait Ratings. Several PEG studies have rated components of writing in addition to overall or holistic scores. Table 9.2 summarizes correlations from two such studies. The correlations of PEG component scores with average human judge scores were considerably stronger than the correlations of these same average judge scores with a separate, single human rater (Shermis et al., 2002), and were equivalent to validity coefficients for average judge scores with a composite of three to four human judges in the NAEP data (Keith, 1998; Page, Lavoie, & Keith, 1996).

TABLE 9.2
Correlations of Components of Writing, as Measured by PEG with
Averages of Human Judges.

Component of Writing	NAEP Data (Page, Lavoie, & Keith, 1996): Correlation with Average of Eight Judges	IUPUI Data (Shermis et al., in press): Correlation with Average of Five Judges
Holistic	.88	.83
Content	.89	.84
Organization	.84	.76
Style	.82	.79
Mechanics	.80	.77
Creativity	.88	.85

Note. NAEP=National Assessment of Educational Progress; IUPUI=Indiana University-Purdue University Indianapolis.

Confirmatory Factor Analyses. The results of confirmatory factor analyses have also been reported on PEG data (Keith, 1998; Shermis et al., 2002). Figure 9.3 displays the basic CFA model (here using the 1995 Praxis data). The model first tests whether and the extent to which human judges are all getting at the same basic construct when they score essays. From a measurement and validity standpoint, that characteristic is the "true score" underlying the essays. The models then test the degree to which PEG scores measure that same underlying construct. As shown in the Figure 9.3, PEG more closely approximated the true essay score in the Praxis data than did pairs of human raters. Other CFA findings are displayed in Table 9.3. Note that PEG factor loadings were relatively constant across different combinations of judges, but judges' scores showed higher factor loadings as additional judges were averaged together. In other words, more judges more closely approximate the "true essay" score.

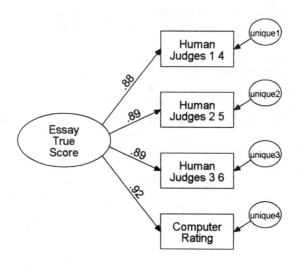

Chi-Squared = 5.189
df = 2
p = .075
GFI = .991
TLI = .991
CFI = .997

FIG. 9.3. Confirmatory factor model of the relative construct validity of AES and human judge pairs. Computer ratings more closely approximated the true essay score than did pairs of human judges.

Convergent and Discriminant Validity. The teacher candidates who completed the Praxis exam also earned scores on multiple–choice tests of writing, reading, and mathematics. PEG scores correlated with these objective scores in the ordering that would be expected if it indeed measures writing skill: .47, .39, and .30, respectively (Petersen, 1997). The PEG–objective writing correlation of .47 compared favorably with the human judge-objective writing correlation of .45.

TABLE 9.3
Confirmatory Factor Analytic Results Comparing the Validity the PEG scores with those from Human Raters

| Study | PEG vs. Single Judge | | vs. Judge Pairs | | vs. 3 Judge Sets | |
	PEG	Judge	PEG	Judge	PEG	Judge
NAEP (Keith, 1998)	.93	.72	.91	.82	.92	.87
Praxis	.92	.81	.92	.89	.92	.91
IUPUI			.89	.86		
(Shermis et al., press)						

TABLE 9.4
The Generalized Validity of PEG. Scoring Formulae Developed from One Set of Essays
Were Applied to Another Set of Essays.

Essay Scored	*Source of Training Formula*							
	Other	GRE	Praxis	IUPUI	High-School	NAEP -90	Write-America	N Judges
Other	**.88**	.82	.81	.78	.77	.81	.79	5
GRE	.79	**.86**	.81	.76	.76	.80	.75	2
Praxis	.77	.81	**.86**	.79	.72	.79	.81	6
IUPUI	.70	.71	.72	**.78**	.68	.70	.72	2
High-School	.78	.79	.78	.80	**.90**	.81	.77	Varied
NAEP-90	.80	.83	.81	.79	.77	**.88**	.76	8
Write-America							**.69**	2
N Judges	5	2	6	2	Varied	8	2	

Note. Columns show the source of the scoring formula, and rows show the set of essays to which they were applied. The diagonal shows the calibration correlation between PEG and human judges. See text for additional detail.

Generalization of Scoring Formulae Across Studies. Do AES programs measure some general, consistent aspect of writing, or do they measure something different for each new set of essays? Table 9.4 (from Keith, 1998) shows the degree of generalization from one set of essays to the next. Using various PEG data sets, the formula from each data set was used to score the essays from other data sets. The table shows the validation correlations in the off-diagonals, and the calibration correlations between PEG and human judges in the diagonal (bolded). So for example, the sixth column of numbers (NAEP-90) and second row of numbers (GRE) shows the results of using the high school level NAEP-generated scoring formula to score the graduate level GREs. The NAEP-generated scores correlated .80 with the human judges' ratings of the GRE essays. All of the correlations are impressively high, and suggest that PEG's AES scores indeed measure some basic, generalizable aspect of writing.

The final column of data (Writ-Am) is also interesting because it suggests the Write America formula is more accurate in predicting judges' scores for *other* essays than for Write America. This finding, in turn, nicely illustrates the effect of predicting a less reliable (Write America) versus more reliable (e.g., Praxis judges) outcome. The finding also suggests that even relatively unreliable judges can be used to produce a valid AES score, although the extent of the validity of that formula may only show up when used to predict a more reliable outcome.

Intellimetric™

Intellimetric™ was developed by Vantage Learning beginning in approximately 1996; the program was commercially available beginning in 1998 (Elliot, this volume). For information on how Intellimetric™ works, see Elliot (Chaper 5, this volume).

Correlations with Human Judges. Elliot presents extensive validity data in chapter 5 in this volume, using a variety of exams, and various numbers of raters. Most such studies appear to focus on calibration samples, however, and cross-validation estimates (which tend to be lower) are not available. In addition, not all studies report correlations. Still, several cross-validated studies are noteworthy, and have demonstrated impressive results. Three such studies are summarized in Table 9.5.

For each study, a larger sample was split into calibration and validation samples, with the correlations reported from the validation subsamples. For each study, the process was repeated with different divisions into calibration and validation samples, and thus the correlations reported are averaged across replications. The average correlations among human judges were not reported for the first study, and it is not clear how many judges were used (data from Elliot, Chapter 5, this volume). For the Kindergarten through 12th grade Persuasive Study, it is likely that the correlation is inflated due to the extended range of the sample; clearly, 12th graders should generally write better essays than elementary students. The effects of such extension are illustrated by the International study. When correlations were averages of separate grade levels, Intellimetric™ showed an average correlation of .74 with single human judges (from the Table). When grade level was not controlled in this fashion (i.e., when the correlation was computed across the entire sample), the correlation increased to an average of .86 (Elliot, 1999, this volume). Despite these caveats, these results show that Intellimetric™ indeed produces valid estimates of writing skill

TABLE 9.5
Correlations of AES scores from Intellimetric™ with Human Judges. All Correlations are from Validation Samples.

Study	One Judge	Two Judges	Average Judge Correlation
Eighth Grade Science (Elliot, this volume)	.88		
K-12 Persuasive (Elliot, 2000)		.82	.84
International, Age 7 (Elliot, 1999)	.68		.76
Age 11	.74		.72
Age 14	.79		.79
Average	.74		.76

Note: K-12 = Kindergarten through 12th grade.

Correlations with Other Measures of Writing. Elliot (1999) reported correlations for the International Study between Intellimetric™ and and scores from an external, multiple choice measure of writing, and an external teacher's estimate of overall writing skill. The data are summarized, by age, in Table 6. The averaged correlations of .60 with the multiple choice test and .64 with teachers' ratings of writing compared well to the correlations of these external criteria with judges' scores (.58 and .60, respectively).In a separate study of college students, Elliot demonstrated differences in mean scores depending on the academic level of their previous writing instruction.

TABLE 9.6

Correlations of Intellimetric™ Scores with External Measures of Writing: A Multiple Choice
Writing Test and Teacher Ratings of Writing Skill.

Sample	Multiple Choice Test	Teacher Rating
International, Age 7	.56 (.46)	.46 (.36)
Age 11	.55 (.58)	.69 (.68)
Age 14	.69 (.70)	.76 (.76)
Average	.60 (.58)	.64 (.60)

Note. Correlations of human judges with the external measures are shown in parentheses.
Data from Elliot, 1999.

Number of Graders and Number of Papers. The Intellimetric™ research reports on
the impact of number of graders and number of papers on correlations between
AES and human scores and is consistent with the graph in Figure 9.2. His research
also suggests that training may be able to be accomplished with as few as 50 essays..
More such research, using multiple samples and multiple variables within the same
study are needed. Intellimetric™, like PEG, has also explored scoring the
components of writing, although only accuracy/agreement statistics are reported in
Elliot (this volume).

Intelligent Essay Assessor

Intelligent Essay Assessor (IEA) was developed by Thomas Landauer, Darrell
Laham, and colleagues beginning in approximately 1996 (Landauer et al., in press),
and uses "Latent Semantic Analysis" (LSA) to assess the similarity between new
essays and pre-scored essays. An overview of how IEA works is available in
Landauer et al. (this volume).

Correlations with Human Judges

Table 9.7 shows correlations between IEA scores and those of human judges for
both standardized tests and classroom essays; all data are from Landauer and
colleagues (in press, this volume). For the standardized tests, correlations are
shown using validation samples only, across which IEA scores averaged
correlations with human judges .85 (single judges) and .88 (judge pairs). For the
classroom essays, only correlations using jackknifed calibration samples were
available. Nevertheless, correlations between IEA classroom scores and judges
were somewhat lower (.70 single, .75 pairs). This difference is likely due, in part, to
the somewhat lower inter-judge correlations for classroom as opposed to
standardized test essays. With classroom essays the actual content of the essays is
likely much more important than for the standardized test essays; this difference in
the importance of content could also affect the correlations.

TABLE 9.7

Averaged Correlations of AES scores from Intelligent Essay Assessor with Human Judges. Except Where Noted, All Correlations are from Validation Samples.

Study	Single Judge	Two Judges	Average Judge Correlation
GMAT-1	.84	.87	.86
GMAT-2	.85	.87	.88
Narrative essay, standardized exam	.87	.90	.86
Various classroom essays[a]	.70 (.54-.78)	.75 (.70-.84)	.65 (.16-.89)

Note: Data are from Landauer, Laham, & Foltz, in press, and Landauer, Laham, & Foltz, this volume. [a]Correlations for classroom essays are from calibration rather than validation samples; for these essays, average correlations and ranges are shown.

Correlations with Other Measures and Other Validity Evidence

IEA researchers have reported a number of other lines of evidence that support the validity of IEA as a measure of writing skill or the content of writing. For one experiment, undergraduates wrote essays about heart anatomy and function before and after instruction. IEA scores correlated well with scores on a short answer test on the topic (.76 versus an average of .77 for human judges), and IEA content scores showed evidence of improvement pre- and post-instruction (Landauer et al., in press). IEA scores on standardized, narrative essays were able to discriminate among the grade levels of student writers in grades four, six and eight with 74% accuracy (modified calibration sample) (Landauer et al., in press).

E-Rater

E-Rater is the AES system developed by Educational Testing Service (ETS). In one of its applications, e-Rater is used, in conjunction with human raters, to score essays on the Graduate Management Admissions Test (GMAT). A description of how *e-rater* works is documented in Burstein (this volume).

Correlations with Human Judges

E-rater research generally uses both calibration and validation samples, and logically focuses on ETS's large-scale assessment exams. In a study of the performance of e-rater in scoring essays on the GMAT, Burstein and colleagues (1998) reported correlations of .822 (averaged) between e-rater and each of two human judges. The correlations were based on validation samples, and compared to correlations between the two judges of .855. Powers and colleagues (2000) reported correlations between e-rater and judge scores (two scores on each of two essays) of .74 for GRE essays (these correlations were based on jackknifed calibration rather than validation samples). E-rater also appears capable of scoring essays by non-native speakers of English. Research with the Test of Written English (TWE) showed correlations between e-rater and single human judges of .693 averaged (Burstein & Chodorow, 1999). More generally, "correlations between e-rater scores and those of a single human reader are about .73; correlations between two human readers are about .75" (Burstein & Chodorow, 1999, p. 2). These data are summarized in Table 9.8.

TABLE 9.8
Correlations of AES scores from E-Rater with Human Judges.

Study	Single Judge	Two Judges	Average Human Judges
GMAT (Burstein et al., 1998)	.822		.855
GRE (Powers et al., 2000)		.74	.84
TWE (Burstein & Chodorow, 1999)	.693	~.75	~.75
"Typical" (Burstein & Chodorow, 1999)	~.73		~.75

Other Validity Evidence. Powers and colleagues (2000) also reported correlations between e-rater and a variety of external evidence of writing skill. Correlations between e-rater scores and these external criteria ranged from .09 to .27. Higher correlations were reported for self-reported grades in writing courses (.27), undergraduate writing samples (.24), and self-evaluations of writing (.16 to .17). The correlations were generally lower than those reported for these same indicators and judges' essay scores, which ranged from .38 to .26 for the individual indicators mentioned above, and from .07 to .38 for all indicators (judge pairs).

VALIDITY OF AES PROGRAMS

Similarities and Differences Across Programs

There are definite similarities across programs. As a first step, electronic versions of essays are generally picked apart by, counters, taggers, and parsers. Numerous aspects of essays are sorted and calculated, ranging from simple (e.g., average word length) to complex (e.g., different parts of speech, measures of word relatedness, averaged measures of quality of structure of sentences, number of subordinating conjunctions are measured in PEG). Essays are assigned scores on each variable, and multiple regression is used to create a prediction equation. Human judges'— often several judges—scores on a (calibration/training) sample of essays serve as the dependent variable, and the variables scored by the AES program are used as the independent variables. This prediction equation is what is to score subsequent essays.

All programs parse essays and count numerous aspects of each essay. Most programs recognize the primacy of human judges as the most important criterion to emulate, although IEA has the capability of scoring essays from other sources of information (ideal essays or learning materials). Most use multiple regression analysis to create an equation that predicts human judges' scores from those aspects of the essay scored by the computer. All score essay content at some level. According to Scott Elliot, Intellimetric™ does not use multiple regression analysis, but instead uses "artificial intelligence" methods (S. M. Elliot, personal communication, November 19, 2001). Because there was not enough information on the mechanics of how Intellimetric™ works, it is not included in the subsequent comparisons of programs.

There are also differences in how the various programs work. Perhaps the biggest difference is how the programs score essay content. PEG has used dictionaries of words, synonyms, and derivations that should appear in essays. E-rater scans words that do appear in good versus poor essays and compares these lists of words to the new essays. IEA uses the most divergent method to score content. IEA also focuses on the words that appear in good versus poor essays, but uses LSA to reduce the words from test essays in almost a factor-analytic fashion, thus attempting to get closer to word meaning in its profiles. The resulting "profiles" of word meanings are used to determine the similarity of each unscored essay to the scored essays. Content scores are created for each essay by determining the correlation (cosine of angle) between each essay and the pre-scored essays.

The programs differ in their use, in the final multiple regression, of composites versus smaller components as the independent variables. IEA generally creates content, style, and mechanics *composite* scores for use in the final regressions. PEG uses all of the smaller counts and tallies in its regressions. E-rater uses some composites and some components. E-rater creates two composite scores for content (by essay and by argument), but uses individual values for all the other aspects of the essay that are scored (e.g., number of discourse-based cure terms).

The programs also differ in their use of multiple regression, with some (e.g., e-rater) using stepwise regression, with others using hierarchical/sequential (IEA) or forced entry/simultaneous regression (PEG). The type of regression used is relevant because with sequential and simultaneous multiple regression the researcher controls which variables enter the regression equation. With stepwise regression, the computer controls which variables enter the equation, not the researcher, and the actual equation may contain only a small number of the originally scored variables. Thus, although e-rater is nominally organized in modules, there is no guarantee that each module will be represented in the final score. However, it is typically the case that each module is represented.

The programs may differ in the simple number of aspects of essays scored. PEG scores over a hundred aspects of essay, whereas several of the other programs suggest that they score 50-75 aspects of essays (e.g., Intellimetric™, e-rater).

VALIDITY OF AES SYSTEMS

Despite these differences, and although there is considerable variability in the validity information available for each program, it is clear that each program is capable of scoring written essays with considerable validity. Cross-validated correlations between the various AES programs generally range from .70 to .90 and are often in the .80 to .85 range. There is, of course, variability across studies, with some of that variability being predictable (see below), and some not. AES scores behave as they should—if they are valid measures of writing skill—when compared to external measures of convergent and divergent criteria, such as objective tests. AES programs appear to measure the same characteristics of writing as human raters, and often do so more validly than do pairs of human raters. Validity pertains to "inferences and actions" (Messick, 1989, p. 13) based on test scores, and it is obvious from this review that those inferences will be as well—or better—informed when using AES information than when only using information from human raters.

The validity coefficients obtained in standard AES validation research (correlations of AES scores with human judges) vary based on a number of characteristics of the study reported. Several of these influences have already been discussed.

Judge Correlation

A perusal of the validation evidence here and elsewhere demonstrates clearly the earlier discussion of the importance of the correlation between the human judges. Other things being equal, the higher the correlation between human judges, the higher the correlation of AES scores with human judges. As discussed previously, however, there may be limits to this effect, in that higher correlations may not always reflect higher inter-judge validities.

The tables of correlations presented for each program's holistic scores also included, when available, the average correlation between human judges. These values were used as estimates of reliability in the formula for correction for attenuation ($r_{tt} = \dfrac{r_{xy}}{\sqrt{r_{xx}r_{yy}}}$) to determine the likely validity coefficients given a perfectly reliable criterion. For all calculations, the reliability of the AES program was estimated at .95. With these corrections, the range of validity coefficients for the various programs were: PEG, .90 -.97 (M=.94 standardized, .90 classroom); Intellimetric™, .80-.92 (M=.88); IEA, .74-.96 (excluding one coefficient greater than 1, M=.94 standardized, .85 classroom), and e-rater, .82-.91 (M=.86, standardized). As might be expected, the lowest values for PEG and IEA were from classroom essays; for e-rater they were from the Test of Written English. (Corrected validities were calculated using the fewest number of judges listed in each table. Thus if information were available for single judge validities and judge pairs, the single judge values were used. Validities were corrected only when the correlations between human judges [reliability estimates] were available.)

Number of Judges

The more judges the better. Increasing the number of judges provides a more reliable and valid criterion for prediction. This effect, like that of judge correlation, is curvilinear, and becomes more important the lower the correlation between judges.

Proponents of AES systems who wish to demonstrate the validity of those systems should ensure that the human judges demonstrate reasonably high intercorrelations. Training of judges may help. It may also be worthwhile to add additional judges, in order to increase the composite judge reliability and validity and to improve the criterion AES scores are designed to predict. It should be noted that although these strategies will likely improve validity estimates, they are not tricks; they simply make it more likely that the validity estimates obtained are good, accurate estimates.

Standardized Tests vs. Classroom Essays

Most AES validity studies have focused on the scoring of large scale standardized tests such as the GRE and the GMAT. Fewer studies have focused on scoring essays from primary, secondary, and post-secondary classrooms (Landauer et al., in press; Page, this volume). To date, somewhat lower validity estimates have been shown with classroom essays (note the data for Write American in Table 1, and for "Various classroom essays" in Table 7). Even when corrected for attenuation, these coefficients tended to be lower than those for standardized tests. It is not clear, however, whether this difference is due primarily to the generally lower reliabilities of the human judges, or some inherent difficulty in scoring localized classroom essays. (Note that the corrected validity estimates correct only for judge unreliability at the validation step. Unreliable judges undoubtedly affect the calibration step, as well.) It may be, for example, that such essays are confounded with the importance of content. That is, such essays may place a heavier premium on knowledge of content over writing skill, and AES programs may be less valid when scores depend heavily on content knowledge. More research on this difference is needed.

Additional Future Research

The preliminary evidence is in, and it is promising: AES programs can indeed provide valid estimates of writing skill, across a variety of systems, ages, prompts, and tasks. The evidence is promising, but incomplete. Although demonstrations of the correlations of AES scores with human judges will continue to be important, broader demonstrations of the validity of AES systems are needed. Additional studies are needed comparing AES scores to objective measures of writing skill and essay content. Convergent/divergent validity studies and factor analyses should be completed. Additional research is needed on the components of writing skills (e.g., Shermis et al., in press), and whether these can be used to improve students' writing. More research is needed on the issue of content scoring. IEA stresses the importance of content; is it therefore better at scoring content-related essays than are other programs, or are they all equivalent? Comparisons of classroom versus standardized test essays are also needed.

A Blind Comparison Test?

Although this review has concluded that the four major AES systems studied have each demonstrated a degree of validity, the question of their relative validity still remains. Based on existing data, I don't believe it is possible to say that one system is more valid than others, but this conclusion may reflect a lack of knowledge as much as a lack of true variability across programs. What is needed to answer this question is a cross-program blind test (or, better, a series of them). The blind test could be set up along the lines of those conducted by Page and Peterson (1995): have a large set of essays scored by multiple judges. Send all essays to the vendors of each of the AES programs, but only send judges' scores for half of those essays (the calibration sample). Each AES program could train on the same set of calibration essays, and use the generated formula to score the other, validation, essays. Each programs' scores for the validation sample would be returned to the neutral party in charge of the blind test. For each program, AES scores would be compared to human judges' scores for the validation sample; the results would provide an empirical test of the relative validity of each program. It would be worthwhile to repeat the test under several conditions—general writing and writing about specific content, different grade levels, and so on—because it may well be that one program is more valid under some conditions versus others. The research would not only answer questions about the relative validity of AES programs, but would undoubtedly improve future programs.

We are beyond the point of asking whether computers can score written essays; the research presented in this volume and elsewhere demonstrates that computer can indeed provide valid scores reflecting the writing skills of those who produce the essays. The inferences one would make from AES-scored essays would be at least, and possibly better, informed as those based on human scoring of those same essays. I look forward to the extension and generalization of these programs to classrooms, individual assessments, and interventions with those needing improvement in writing skills.

REFERENCES

Ajay, H.B., Tillett, P.I., and Page, E.B. (Principal Investigator) (1973, December). *Analysis of essays by computer (AEC-II) (8-0102). Final Report to the National Center for Educational Research and Development.* Washington, DC: U.S. Dept. of Health, Education, and Welfare, Office of Education, National Center for Educational Research and Development.

Burstein, J. (this volume). The e-rater scoring engine: Automated essay scoring with natural language processing. In M. D. Shermis, & J. Burstein (Eds.). Automated essay scoring: A cross-disciplinary perspective. Mahwah, NJ: Erlbaum.

Burstein, J. & Chodorow, M. (1999, June). *Automated essay scoring for nonnative English speakers.* Joint Symposium of the Association of Computational Linguistics and the International Association of Language Learning Technologies, Workshop on Computer-Mediated Language Assessment and Evaluation of Natural Language Processing, College Park , MD.

Burstein, J., Kukich, K., Wolff, S., Lu, C., & Chodorow, M. (1998, April). *Computer analysis of essays.* NCME Symposium on Automated Scoring.

Cohen, J. (1983). The cost of dichotomization. *Applied Psychological Measurement, 7,* 249-253.

Elliot, S. M. (1999). *Construct validity of Intellimetric™™ with international assessment.* Yardley, PA: Vantage Technologies (RB-323).

Elliot, S. M. (2000). *Applying Intellimetric™™ technology to the scoring of K-12 persuasive writing: A subsample cross validation study.* Yardley, PA: Vantage Technologies (RB-424).

Elliot, S. M. (this volume). *Intellimetric™: From here to validity.* In M. D. Shermis, & J. C. Burstein (Eds.). *Automated essay scoring: A cross-disciplinary perspective.* Mahwah, NJ: Erlbaum.

Keith, T. Z. (1996, April). Types of construct validity in PEG measures. In E. B. Page (Moderator), J. W. Asher, B. S. Plake, & D. Lubinski (Discussants), *Grading essays by computer: Qualitative and quantitative grading in large programs and in classrooms.* Invited symposium at the annual meeting of the National Council for Measurement in Education, New York.

Keith, T. Z. (1998, April). *Construct validity of PEG.* Paper presented at the American Educational Research Association, San Diego, CA.

Landauer, T. K., Laham, D., & Foltz, P. (in press). Automatic essay assessment with latent semantic analysis. *Journal of Applied Educational Measurement.*

Landauer, T. K., Laham, D., & Foltz, P. (this volume). Automated scoring and annotation of essays with the intelligent essay assessor. In M. D. Shermis, & J. C. Burstein (Eds.). *Automated essay scoring: A cross-disciplinary perspective.* Mahwah, NJ: Erlbaum.

Messick, S (1989). Validity. In R. L. Linn (Ed.), *Educational measurement* (pp. 13-103). New York: Macmillan.

Page, E. B. (1966). The imminence of grading essays by computer. *Phi Delta Kappan, 48,* 238-243.

Page, E. B. (1994). Computer grading of student prose, using modern concepts and software. *Journal of Experimental Education, 62(2),* 27-142.

Page, E. B. (this volume). Project essay grade: PEG. In M. D. Shermis, & J. C. Burstein (Eds.). *Automated essay scoring: A cross-disciplinary perspective.* Mahwah, NJ: Erlbaum.

Page, E. B., Lavoie, M. J., & Keith, T. Z. (1996, April). *Computer grading of essay traits in student writing.* Paper presented at the annual meeting of the National Council on Measurement in Education, New York, NY.

Page, E.B. & Petersen, N.S. (1995). The computer moves into essay grading: Updating the ancient test. *Phi Delta Kappan, 76(7),* 561-565.

Page, E.B. (1997, March). *The second blind test with ETS: PEG predicts the Graduate Record Exams.* Handout for AERA/NCME Symposium, Chicago.

Peterson, N. S. (1997, March). Automated scoring of writing essays: Can such scores be valid? Paper presented at the annual meeting of the National Council on Education, Chicago.

Powers, D.E., Burstein, J.C., Chodorow, M., Fowles, M.E., & Kukich, K. (2000). Comparing the validity of automated and human essay scoring (GRE No. 98-08aR). Princeton, NJ: Educational Testing Service.

Shermis, M. D., & Daniels, K. E. (this volume). Norming and scaling for automated essay scoring. In M. D. Shermis, & J. C. Burstein (Eds.). *Automated essay scoring: A cross-disciplinary perspective.* Mahwah, NJ: Erlbaum.

Shermis, M.D., Koch, C.M., Page, E.B., Keith, T.Z.,& Harrington, S. (in press). Trait ratings for automated essay grading. *Educational and Psychological Measurement.*

10

Norming and Scaling for Automated Essay Scoring

Mark D. Shermis
Florida International University
Kathryn Daniels
Indiana University Purdue University Indianapolis

Scores on essays, as is the case with other types of assessments, reflect a set of numbers assigned to individuals on the basis of performance, in which higher numbers reflect better performance (Peterson, Kolen, & Hoover, 1989). Depending on how the scores are derived, the numbers may reflect assignments given at the ordinal, interval, or ratio scale. With ordinally–scaled numbers, the higher the number, the more of the underlying trait or characteristic one possesses. However, the distances between the numbers on the scale are not assumed to be equal. For example, if one uses a writing rubric on a 5–point scale, it likely that the trait discrepancies in performance between a "1" and a "2" are different than between a "2" and a "3," although the numeric result in both cases reflects 1 point. The exception to this definition comes in the form of "rank–ordered numbers," in which the lower the number, the more of the trait or characteristic one possesses. So, for instance, being ranked first in your high school is better than being ranked 16th.

With intervally–scaled numbers, the differences among the numbers are assumed to be equal, though there is no true zero point. So, although one might like to characterize an uncooperative colleague as having "no intelligence," this would technically be inaccurate. What we say is that our intelligence measure is insensitive at the extremes of the cognitive ability spectrum. With ratio–scaled numbers, however, there is a true zero point. For example, it is possible to have "no money." Therefore, money is considered to be on a ratio–scale. Sometimes the true zero point cannot be obtained under normal conditions. One can obtain a state of weightlessness in space, but not on earth.

If the assignment of numbers is arbitrary, but consistently applied to categories of performance, then the measurement is said to be at the nominal scale. In this situation, the numbers have no inherent meaning in that we can apply a score of, say, "1" to "nonmasters" and "2" to "masters," or vice versa. In this example it doesn't matter how we make the assignment, just as long as we do it in a consistent fashion. Some authors argue that the nominal scale is not really a scale of measurement because no underlying trait is being measured, but rather it is a classification scheme (Glass & Hopkins, 1996).

SCORING AND SCALING

There are three basic approaches to scoring and scaling essays. The most common approach is to define performance through the use of a rubric or a group of standards. The key feature of this approach is that the writing is compared to a set of criteria against which the essay is judged, and would be an example of criterion–referenced performance assessment. This method is often mixed with normative scaling, the second approach. The rubric is used as a guideline for instructing raters, but the actual evaluation of essay performance is based on a set of norms established for making essay comparisons. The higher the score one obtains, the higher the relative performance on the essay writing task. The last technique, which employs Item Response Theory (IRT), examines the relation between ability and the probability of obtaining a particular score on the essay.

CRITERION–REFERENCED PERFORMANCE ASSESSMENT

The problem with writing is that while we appear to know good writing when we see it, we may come to these conclusions about essays for different reasons. One way to begin articulating the dimensions of writing through which some consensus among writers might be obtained is by using a rubric.

Rubrics are a set of rules that describe the parameters of score boundaries in performance assessment. In the evaluation of writing, one may choose to use a single overall score (holistic), a score based on attributes or skills that we care about (analytic), or on inherent characteristics of writing itself (trait). Analytical scoring focuses on the component parts of writing (e.g., ideas, wording) whereas trait scoring evaluates the attributes of performance for a particular audience and writing purpose (Harrington, Shermis, & Rollins, 2000). Because traits and attributes of writing may overlap, there is a perception that the distinction between analytic and trait ratings is vague. A good rubric will define the trait of interest and then provide operational definitions of different levels of performance.

A number of studies (Page, Lavoie, & Keith; 1996, Page, Poggio, & Keith, 1997; Shermis, Koch, Page, Keith & Harrington, 2002) have employed the so–called big five traits for evaluating English essays. These traits include content, creativity, style, mechanics, and organization. Their emergence stems from a distillation of results across a wide array of empirical studies. The hope is that the use of traits would serve to inform writers what characteristics or dimensions of their writing form the basis for rater judgments. However, in one study by Shermis, Koch, Page, Keith, and Harrington (2002), the big five traits didn't discriminate writing performance any better than the use of a holistic evaluation scheme alone. It should be noted in that study that the ratings on content and creativity cut across a number of different topics.

Page, Poggio, and Keith (Page, et al 1997) argued that the value of a trait score lies with the ability to portray relative strengths of the writer in much the same way that a broad achievement test in reading can provide a similar diagnosis. It could be, however, that the use of the big five traits is restricted to models based on single topics. If this is the case, then the big five traits would have restricted utility for automated essay scoring.

Northwest Regional Educational Laboratory Rubric

One of the more popular rubrics was developed by the Northwest Educational Research Laboratory in Portland, OR. The "6+1" Traits model for assessing and teaching writing is made up of six key qualities (traits) that define strong writing [NWREL, 1999]. These traits are: (a) ideas, the heart of the message; (b) organization, the internal structure of the piece; (c) voice, the personal tone and flavor of the author's message; (d) word choice, the vocabulary a writer chooses to convey meaning; (e) sentence fluency, the rhythm and flow of the language; (f) conventions, the mechanical correctness; and Presentation, how the writing actually looks on the page (NWREL, 1999).

TABLE 10.1
6+1 Traits™. Source: Northwest Educational Research Laboratory, Portland, OR. Used by permission. 6+1 Traits™ and Six–trait Writing™ are trademarks of the Northwest Educational Research Laboratory.

Trait	Definition
Ideas	The Ideas are the heart of the message, the content of the piece, the main theme, together with all the details that enrich and develop that theme. The ideas are strong when the message is clear, not garbled. The writer chooses details that are interesting, important, and informative– often the kinds of details the reader would not normally anticipate or predict. Successful writers do not tell readers things they already know; e.g., "It was a sunny day, and the sky was blue, the clouds were fluffy white." They notice what others overlook, seek out the extraordinary, the unusual, the bits and pieces of life that others might not see.
Organization	Organization is the internal structure of a piece of writing, the thread of central meaning, the pattern, so long as it fits the central idea. Organizational structure can be based on comparison-contrast, deductive logic, point-by-point analysis, development of a central theme, chronological history of an event, or any of a dozen other identifiable patterns. When the organization is strong, the piece begins meaningfully and creates in the writer a sense of anticipation that is, ultimately, systematically fulfilled. Events proceed logically; information is given to the reader in the right doses at the right times so that the reader never loses interest. Connections are strong, which is another way of saying that bridges from one idea to the next hold up. The piece closes with a sense of resolution, tying up loose ends, bringing things to closure, answering important questions while still leaving the reader something to think about.
Voice	The Voice is the writer coming through the words, the sense that a real person is speaking to us and cares about the message. It is the heart and soul of the writing, the magic, the wit, the feeling, the life and breath. When the writer is engaged personally with the topic, he/she imparts a

	personal tone and flavor to the piece that is unmistakably his/hers alone. And it is that individual something–different from the mark of all other writers–that we call voice.
Word Choice	Word Choice is the use of rich, colorful, precise language that communicates not just in a functional way, but in a way that moves and enlightens the reader. In good descriptive writing, strong word choice clarifies and expands ideas. In persuasive writing, careful word choice moves the reader to a new vision of things. Strong word choice is characterized not so much by an exceptional vocabulary that impresses the reader, but more by the skill to use everyday words well.
Sentence Fluency	Sentence Fluency is the rhythm and flow of the language, the sound of word patterns, the way in which the writing plays to the ear, not just to the eye. How does it sound when read aloud? That's the test. Fluent writing has cadence, power, rhythm, and movement. It is free of awkward word patterns that slow the reader's progress. Sentences vary in length and style, and are so well crafted that the writer moves through the piece with ease.
Conventions	Conventions are the mechanical correctness of the piece–spelling, grammar and usage, paragraphing (indenting at the appropriate spots), use of capitals, and punctuation. Writing that is strong in conventions has been proofread and edited with care. Handwriting and neatness are not part of this trait. Since this trait has so many pieces to it, it's almost a holistic trait within an analytic system. As you assess a piece for convention, ask yourself: "How much work would a copy editor need to do to prepare the piece for publication?" This will keep all of the elements in conventions equally in play. Conventions is the only trait where we make specific grade level accommodations.
Presentation	Presentation combines both visual and verbal elements. It is the way we "exhibit" our message on paper. Even if our ideas, words, and sentences are vivid, precise, and well constructed, the piece will not be inviting to read unless the guidelines of presentation are present. Think about examples of text and presentation in your environment. Which signs and billboards attract your attention? Why do you reach for one CD over another? All great writers are aware of the necessity of presentation, particularly technical writers who must include graphs, maps, and visual instructions along with their text.

(Table 10.1 shows the trait label and its associated definition. The traits are rated on a 1 to 5 scale ranging from "Not Yet" to "Strong".)

Although the research on this rubric is still emerging, early research on it has been promising (Jaimer, Kozol, Nelson, & Salsberry, 2000). Also, the developers have created workshops, materials, and other support measures to make the rubric easy to adopt.

NORM–REFERENCED ASSESSMENT

Holistic ratings, which typically employ a norm–referenced approach, are another common way to evaluate essays. In assigning essay scores, most studies or projects will employ between two to six raters. Using this method, an averaged essay score is compared to the distribution of other essay ratings. A chief drawback of this method is inherent in any enterprise that uses classical test theory—the norms may only be good for a particular set of examinees, at a particular time, for a particular purpose, or in a particular setting. Vigilance is required so that the attributes of validity for the norms is maintained in a changing world.

HOW SCORES ARE FORMED

There are several ways to create scores for Automated Essay Scoring (AES). All of the grading engines use some sort of a regression approach in making predictions about a particular essay. Usually, the essay grading engine parses the text and tags it according to an a priori variable set. For example, the parser might look and tag such things as the number of sentences, the use of conjunctions, the order of certain words, and so forth. We discuss the types of classifications a parser might make in the following section. Once the parser has done its work, the variables are summarized. To create a prediction equation, the variables are then regressed against the evaluations provided by the raters for a set of essays randomly selected for model building. In this case, the evaluations from the raters serve as the criterion. The exception to this approach is embodied in the Intelligent Essay Assessor (IEA) in that it uses Latent Semantic Analysis (LSA; Landauer, Latham, & Foltz, 1998) as a primary evaluation mechanism. With LSA, content is evaluated by looking at the document's propensity to contain keywords and synonyms and comparing their Euclidean distance to words contained in a master list. With IEA, other attributes of writing are evaluated in a manner similar to the other essay grading engines.

Most studies create models using two data sets—one randomly–selected for model building and the other randomly–selected for validating the model. Those variables that are flagged as significant predictors are retained for the model. The number of variables used by a model varies from parser to parser. For example, the parser in Project Essay Grade can classify over 200 variables, but only about 30 to 40 of them are typically identified as significant predictors in a multiple–regression equation. A randomly selected second set of data is then used to validate the multiple regression equation developed for the first data set (Page & Petersen, 1995; Shermis, Mzumara, Olson & Harrington, et al 2001; Shermis, 2002). Under classical test theory, models developed for one sample tend to predict less well when a second sample of essays is applied to them. This loss of precision accuracy is referred to as "shrinkage" (Cohen & Swerdlik, 1999).

Although it may vary, most rating rubrics result in human ratings ranging from 1 to 5 or 1 to 6. If a nonstandardized multiple regression is used for model building, then scores that are returned from a computer model will (after truncation) be on the same scale. If a standardized multiple regression is used, then resulting mean of the distribution will be 0 with a standard deviation of 1. The nonstandardized scores are what end–users desire whereas the standardized scores are often used for research purposes. However, Page developed a "modified T–score," based on the standardized multiple regression, where the mean is transformed to 70 rather than 50 and the standard deviation remains at 10. The score that a student receives from the automated essay scorer has a range of 40 to 100 and is analogous to what a teacher might assign for a classroom–based essay or assignment.

Proxes and Trins

A rubric can help raters make valid judgments by identifying the salient features of writing that have value in the assessment context. Inherent in the process is that some aspects of writing will be ignored or undervalued, generally those features that the developers of the rubric think are less–important or unimportant. In formulating a rubric, the developers identify those characteristics that can be readily observed and use these characteristics as a placeholder for some intrinsic feature of the writing that is not so easily discernable. In the social science context, this would be analogous to the observed or latent distinction that is made in formulating models of systems or behaviors. Observed variables are ones that we measure whereas latent variables are the "real" traits or characteristics that we are interested. Our measurement of a trait is hampered by the unreliability or invalidity of the observed variables that we are constrained to use.

In the world of AES, this same distinction was coined by Page and Peterson, 1995 as the difference between trins and proxes. Trins are intrinsic characteristics of interest whereas proxes are approximations of those characteristics (observed variables). At first glance, it may appear as if some of the proxes are rather superficial, but on closer inspection they may in fact reflect sophisticated thinking. For example, one of the grading engines counts the number of times "but" appears in the writing sample. From a grammatical standpoint, "but" is a simple conjunction and may not contribute all that much to our understanding of the writing. However, "but" is often used at the beginning of a dependent clause which occurs in the context of more complex writing. It could be that "but" is an appropriate proxy for the writing sophistication or sentence complexity.

The point to keep in mind is that a proxy may act as good or better indicator of quality than more authentic procedures for two basic reasons. First, one should be able to better train raters on observable features of the writing than on their intrinsic characteristics. Second, one has a better chance of obtaining expert consensus on the observable variables rather than arguing about the inherent features of the writing product.

If you wanted to navigate the fjords of Norway, you could either take your triangulated measurements from lookouts perched on each side of your ship or obtain them from the measurements generated off a radar screen. Those lookouts might represent the "authentic" way of navigating a sea channel. And, all other things being equal, most sea–farers would prefer to use both sources of information, but can perform reasonably well with just the radar scope. In this case the proxy (i.e., the radar scope) is a viable alternative to actually seeing the glacial remnants of northern Norway.

ADJUSTMENT OF SCORES BASED ON NEEDS OF CLIENTS

One of the problems of using the raters as the criterion measure is that they may provide ratings not ideally aligned with the rubrics underlying them. This can occur in spite of instruction and training to the contrary. For example, one commonly made observation is that raters more heavily weight the expression of nonstandard English than is sometimes desired. That is, when raters encounter nonstandard English expressions, they tend to undervalue the text although it may contain all the other ingredients that address well the rubric that is being used. When this occurs, it may be possible to reweight the predictors to better reflect what was intended by the original rubric. This can be accomplished if the predictors embodied in the grading engine have clear counterparts related to the elements of nonstandard English. Thus AES might be used to compensate for known bias in the human rating process.

Taken to an extreme, the AES scoring model itself can be formulated without empirical input. For example, let's say that an "ideal" answer was constructed based on theoretical considerations or "best practice" by an expert or a group of experts. One could form the statistical model for AES on the "ideal" and evaluate candidate essays based on this rather than on an empirical model developed over hundreds of essays. Most AES scoring engines could accommodate this approach quite easily.

Norms

The norm–referenced approach has as its basis the comparison of a test score to the distribution of a particular reference group. National norms would be based on a nationally representative sample of writing. Shermis (Shermis, 2000) has proposed the establishment of norms for electronic portfolio documents that would be scored through AES. Documents that would be included in the norming procedure would be drawn from four writing genre: reports of empirical research, technical reports, historical narratives, and works of fiction. This application is based on previous research with shorter (i.e., less than 500 words) essays in which computers have surpassed both the reliability and validity of human raters. The approach uses the evaluation of human raters as the ultimate criterion, and regression models of writing are based on large numbers of essays and raters. To build the statistical models to evaluate the writing, approximately 15 institutions across the country, representing a range of Carnegie classifications, have agreed to provide 300 to 550 documents each that are reflective of their current electronic portfolios. Six raters will evaluate each document and provide both holistic and trait ratings. Vantage Learning, Inc. has agreed to provide their Intellimetric parser for both model building and actual implementation of the project. Postecondary institutions that are moving toward electronic portfolios could benefit from having access to the comparative information. Moreover, establishing norms would allow a college to examine writing development of students over time. Finally, the software could be used in a formative manner, allowing students to preview their writing evaluations in order to improve writing or make better document selections. Figure 10.1 shows a screenshot for the demonstration site for this project which can be reached at http://coeweb.fiu.edu/fipsedemo.

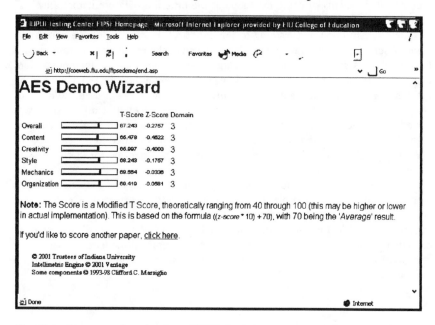

Fig. 10.1 Demonstration site for a FIPSE-funded project that will establish norms for longer essays.

The problem for establishing norms in this national study is that although samples of student writing are probably relatively stable from year to year, the number and scope of institutions that are adopting electronic portfolios will likely change in the near future. The sample that may be representative today may in a few years no longer be reflective of those institutions using electronic portfolios in the future.

Alternate Norms

If one is concerned that examinee performance will be linked to some demographic or characteristic of concern, then a test constructor might create developmental norms or, alternatively different forms of the test to match with the different characteristic levels (Peterson, et al, 1989). The most common demographics used for achievement tests are those of "age" and "grade." In AES, the norms developed for entering college students may not extrapolate well to middle school students. Consequently, norms may have to be developed at multiple grade levels, depending on the purpose of the test. Age norms can also be helpful. For example, if a student skips a grade level in school, she or he may write at an "average" level for the grade, but be in the "superior" group by age.

Occasionally one might extrapolate norms to look for development over time using the same empirical model. If one measured the same individual at different points in time with different essays (and it was appropriate to measure the different essays with the same model), then the differences in normal curve percentiles might represent a shift in developmental performance (positive or negative). This would be a way to document writing growth.

To date, little research has been conducted on the use of automated essay scorers for English as a Second Language subgroup. From a teaching perspective, it is quite possible that the use of AES can provide a helpful feedback mechanism that can accelerate learning, but the evaluation of such students using norms based on an English as a First Language sample may be inappropriate. Norms for gender and ethnicity may also be appropriate or at least warrant study. Because most AES engines use an empirical base for modeling, this pattern is likely to be replicated through automated scoring. If the differences are based on rater bias, then it would be desirable to eliminate them. If not, then it would be desirable to identify the variables or combination of factors for which the differences exist.

Equating

Equating is a statistical technique that is used to ensure that different versions of the test (prompts) are equivalent. As is true with objective tests, it is quite likely that the difficulty level of prompts differ from one prompt to the next (Shermis, Rasmessen, Rajecki, Olson, & Marsiglio, 2001). Although some of the AES engines may use a separate model for each prompt, it is likely that from one test group to the next, the prompts would be treated as being equal unless either the prompts or the models to score the prompts were equated.

Shermis, Rasmussen, Rajecki, Olson, & Marsiglio (2001) investigated the equivalency of prompts using both Project Essay Grade and Multiple Content Classification Analysis (MCCA), a content analysis package that had been used to evaluate the content of television ads for children (Rajecki, Darne, Creek, Barrickman, (1993). Based on the Project Essay Grade model that involved 1,200 essays, each with four raters (800 essays for model building and 400 for validation; Shermis, Mzumara, Page, Olson, & Harrington, 2001). One thousand essays were randomly selected and analyzed using MCCA. The essays included ratings across 20 different prompts. These researchers concluded that essays which were oriented more toward "analytical" responses were rated higher than prompts which elicited "emotional" responses. That is, raters had a bias for the "analytical" themes. The authors concluded that prompts might be differentially weighted in much the same way that dives in a swimming competition are assigned a variety of difficulty levels.

Finally, little research has been done on trying to incorporate IRT in the calibration of AES models, although some foundational work has been performed in IRT calibration of human rating respones (de Ayala, Dodd, & Koch, 1991; Tate

& Heidorn, 1998). For example, de Ayala et al. (1991) used an IRT partial credit model of direct writing assessment to demonstrate that expository items tended to yield more information than did the average holistic rating scale. Tate and Heidorn (1998) employed an IRT polytomous model to study the reliability of performance differences among schools of various sizes.

The hope is that future theoretical research would permit the formulation of graded response or polytomous models to AES formulations. The purpose would be to create models that are more robust to changes in time, populations, or locations. One might also speculate that IRT could also help address the sticky issue of creating a separate model for each content prompt in those engines that focus on content. A major challenge in applying IRT techniques to AES has to do with the underlying assumptions regarding the models (e.g., unidimensionality).

Differential Item Functioning

Differential Item Functioning (DIF) exists when examinees of comparable ability, but different groups, perform differently on an item (Penfield & Lam, 2000). Bias is attributed when something other than the construct being measured manifests itself on the test score. Because performance on writing may be contingent on mastery of several skills (i.e., it is not unidimensional) and be influenced by rating biases, it is a good practice to check for DIF in AES.

Use of performance ratings does not lend itself to dichotomous analysis of DIF. Dichotomous items are usually scored as zero for incorrect items and 1 for correct items. Polytomous items are usually scaled where increasing credit is given to better performance (e.g., a score rating from 1 to 5 on a written essay). However, there are at least three problems limiting the use of polytomous DIF measures: (a) low reliability of polytomous scores, (b) the need to define an estimate of ability to match examinees from different demographic groups, and (c) the requirement of creating a measure of item performance for the multiple categories of polytomous scores (Penfield & Lam, 2000).

For the moment, no single method will address all types of possible DIF under all possible situations (e.g., uniform & nonuniform DIF). Penfield and Lam (2000) recommend using three approaches: Standardized Mean Difference, SIBTEST, and Logistic Regression. All of these approaches, with perhaps the exception of Logistic Regression, require a fairly sophisticated statistical and measurement expertise. Standardized Mean Difference is conceptually simple and performs reliably with well-behaved items. SIBTEST, although computationally complex, is robust to departures from the equality of the mean abilities. Finally, with Logistical Regression is generally more familiar to consumers and developers of tests than are some of the feasible alternatives (e.g., discriminant function analysis; French & Miller, 1996).

In this chapter we have attempted to lay out some of the norming and scaling concerns that face AES researchers as they try to gain wider acceptance of the new technology. A few of the challenges will be unique because AES is a type of performance assessment that utilizes human ratings as a typical criterion measure. Even with extensive training and experience, raters have been known not to conform to the specifications of their rubrics or to introduce biases into their evaluations. When this is the case, it is important to check the ratings for differential item performance.

REFERENCES

Cohen, R. J., & Swenlik, M. E. (1999). *Psychological testing and assessment.* (4th ed). Mountain View, CA: Mayfield Publishing Company.

de Ayala, R. J., Dodd, B. G., & Koch, W. R. (1991). Partial credit analysis of writing ability. *Educational and Psychological Measurement, 51*,103–114.

French, A. W., & Miller, T. R. (1996). Logistic regression and its use in detecting differentially item functioning in polytomous items. *Journal of Educational Measurement, 33*, 315–332.

Glass, G. V., & Hopkins, K. D. (1996). *Statistical methods in education and psychology.* Needham Heights, MA: Allyn & Bacon.

Harrington, S., Shermis, M. D., & Rollins, A. (2000). The influence of word processing on English placement test results. *Computers and Composition, 17*, 197–210.

Jarmer, D., Kozel, M., Nelson, S., & Salsberry, T. (2000). Six-trait writing model improves scores at Jennie Wilson Elemenary. *Journal of School Improvement, 1.* Retrieved from http://www.hcacasi.org/jsi/2000v1i2/six-trait-model.adp.

Landauer, T., Laham, D., & Foltz, P. (1998). *The Goldilocks principle for vocabulary acquisition and learning: Latent semantic analysis theory and applications.* Paper presented at the American Educational Research Association, San Diego, CA.

Northwest Educational Research Laboratories (MWREL). (1999, December). *6+1 Traits of writing rubic* [website]. http://www.nwrel.org/eval/pdfs/6plus1traits.pdf

Page, E. B. (1966). The imminence of grading essays by computer. *Phi Delta Kappan, 48*, 238–243.

Page, E. B., Keith, T., & Lavoie, M. J. (1995, August). *Construct validity in the computer grading of essays.* Paper presented at the annual meeting of the American Psychological Association, New York.

Page, E. B., Lavoie, M. J., & Keith, T. Z. (1996, April). *Computer grading of essay traits in student writing.* Paper presented at the annual meeting of the National Council on Measurement in Education, New York.

Page, E. B., & Petersen, N. S. (1995). The computer moves into essay grading: Updating the ancient test. *Phi Delta Kappan, 76*, 561–565.

Page, E. B., Poggio, J. P., & Keith, T. Z. (1997, March). *Computer analysis of student essays: Finding trait differences in the student profile.* Paper presented at the annual meeting of the American Educational Research Association, Chicago.

Penfield, R. D., & Lam, T. C. M. (2000). Assessing differential item functioning in performance assessment: Review and recommendations. *Educational Measurement: Issues and Practice, 19*(3), 5–15.

Petersen, N. S., & Page, E. B. (April, 1997). *New developments in Project Essay Grade: Second ETS blind test with GRE essays.* Paper presented at the American Educational Research Association, Chicago, IL.

Peterson, N. S., Kolen, M. J., & Hoover, H. D. (1989). Scaling, norming, and equating. In R. L. Linn (Ed.), *Educational measurement* (3rd ed., pp. 221–262). New York: MacMillan.

Rajecki, D. W., Dame, J. A., Creek, K. J., Barrickman, P. J., Reid, C. A., & Appleby, D. C. (1993). Gender casting in television toy advertisements: Distributions, message content analysis, and evaluations. *Journal of Consumer Psychology, 2,* 307-327.

Shermis, M. D. (2000). *Automated essay grading for electronic portfolios.* Washington, D.C.: Fund for the Improvement of Post-Secondary Education (funded grant proposal).

Shermis, M. D., Koch, C. M., Page, E. B., Keith, T., & Harrington, S. (2002). Trait ratings for automated essay grading. *Educational and Psychological Measurement, 62*(1), 5–18.

Shermis, M. D., Mzumara, H. R., Olson, J., & Harrington, S. (2001). On–line grading of student essays: PEG goes on the web at IUPUI. *Assessment & Evaluation in Higher Education, 26,* 247–259.

Shermis, M. D., Rasmussen, J. L., Rajecki, D. W., Olson, J., & Marsiglio, C. (2001). All prompts are created equal, but some prompts are more equal than others. *Journal of Applied Measurement, 2,* 154-170.

Tate, R., & Heidorn, M. (1998). School–level IRT scaling of writing assessment data. *Appled Measurement in Education, 11,* 371–383.

11

Bayesian Analysis of Essay Grading

Steve Ponisciak
Valen Johnson
Duke University

The scoring of essays by multiple raters is an obvious area of application for hierarchical models. We can include effects for the writers, the raters, and the characteristics of the essay that are rated. Bayesian methodology is especially useful because it allows one to include previous knowledge about the parameters. As explained in Johnson and Albert (1999), the situation that arises when multiple raters grade an essay is like the person who has more than one watch – if the watches don't show the same time, that person can't be sure what time it is. Similarly, the essay raters may not agree on the quality of the essay; each rater may have a different opinion of the quality and relative importance of certain characteristics of any given essay. Some raters are more stringent than others, whereas others may have less well–defined standards. In order to determine the overall quality of the essay, one may want to pool the ratings in some way. Bayesian methods make this process easy. In our analysis of a dataset that includes multiple ratings of essays by multiple raters, we examine the differences between the raters and the categories in which the ratings are assessed. In the end, we are most interested in the differences in the precision of the raters (as measured by their variances) and the relationships between the ratings.

Our dataset consists of ratings assigned to essays written by 1,200 individuals. Each essay received 6 ratings, each on a scale of one to 6 (with 6 as the highest rating), from each of 6 raters. Each rater gave an overall rating and five subratings; the categories in which the essays were rated were content, creativity, style, mechanics, and organization. Each essay was rated in all six categories by all six raters, so the data constitutes a full matrix. Histograms of the grades assigned by one rater in each category are shown in Fig. 11.1 to illustrate some of the differences among the raters and categories. One can see in Fig. 11.1a and 11.1b that the first and second raters rate very few essays higher than 4. As another illustration, the graph in Fig. 11.1d shows that in the creativity category, the fourth rater rates a higher proportion of essays at 5 or 6, and probably has a larger variance. The graph in Fig. 11.1c, for Rater Three, is somewhat skewed, and shows little variability.

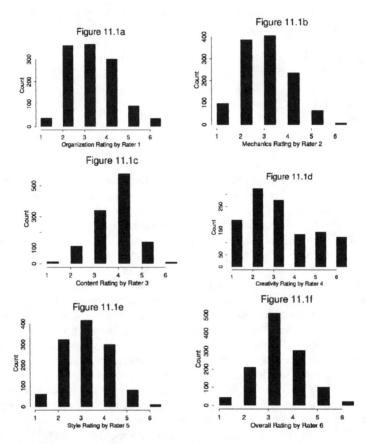

FIG. 11.1 Histograms of the scores assigned in one category by each rater. a) Organization rating by Rater 1, b) Mechanics rating by Rater Two. c) Content rating by Rater Three. d) Creativity rating by Rater Four. e) Style rating by Rater Five. f) Overall rating by Rater Six.

In Fig. 11.1e and 11.1f, one can see that Raters Five and Six tend to rate items more similarly to each other than to Rater Four. The essay ratings for all pairs of categories for a given rater are all positively correlated, as shown in Table 11.1. The correlations are least variable for Rater Four, ranging from 0.889 to 0.982, and most variable for Rater Five, ranging from 0.577 to 0.895. One can conclude from these values that there is a relationship between the category ratings. For Raters one, three, and five the lowest correlation is observed for the ratings of mechanics and creativity, and the highest, for content and the overall rating.

TABLE 11.1
Range of Intra-rater Correlations

	1	2	3	4	5	6
Lowest	0.797	0.794	0.687	0.889	0.577	0.750
Highest	0.928	0.971	0.888	0.982	0.895	0.924

The relationship between any two raters within a given category is not as strong, as shown in Table 11.2. The lowest correlation in four of the six categories is for Raters 4 and 5, suggesting that these are the most dissimilar raters. The highest correlation in four of the six categories is for Raters 1 and 2.

TABLE 11.2
Range of Intra–Category Correlations
Rating

Correlation		Content	Creativity	Style Mechanics	Organization	Overall
Lowest	0.409	0.434	0.318	0.280	0.352	0.413
Highest	0.651	0.643	0.581	0.639	0.666	0.67

The between–rater, between–category correlations range from 0.258 (for Rater 4, content, and Rater 5, mechanics) to 0.683 (Rater 1, content, and Rater 2, overall). The relation among the intracategory and between–rater, between–category ratings is evidently not as strong as the relation among the ratings given by an individual rater, as we might expect. In the graphs that follow, these relation are illustrated. Noise has been added to each data point to provide a sense of density.

One can see in Figure 11.2 that some pairs of ratings are more highly correlated than others. In Figure 11.2a, the overall rating given by Rater 5 does not differ from the rating in content by more than two grades, with very few exceptions. In Figure 11.2b, one can see substantially more disagreement between the fifth rater's assessments of the writer's ability in creativity and mechanics.

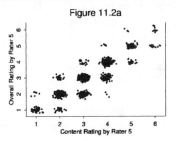
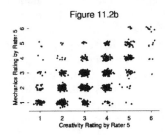

FIG. 11.2 Intrarater comparisons. a) Overall versus content rating for Rater 5. b) Mechanics versus creativity rating for Rater 5.

In Fig. 11.3, one can see that different raters do not always agree on their ratings within the same category. Fig. 11.3a shows the overall rating given by Rater 5 against the overall rating by Rater 4. Fig. 11.3b shows the fourth rater's assessment of the essay's style against the same category for Rater 3. The plots reveal different assessments of the quality of the essay in the chosen categories, consistent with the range of intra–category correlations displayed in Table 11.2.

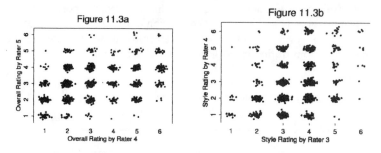

FIG. 11.3 Intracategory comparisons a) Rater 5 versus Rater 4, overall rating. B) Rater 4 versus Rater 3, style rating.

METHODS

Our analysis employs hierarchical statistical methods with a random effect for each writer in each category (Johnson, 1996; Johnson & Albert, 1999) to examine the relation between the subratings and the overall rating, and to study the differences between raters.

A three–stage hierarchical model is employed with the rating y_{ijk} of essay i by Rater j in category k as the outcome. An individual essay will receive this rating if, in the opinion of Rater j, the essay's quality falls within that rater's unobserved interval for that rating. This strategy can be interpreted in the same way as academic grading, where a student receives a letter grade of "B" in a class if his or her average test score (for example) falls in the range (83 to 90). These cutoffs may or may not be known by the student. A continuous variable Z_{ijk}, which will be termed the "observed" latent variable, is associated with each rating y_{ijk}. The variable Z_{ijk} is Rater j's perception of the quality of essay i in category k, and it must fall within the interval $(\gamma_{c-1, jk}, \gamma_{cjk})$ for writer i to receive the grade c. For any two ratings (y_{ijk}, y_{mjk}), if $y_{ijk} < y_{mjk}$ then $Z_{ijk} < Z_{mjk}$. Under these assumptions, we reconstruct the rating cutoffs while assessing the accuracy and severity of the raters by examining the variance specific to that rater and category.

Explicitly, the probability that writer i receives rating c from Rater j in category k is

$$P_{ijkc} = \int_{\gamma_{c-1, jk}}^{\gamma_{cjk}} f\left(\frac{z - a_{ik}}{\sigma_{jk}}\right) dz = \Pr(\gamma_{c-1, jk} \leq Z_{ijk} < \gamma_{cjk}) = F\left(\frac{\gamma_{cjk} - a_{ik}}{\sigma_{jk}}\right) - F\left(\frac{\gamma_{c-1, jk} - a_{ik}}{\sigma_{jk}}\right)$$

where $f()$ is the standard normal probability density function, and $F()$ is the cumulative standard normal distribution function. Because it is interpreted as Rater j's assessment of the ability of writer i in category k, the value Z_{ijk} is assumed to have the writer's "true" ability variable a_{ik} as its mean. This value is observed with a precision $\tau_{jk}=1/\sigma_{jk}^2$ that is specific to each rater in each category. We assume the raters assign ratings independently of each other.

We further assume that the "true" ability variables $\{a_{ik}\}$ for each writer i are distributed as dependent multivariate normal vectors, with mean 0 and covariance matrix Λ_0. Λ_0 is required to have the form of a correlation matrix. That is, it has 1 on its diagonal, and values in $[-1,1]$ off its diagonal, and it is positive definite. This step is taken in order to establish a scale for the latent variables. The variables $\{a_{ik}\}$ are therefore assumed to be marginally distributed as normal $(0,1)$ random variables.

The variables Z_{ijk} and a_{ik} are latent variables, which means that they are not directly observed. As explained in Johnson and Albert (1999, p. 127) the most natural way to view ordinal data [such as essay ratings] is to postulate the existence of an underlying latent (unobserved) variable associated with each response." Such variables are often assumed to be drawn from a continuous distribution centered on a mean value that varies from individual to individual. Often, this mean value is modeled as a linear function of the respondent's covariate vector." In our model, we assign a latent performance variable Z_{ijk} to each essay in each of the K categories for each of the J raters. We assume that this unobserved variable has some known distribution whose mean value is a random effect a_{ik} reflecting the quality of the essay in that category. No covariate information is used. We use uniform prior distributions for all of the grade cutoffs γ_{cjk}, subject only to the constraint $\gamma_{c-1,jk} < \gamma_{cjk}$ for all combinations (c, j, k) of grades, raters and categories, and $\gamma_{0jk} = -\infty$, $\gamma_{Cjk} = \infty$. We also assume that the precisions τ_{jk} for all raters $j=1,...,J$ within a given category k are drawn from the same distribution, a Gamma distribution with mean μ_k and variance μ_k^2/v_k.

We assume inverse gamma prior distributions on the parameters v_k and μ_k:

$$v_k \sim Inv-Gamma(\alpha_v, \beta_v)$$
$$\mu_k \sim Inv-Gamma(\alpha_\mu, \beta_\mu)$$

The selection of the parameters $(\alpha_v, \beta_v, \alpha_\mu, \beta_\mu)$ of these inverse gamma distributions follows the methods used in Johnson and Albert (1999), so that on average, the prior mean of each rater–category precision is 2.0, and its prior variance is 20.0. Therefore, the prior density for each of the rater–category variances has most of its mass in the region (0.01, 4.0). The likelihood can also be expressed without using the latent variables Z, as a product of differences in standard normal cumulative distribution functions,

These modeling assumptions lead to the following likelihood function, where $f()$ is the standard normal probability density function and $1(a < x < b)$ is an indicator variable that takes the value 1 when $a < x < b$ and 0 otherwise:

$$p(y \mid \gamma, Z, a, \tau) = L(\gamma, Z, a, \tau) = \prod_{i=1}^{n} \prod_{j=1}^{J} \prod_{k=1}^{K} f(\frac{Z_{ijk} - a_{ik}}{\sigma_{jk}}) 1(\gamma_{y_{ijk}-1,jk} \leq Z_{ijk} < \gamma_{y_{ijk},jk})$$

This likelihood function is just a product of indicators multiplied by standard normal probability density functions.

as $p(y \mid \gamma, a, \tau) = L(\gamma, a, \tau) = \prod_{i=1}^{n} \prod_{j=1}^{J} \prod_{k=1}^{K} F\left(\frac{\gamma_{y_{ijk}jk} - a_{ik}}{\sigma_{jk}} \right) - F\left(\frac{\gamma_{y_{ijk}-1,jk} - a_{ik}}{\sigma_{jk}} \right)$ w

here $F()$ is the standard normal cumulative distribution function and

$\sigma_{jk} = \dfrac{1}{\sqrt{\tau_{jk}}}$ is the standard deviation specific to Rater j in category k.

POSTERIOR DISTRIBUTION

We can express the posterior distribution as the product of the likelihood and the prior distribution

$$p(\gamma, Z, a, \tau, v, \mu, \Lambda_0 \mid y) \propto L(\gamma, Z, a, \tau) p(a \mid \Lambda_0) p(\Lambda_0) p(\tau \mid v, \mu) p(v) p(\mu)$$

With this expression, one can calculate the full conditional distribution for each variable. The index $i = 1, ..., n$ indicates the essay, $j = 1, ..., J$ the rater, and $k = 1, ..., K$ the category in which the essay is rated. The full conditional distribution is easy to calculate for each of the variables except Λ_0 and $\{v_k, k=1,..., K\}$, so that Gibbs sampling can be used for all variables except these.

To sample from the posterior distributions of Λ_0 and $\{v_k, k = 1, ..., K\}$, alternative (non–Gibbs) methods must be used, because the full conditional distributions for these variables are intractable (that is, they cannot be sampled in a simple way). A Metropolis–Hastings step can be employed to draw from the posterior distribution of $\{v_k, k = 1, ..., K\}$. To sample Λ_0, we will use a method developed by Barnard, McCulloch, and Meng (1997).

In our prior for a_i, we assumed

$$a_i = \{a_{ik}\} \sim MVNormal(0, \Lambda_0)$$

Recall that Λ_0 has the form of a correlation matrix, because in our prior, we want each writer's "true" ability variable a_{ik} to be marginally normal $(0,1)$. If S is a diagonal matrix containing entries $S_{ii} = \sqrt{w_{ii}}$, where w_{ii} are the diagonal entries in the matrix W, we can express Λ_0 as the product $S^{-1}WS^{-1}$, where W is drawn from an inverse–Wishart distribution with v degrees of freedom and the identity as its scale matrix. With these assumptions, the prior for Λ_0 can be written as a function of the degrees of freedom ν only, because the other elements can be integrated out of the equation. We can write

$$p(\Lambda_0 \mid \nu) \propto \mid \Lambda_0 \mid^{0.5(\nu-1)(K-1)-1} \prod_{k=1}^{K} \mid \Lambda_{kk} \mid^{-0.5\nu}$$

where Λ_{kk} is the kth principal submatrix of Λ_0. We use $\nu = K + 1$ to achieve a marginally uniform prior on each element of Λ_0.

For each unique non–unit element λ_{ij} of Λ_0, the interval *(low, high)* can be calculated such that the restriction *(low $\leq \lambda_{ij} \leq$ high)* maintains the positive definiteness of the covariance matrix Λ_0, conditional on the other elements $\{\lambda_{ij}\}$. Therefore, for each element λ_{ij}:

1. Calculate the interval *(low, high)*:
    a) Calculate the determinant $f(r) = \mid \Lambda_0(r) \mid = ar^2 + br + c$, where $\Lambda_0(r)$ is the covariance matrix with the ij^{th} and ji^{th} elements replaced by r.
    b) Solve the quadratic equation $f(r) = 0$ – the roots give the endpoints (low, high).
    c) The coefficients are $a = ((f(1) + f(-1) - 2f(0))/2, b = ((f(1) - f(-1))/2, c = f(0)$.
2. Generate a candidate λ_{ij}^* from the proposal distribution $q(\lambda_{ij}^* \mid \lambda_{ij}) = $ *Normal* (λ_{ij}, σ^2) truncated to the interval (low, high).
3.   Accept the candidate λ_{ij}^* with

$$\text{probability } \alpha = \min \left(1, \frac{q(\lambda_{ij} \mid \lambda_{ij}^*)p(\Lambda_0^*)\prod_{i=1}^{n} p(a_i \mid \Lambda_0^*)}{q(\lambda_{ij}^* \mid \lambda_{ij})p(\Lambda_0)\prod_{i=1}^{n} p(a_i \mid \Lambda_0)} \right)$$

where Λ_0^* is the correlation matrix with the proposed value entered in the ij^{th} and ji^{th} components. This is a Metropolis–Hastings step for each element λ_{ij}. See Barnard, McCulloch and Meng (1997) for further details.

We chose the multivariate normal $(0, \Lambda_0)$ prior for the "true" ability vectors $\{a_i\}$ in order to establish a scale for the problem, and because it can be expressed as a regression. For each essay, the overall rating and five sub–ratings are available. The model updates the set $\{a_{ik}\}$ all at once for each essay i. Of particular interest is the relationship between the sub–ratings and the global rating, which is determined as follows:

$$a_{i,global} \mid \mathbf{a}_{i,others}, \Lambda_0 \sim Normal(\mu_1 + \Lambda_{12}\Lambda_{22}^{-1}(\mathbf{a}_{i,others} - \mu_2), \Lambda_{11} - \Lambda_{12}\Lambda_{22}^{-1}\Lambda_{21})$$

$$\mu = \begin{pmatrix} 0 \\ \mathbf{0} \end{pmatrix} = \begin{pmatrix} \mu_1 \\ \mu_2 \end{pmatrix}, \Lambda_0 = \begin{pmatrix} \Lambda_{11} & \Lambda_{12} \\ \Lambda_{21} & \Lambda_{22} \end{pmatrix}$$

Therefore we can write the following:

$$a_{i,global} \mid a_{i,others}, \Lambda_0 \sim Normal(\beta_0 + \beta a_{i,others}, \sigma^2)$$

where $\beta = \Lambda_{12}\Lambda_{22}^{-1}, \beta_0 = \mu_1 - \Lambda_{12}\Lambda_{22}^{-1}\mu_2, \sigma^2 = \Lambda_{11} - \Lambda_{12}\Lambda_{22}^{-1}\Lambda_{21})$.

RESULTS

One can see from Table 11.3 that organization has the largest coefficient in the regression, with a median of 0.2546, while mechanics has the smallest, with a median of 0.1467. The median of each of the coefficients is positive, but none of the characteristics seems to have an overwhelming impact on an essay's overall grade, and in general, the effect of each characteristic is as we would expect it to be – anincrease in ability in one of the sub–categories is associated with a small increase in overall ability.

TABLE 11.3
Summary of Regression Parameters

Coefficient	Minimum	1st Quartile	Median	Mean	3rd Quartile	Maximum
Content	–0.2214	0.1396	0.2427	0.2478	0.3518	0.8202
Creativity	–0.4413	0.0794	0.1829	0.1821	0.2873	0.7535
Style	–0.2575	0.0814	0.1717	0.1739	0.2697	0.6156
Mechanics	–0.1224	0.0932	0.1467	0.1464	0.2030	0.4120
Organization	–0.1280	0.1916	0.2546	0.2559	0.3207	0.5847
Variance	0.0039	0.0065	0.0073	0.0074	0.0083	0.0124

Posterior Distributions of Coefficients (and Variance)

Analyses were performed with a program written in C on a Digital Personal WorkStation 600. We discarded 200,000 iterations of burn–in, after which an additional 200000 iterations were run to obtain samples from the posterior distributions; this run required 60 hours. Every 200th draw was retained for subsequent analysis. Convergence was assessed by means of trace plots in S–Plus version 6.0. Figure 11.4 shows the posterior distribution of each of the coefficients summarized in Table 11.3. One can see in each graph of the coefficients of the abilities that most of the posterior mass sits to the right of 0. The variance term is the conditional variance of the writer's global (overall) ability given the other ability variables and the covariance matrix Λ_0. We would expect this variance term to be small, and with a median of 0.0073, it meets our expectations.

In Table 11.4, we see that the posterior mean for each of the elements of the covariance matrix Λ_0 is above 0.93. This result, as well as the related result from the expression of the multivariate normal as a regression, tells us that although raters may disagree about the quality of an essay in a given category, the essay writer's true underlying ability is related to his or her ability in each of the categories. In the "pair" column of Table 11.4, 1 represents content, 2 is for creativity, 3 is for style, 4 is for mechanics, 5 is for organization, and 6 is for the overall ability.

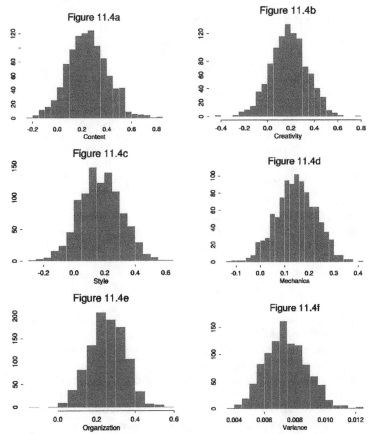

FIG. 11.4 Posterior distributions of regression parameters. a) content, b) creativity, c) style, d) mechanics, e) organization, f) variance.

Another area of inquiry in the area of essay grading is the differences between the raters, namely, how consistently do they tend to assess their ratings? In order to answer this question, one must examine the posterior distributions of the rater–category variances. In fact, the order or the raters from largest to smallest variance is the same for the ratings of content, creativity, mechanics, organization, and overall: Rater 4 has the largest variance, followed by raters 5, 6, 3, 2, and 1. For category 3 (style), the order is 4, 5, 3, 6, 1, and 2. There does not appear to be a trend for variances to be higher in any one particular category, although all raters tend to exhibit the highest degree of agreement for their overall ratings.

TABLE 11.4
Summary of Posterior Distributions of Unique Elements of Covariance Matrix

Pair	Minimum	1st Quartile	Median	Mean	3rd Quartile	Maximum
1,2	0.9922	0.9954	0.9961	0.9960	0.9967	0.9983
1,3	0.9671	0.9765	0.9794	0.9792	0.9820	0.9896
1,4	0.9151	0.9318	0.9370	0.9374	0.9431	0.9586
1,5	0.9730	0.9822	0.9840	0.9838	0.9858	0.9912
1,6	0.9823	0.9872	0.9885	0.9884	0.9897	0.9949
2,3	0.9679	0.9778	0.9808	0.9804	0.9832	0.9892
2,4	0.9075	0.9339	0.9394	0.9389	0.9448	0.9602
2,5	0.9719	0.9808	0.9828	0.9828	0.9849	0.9916
2,6	0.9820	0.9869	0.9883	0.9883	0.9898	0.9932
3,4	0.9663	0.9764	0.9789	0.9787	0.9811	0.9893
3,5	0.9740	0.9825	0.9847	0.9844	0.9865	0.9930
3,6	0.9846	0.9892	0.9904	0.9903	0.9915	0.9953
4,5	0.9356	0.9566	0.9605	0.9603	0.9641	0.9753
4,6	0.9508	0.9625	0.9657	0.9657	0.9689	0.9811
5,6	0.9839	0.9893	0.9905	0.9904	0.9916	0.9952

CONCLUSIONS

We examined the relation among scores across raters and categories. We saw that the relationship between category ratings for a given rater is stronger than the relationship between raters for a fixed category. We illustrated this relationship further by demonstrating that for a given rater, ratings in any pair of categories are usually within one or two units. However, for a fixed category, there was no such consistency across raters. We implemented a latent variable model with a random effect for each essay in each category, and found that if we assume *a priori* that the writer's ability vector is multivariate normal $(0, \Lambda_0)$, an increase in quality in any of the categories is linked to a smaller increase in the overall quality of the writer. We found that the underlying ability variables $\{a_{ik}\}$ are highly correlated. Finally, we found, with the exception of the sub–category "style," the order of raters by their variance is the same in each category.

REFERENCES

Barnard, J., McCulloch, R., and Meng, X. (1997), "Modeling Covariance Matrices in Terms of Standard Deviations and Correlations, with Applications to Shrinkage," University of Chicago Press (Tec. Rep. No. 438).

Chib, S., and Greenberg, E. (1995), "Understanding the Metropolis–Hastings Algorithm," *American Statistician*, 49, 327–335.

Johnson, V.E., and Albert, J.H. (1999), *Ordinal Data Modeling*, New York: Springer.

Johnson,V.E. (1997), "On Bayesian Analysis of Multi-rater Ordinal Data," *Journal of the American Statistical Association*, 91, 42–51.

Weisberg, S. (1985), *Applied linear regression*, New York: Wiley.

V.   Current Innovation in Automated Essay Evaluation

12

Automated Grammatical Error Detection

Claudia Leacock
ETS Technologies, Inc.
Martin Chodorow
Hunter College and ETS Technologies, Inc.

An automated grammatical error detection system called ALEK (Assessment of Lexical Knowledge) is being developed as part of a suite of tools to provide diagnostic feedback to students. ALEK's goal is to identify students' grammatical errors in essays so that they can correct them. Its approach is corpus–based and statistical. ALEK learns the distributional properties of English from a very large corpus of edited text, and then searches student essays for sequences of words that occur much less often than expected based on the frequencies found in its training. ALEK is designed to be sensitive to two classes of errors. The first error class consists of violations of general rules of English syntax. An example would be agreement errors such as determiner–noun agreement violations ("this conclusions") or verb formation errors ("people would said"). In this chapter, we address how ALEK recognizes violations of this type. The second error class is comprised of word–specific usage errors, for example, whether a noun is a mass noun ("pollutions") or what preposition a word selects ("knowledge at math" as opposed to "knowledge of math"). ALEK's detection of this class of errors is discussed in Chodorow and Leacock (2000) and in Leacock and Chodorow (2001).

For an automated error detection system to be successful in providing diagnostic feedback to students, the following three questions need to be answered affirmatively:

1. Can a system accurately detect the occurrence of an error by looking for unexpected sequences of words, as ALEK does?
2. Once an error is detected, can the system identify to the student the type of error that has been made? Feedback that reports "this is an agreement problem" would be far more useful than simply reporting that "something is wrong here."
3. Does the system detect errors that are related to the quality of writing, that is, are the errors correlated with the essay's overall score?

In this chapter, it is our goal to begin answering these questions.

BACKGROUND

Approaches to detecting grammar errors are typically rule–based. This generally means that essays written by students (often English as a Second Language students) are collected, and researchers examine them for grammatical errors. Parsers that automatically analyze each sentence are then adapted to identify the specific error types found in the essay collection. Schneider and McCoy (1998) developed a system tailored to the error productions of American Sign Language signers. It was tested on 79 sentences containing determiner and agreement errors, and 101 grammatical sentences. We calculate from their reported results that 78% of the constructions that the system identified as being errors were actually errors (.78 precision) and 54% of the actual errors in the test set were identified as such (.54 recall),[1] whereas the remaining 46% of the errors were accepted as well-formed. Park, Palmer, and Washburn (1997) adapted a categorial grammar to recognize "classes of errors [that] dominate" in the nine essays they inspected. Their system was tested on an additional eight essays, but precision and recall figures were not reported. To date, the rule–based engines that are reported in the literature have been similarly limited in scope.

These and other rule–based approaches are based on negative evidence, in the form of a collection of annotated ill–formed sentences produced by writers. Negative evidence is time-consuming, and therefore expensive, to collect and classify. This may, in part, explain why the research of Schneider and McCoy (1998) and of Park, Palmer, and Washburn (1997) is limited. In addition, the results may not be general because the kinds of errors found depend on the native languages and English proficiency of the writers who generated error data. In contrast, from the inception of our research, we have required that ALEK not make explicit use of this type of negative evidence but rather base its decisions on deviations from a model of well–formed English.

Golding (1995) showed how statistical methods (in particular, decision lists and Bayesian classifiers) could be used to detect grammatical errors resulting from common spelling confusions among sets of homonyms (or near–homonyms) such as "then" and "than." He extracted contexts of correct usage for each confusable word from a large corpus and built models for each word's usage (i.e., a model of the context in which "then" is found and another model of the context in which "than" is found). A new occurrence of a confusable word was subsequently classified as an error when its context more closely resembled the usage model of its homonym than its own model. For example, if the context for a novel occurrence of "than" more closely matched the model for "then," the usage was identified as being an error.

However, most grammatical errors are not the result of simple word confusions. Other types of errors greatly complicate the task of building a model of incorrect usage because there are too many potential errors to put into the model.

---

[1] The formula for precision is number of hits divided by the sum of hits and false positives where a "hit" is the correct identification of an error and a false positive is labeling a correct usage as an error. The formula for recall is number of hits divided by number of errors.

In addition, an example of a word usage error is often very similar to the model of appropriate usage. For example, an incorrect usage can contain two or three salient contextual cues as well as a single anomalous element — the context to the right of "saw" in "me saw him" is perfectly well-formed, whereas the context to the left is not. Therefore, to detect the majority of grammatical errors, a somewhat different approach from Golding's (1995) is warranted. The problem of error detection does not entail finding similarities to correct usage; rather, it requires identifying one single element among the entire set of contextual cues that simply does not fit.

ALEK

ALEK's corpus–based approach characterizes English usage as discovered from a large body of well–formed, professionally copyedited text — a training corpus of about 30 million words of running text collected from North American newspapers. ALEK uses nothing else as evidence when building a statistical language model based on sequences of two adjacent elements (bigrams). Bigram sequences in the student essays are compared to the model, but before the model can be built, the corpus must be preprocessed using natural language processing (NLP) tools in a series of automated steps.

Preprocessing

Preprocessing is required to make explicit the elements that carry the grammatical information in a sentence. This information includes a word's part of speech, inflection, case, definiteness, number, and whether it is a function word. Later, we step through preprocessing using an example from the training corpus. Preprocessing for the student essays is the same as for the training, unless otherwise noted.

Step 1. Identify And Extract Sentences From A Machine–Readable Corpus—To build the model of English, sentences are identified and extracted from a corpus of newspaper text. The sentences are filtered to exclude headlines, tables, listings of sports scores, birth and death announcements, and the like. For example, "Friends counseled Mitchard to get a full–time job, but she concentrated instead on her writing."

Step 2. Tokenize Words And Punctuation.— Separate words and punctuation with white space. For example, "Friends counseled Mitchard to get a full–time job , but she concentrated instead on her writing ."

Step 3. Assign A Part–Of–Speech Tag To Each Word Using An Automated Part–Of–Speech Tagger—An automatic part–of–speech tagger labels each word in the sentence with its syntactic category (noun, verb, preposition, etc.) and related information such as number (singular or plural), tense, and whether an adjective is comparative or superlative. In the example that follows, parts of speech have been marked using the MXPOST part–of–speech tagger (Ratnaparkhi, 1996). Plural nouns are tagged with NNS, proper names with NNP, adjectives with JJ, adverbs with RB, past tense verbs with VBD, and so on. For some closed–class categories, these tags are supplemented with an "enriched" tag set that was adapted from Francis and Kučera (1982) that encodes more information about number and case. For example, where appropriate, AT (singular determiner) replaces DT, a more general label that is used for all determiners in the original tag set. For example, "Friends/NNS counseled/VBD Mitchard/NNP to/TO get/VB a/AT full–time/JJ job/NN ,/, but/CC she/PPS concentrated/VBD instead/RB on/IN her/PRP$ writing/VBG ./."

After the sentences are preprocessed, ALEK collects statistics on bigrams consisting of part–of–speech tags and function words (e.g., determiners, prepositions, pronouns). The sequence *a/AT full–time/JJ job/NN* contributes one occurrence each to the bigrams AT + JJ, a + JJ, and JJ + NN. Each individual tag and function word also contributes to its own single element (unigram) count. ALEK does not count frequencies for open–class words (i.e., nouns, verbs, adjectives, and adverbs) such as "full–time" or "job" because these data would be too sparse to be reliable even if much larger corpora were used for training. Instead, counts are collected only for the tags of open–class words (i.e., JJ and NN in the example). These frequencies form the basis of the error detection measures.

Measures of Association

To detect violations of general rules of English, ALEK compares observed and expected frequencies in the general corpus. The statistical methods it uses are commonly employed in finding word combinations, such as collocations and phrasal verbs that occur more often than one would expect if the words were unassociated (independent). For example, the collocation "disk drive" can be shown to occur much more often than we would expect based on the relative frequency of "disk," the relative frequency of "drive," and the assumption that when the two words occur together they do so only by chance. Testing and rejecting the hypothesis of chance co–occurrence enables us to conclude that the words are not independently distributed but instead are associated with each other. ALEK uses the same kinds of statistical measures but for the opposite purpose — to find combinations that occur much less often than expected by chance, indicating dissociation between the elements.

One such measure is pointwise mutual information (MI) (Church & Hanks, 1990), which compares the relative frequency of bigrams in the general corpus to the relative frequency that is expected based on the assumption of independence, as shown below:

$$MI = \log_2 \left(\frac{P(AB)}{P(A) \times P(B)} \right)$$

Here, P(AB) is the probability of the occurrence of the AB bigram, estimated from its relative frequency in the general corpus, and P(A) and P(B) are the unigram probabilities of the first and second elements of the bigram, also estimated from the general corpus. For example, in our training corpus, singular determiners (AT) have a relative frequency of .03 (about once every 33 words), and plural nouns (NNS) have a relative frequency of .07 (about once every 14 words). If AT and NNS are independent, we would expect them to form the sequence AT + NNS, just by chance, with relative frequency .0021 (the joint probability of independent events is the product of the individual event probabilities). Instead, AT + NNS sequences, such as *a/AT desks/NNS* ("a desks"), occur only .00009 of the time, much less often than expected. The mutual information value is the base 2 logarithm of the ratio .00009: .0021, the actual relative frequency of the sequence in the corpus divided by the expected relative frequency. Ungrammatical sequences such as this have ratios less than 1, and therefore the value of the mutual information measure is negative (the log of a number less than 1 is negative). Extreme negative values of MI often indicate dissociation and therefore ungrammaticality. By contrast, the bigram AT + NN, as in a/AT desk/NN ("a desk"), occurs much more often than expected by chance and so its mutual information value is positive.

The log–likelihood ratio can also be used to monitor for errors. It compares the likelihood that the elements of a bigram are independent to the likelihood that they are not. Because extreme values indicate that the null hypothesis of independence can be rejected (Manning & Schütze, 1999), this measure can be used to detect collocations or to look for dissociated elements that might signal an ungrammatical string.

Based on a suggestion by D. Lin (personal communication, May 2, 2000), we have incorporated into ALEK both mutual information and the log–likelihood ratio because the two measures are complementary. Mutual information gives the direction of association (whether a bigram occurs more often or less often than expected), but it is unreliable with sparse data (Manning & Schütze, 1999). The log–likelihood ratio indicates whether a sequence's relative frequency differs from the expected value, and it performs better with sparse data than does mutual information, but the log likelihood ratio does not indicate if a bigram occurs more often or less often than expected. By using both statistical measures, ALEK gets the degree and the direction of association, as well as better performance when the data are limited. We refer to bigrams as having "low probability" when their mutual information values are negative and their log-likelihood ratios are extreme.

Generalization and Filtering

For this study, ALEK extracted sentences with low–probability bigrams from about 2,000 English Placement Test (EPT) essays that were written by entering college freshmen in the California State University System in response to five different essay questions (prompts). We then generalized these manually so that similar or related bigrams were merged into a single representation whenever possible. For example, because both definite and indefinite singular determiners followed by a plural noun are identified as low–probability bigrams, they were merged into a single generalized bigram, shown here in the form of a regular expression:

$$AT+NNS, DT+NNS \rightarrow [AD]T+NNS$$

The motivation for generalizing was primarily to facilitate the development of bigram filters.

Obviously, no bigram model is adequate to capture English grammar. This is especially true here where we restrict ourselves to a window of two elements, so filters are needed to prevent low–probability, but nonetheless grammatical, sequences from being misclassified as errors. We examined a random sample of the sentences with low–probability bigrams that ALEK had found in the development set of 2,000 essays, and wrote filters to recognize structures that were probably well-formed. In creating these filters, we chose to err on the side of precision over recall, preferring to miss an error rather than tell the student that a perfectly well-formed construction was a mistake.

As an example of a filter, the complementizer "that" is often (mis)tagged as a determiner as in, "I understand that/DT laws are necessary." To prevent this use of a complementizer from being identified as a determiner–noun agreement error, when ALEK finds a singular determiner followed by a plural noun, a filter checks that the determiner isn't the token "that." Filters can be quite complex. Bigrams that might indicate agreement problems must be filtered to eliminate those where the first element of the bigram is the object of a prepositional phrase or relative clause as in, "My friends in college assume that ...". Similarly, in the case of "me saw," a filter is needed to block instances in which "me" is the object of a prepositional phrase as in, "the person in front of me saw him."

For this study, we evaluated 21 of these generalized bigrams, taken from a larger set that showed very strong evidence of dissociation. Some low–probability bigrams were eliminated because of the mismatch between student essays and the newspaper articles from which the model of English was built. For example, newspapers rarely contain questions, so the sequence "SENT were" (where SENT represents a sentence boundary) as in "Were my actions mature?" was identified as a low–probability bigram. Others were eliminated due to consistent part–of–speech tagger errors. Again, this is a result of the mismatch between the *Wall Street Journal*, on which the part–of–speech tagger was trained, and the student essays that were subsequently tagged.[2] Finally, there were not enough examples of many of the low–probability bigrams in the sample of 2,000 essays to evaluate their reliability as predictors of grammatical errors, and they were therefore excluded from the study.

---

[2] The publicly available MXPOST part–of–speech tagger was trained on a relatively small sample of 1 million words from the *Wall Street Journal*. In this sample, there are apparently reports about graduate students but not about graduating because even in the sequence "she would graduate," graduate is tagged as an adjective. The same tagging problem occurs with many other adjective–verb pairs. As a result, low–probability bigrams that contained adjectives were unreliable and could not be used.

CAN ALEK ACCURATELY DETECT ERRORS?

A grammatical error detection system that is unreliable is not very useful. Error detection systems can make two kinds of mistakes: false positives, where a grammatical error is "identified" in a well–formed construction, and misses, where the system fails to identify an error. In automated natural language processing systems, there is always a trade–off between the number of false positives (precision) and the number of misses (recall). If one keeps the number of false positives low, the number of misses will inevitably rise. Conversely, if one keeps the misses low, so as to catch as many errors as possible, then the number of false positives will, in turn, increase. As noted earlier, we have chosen to keep false positives to a minimum, at the cost of failing to identify some grammatical errors.

Can the system accurately detect errors? To answer this question, ALEK was tested on an evaluation set, a new sample of 3,300 essays written by a group similar to the group of individuals who wrote the essays in the development set. The evaluation essays were written in response to English Proficiency Test (EPT), National Assessment of Educational Progress (NAEP), and Professional Assessments for Beginning Teachers (PRAXIS) prompts by high school students in the United States using the *Criterion*[SM3] interface. The primary difference between the development and evaluation sets is that, whereas the development set was administered with paper and pencil and then professionally transcribed, the evaluation set consisted of essays that were composed by students at a computer keyboard and entered directly into a computer.

ALEK searched the evaluation essays for low–probability generalized bigrams, and sentences containing these bigrams were extracted and filtered. To evaluate performance, for each low–probability bigram, we manually evaluated 100 randomly–selected sentences that had not been removed by filtering, or all of the sentences that remained after filtering if there were fewer than 100 occurrences of the bigram in the evaluation set. Table 12.1 shows the performance of two of the best-performing and the two worst-performing bigrams. The first column gives ALEK's precision in error detection using the bigram. As can be seen, some patterns detect errors perfectly, others are much less accurate.

False positives, good constructions that ALEK diagnosed as being errors, fell into two categories: tagger error and inadequate filter. A tagger error was identified when an incorrect part–of–speech tag contributed to the formation of the low–probability bigram. The rate of these tagging errors can be very high — as high as 22% in one case. Most of the tagger errors were due to a bad fit between the corpus on which the tagger was trained and the student essays. This mismatch is manifested in two ways: vocabulary limitations and syntactic limitations.

---

[3] Criterion[SM] is a web–based online writing evaluation service. A demonstration is located at http://www.etstechnologies.com/criterion.

TABLE 12.1
Error Identification and False Positives for Two of the Best Performing Bigrams and the
Two Worst Performing Bigrams.

Generalized Bigram	Percentage of Correct Error Identification	Percentage of False Positives Due to Tagger Error	Percentage of False Positives Due to Inadequate Filter
There + noun	100	0	0
Pronoun + to	100	0	0
...	...	...	...
Determiner + verb	72	22	5
Singular noun + non-finite verb	71	12	17
Weighted mean	80	11	9

Vocabulary limitations are implicated when the tagger sees a word used in only one part of speech in training. It will subsequently assign that part of speech to the word, even in the face of very strong contextual evidence to the contrary. As an example of syntactic limitations, newspapers rarely, if ever, use imperatives. Therefore, the tagger tends to mark most of the verbs that begin imperatives as nouns (e.g., "Make/NN sure it is hot"). A subsequent project consists of retraining the part–of–speech tagger on essays (rather than newspapers) and with a much larger vocabulary. The goal is to eliminate many of the false positives that are due to incorrect part–of–speech tags. There will, however, always be some tagging errors.

An inadequate filter error results when a false positive is due to a filtering problem. In the case of a singular noun followed by a nonfinite verb, many of the false positives were caused by an inadequate filter for inversion in questions (e.g. "Does this system have ...?"). Obviously, these filters can be improved, but they too will never work perfectly. The hardest constructions to filter have proven to be reduced relative clauses, as in "the responsibilities adulthood brings."

Mean precision for 21 bigrams is shown at the bottom of Table 12.1. The answer to the question, "Can the system accurately detect errors?" is that, when ALEK identified errors in this study, it was correct about 80% of the time. In addition to retraining the part–of–speech tagger on student essays, we hope to reduce the error rates by refining the filters.

CAN ALEK DIAGNOSE THE ERROR TYPE?

The value of error diagnosis for the student depends in part on how specific and informative it is. Indicating that the error is one of agreement is far more useful than reporting "something is wrong here." This is especially true with remedial students who could benefit most from specific tutorials linked to error types. When sentences containing the 21 bigrams were manually categorized into error type, the errors fell into six major categories:

1. Agreement errors that show problems with agreement ("My best friend meet his guy") or determiner–noun agreement ("This things would help us").
2. Verb formation errors that include ill–formed participles ("their parents are expect good grades"), infinitives ("is able to began a family") and modals ("People would said").
3. "Wrong word," where the wrong syntactic form of a word is used, as when the nominal form is used instead the verbal form; for example, using the verb "chose" when the noun "choice" would have been appropriate ("the chose I had to make").
4. Confused words which indicate a confusion with the spelling of a homophone; for example, using "there" instead of "their" ("some of there grades").
5. Punctuation errors, such as the omission of a comma ("Without grades students will") or a missing apostrophe ("My parents consent").
6. Typing or editing errors such as two determiners in a row ("a the" or "the the").

Table 12.2 shows the distribution of error types in the evaluation set for the eight most frequently occurring bigrams of the 21 tested. The category of spelling errors was added to indicate when the low–probability bigram was the result of a spelling mistake. For example, four different students typed "nowadays" as three words "now a days" instead of one, creating the SINGULAR DETERMINER + PLURAL NOUN bigram for a/AT days/NNS.

The least consistent mapping between bigram and error type is for SINGULAR DETERMINER + PLURAL NOUN, where the errors split about 2:1 between determiner–noun agreement ("a thousands") and a missing possessive marker ("every girls vote"). For the other bigrams, the error diagnosis is generally straightforward: DETERMINER + VERB is a wrong word ("have a chose to drink"). A MODAL + OF, as in "would of" and "could of," is always a confusion between "have" and "of." A MODAL + FINITE VERB is indicative of a problem with verb formation ("anybody can became president"). A SINGULAR NOUN + NONFINITE VERB usually indicates an agreement problem, ("an adult have"), although occasionally it indicates a missing comma ("For example try to ...".) A PLURAL NOUN + SINGULAR NOUN is always a punctuation problem. It usually indicates a missing apostrophe, as in "my parents consent" and, less often, a missing comma from an introductory phrase as in "Without grades students will." A PLURAL NOUN + FINITE VERB is a subject-verb agreement problem ("friends is one thing"). The expletive THERE + NOUN signals a confusion between "there" and "their."

Table 12.2 shows that the category of error can, for the most part, be predicted accurately from the low–probability bigrams which the error type produces. In the few cases where the correspondence is not as clear, further work will be needed to diagnose the error.

TABLE 12.2
Distribution of Error Types With Eight Bigrams

Bigram	Percentage of Verb Formation Errors	Percentage of Agreement Errors	Percentage of Wrong or Confused Words	Percentage of Missing Punctuation Errors	Percentage of Spelling Errors
Singular determiner + plural noun	—	32	—	64	4
Determiner + verb	—	—	90	—	10
Modal + of	—	—	100	—	—
Modal + finite verb	89	—	—	—	11
Singular noun + nonfinite verb	—	71	—	8	21
Plural noun + singular noun	—	—	—	100	—
Plural noun + finite verb	—	93	—	—	7
There + sing noun	—	—	100	—	—

Do Low-Probability Bigrams Correlate With Essay Scores?

One way to evaluate if the errors that ALEK finds are important to teachers is to see whether there is a correlation between the presence of error indicators (the low–probability bigrams) and the essays' scores. Table 12.3 shows the part of the EPT holistic rubric pertaining to grammatical usage.[4] At the high end of the scale, few, if any, grammatical errors are expected, whereas at the low end of the scale, many errors are expected.

We used about 1,500 essays from the development set, representing five different EPT prompts, to look for the correlation. Each essay was scored by two trained ETS readers to normalize for differences in essay length, the number of low–probability bigram occurrences (i.e., tokens) was divided by the number of words in the essay to produce a bigram token ratio. The correlation between this token ratio and essay score was statistically significant ($r = -0.41$, $p < .001$). We also wondered whether the variety of errors found in an essay would be related to

---

[4] The complete rubric is available at
http://www.miracosta.cc.ca.us/home/gfloren/holistic.htm

its score, and so we counted the number of different low–probability bigram types that each essay contained. In computing the type count, only the first occurrence of each kind of bigram was counted. For example, if an essay had three tokens of DETERMINER + VERB, the type count would only be incremented once for this bigram. To normalize for length, the bigram type count was divided by the essay length to form a type ratio. Essay score and bigram type ratio were significantly correlated ($r = -0.46$, $p < .001$). Because the two ratio measures were strongly correlated with each other ($r = 0.87$), partial correlations were computed to assess the independent contributions of each to score.

TABLE 12.3

Section of English Profiency Test (EPT) Rubric That is Relevant to Grammatical Usage

Relevant EPT Rubric Section
An essay in this category is generally free from errors in mechanics, usage, and sentence structure.
An essay in this category may have a few errors in mechanics, usage, and sentence structure.
An essay in this category may have some errors but generally demonstrates control of mechanics, usage, and sentence structure.
An essay in this category has an accumulation of errors in mechanics, usage, and sentence structure.
An essay in this category is marred by numerous errors in mechanics, usage, and sentence structure.
An essay in this category has serious and persistent errors in word choice, mechanics, usage, and sentence structure.

When bigram types were controlled for "partial out of the correlation", there was no significant relation between bigram token ratio and essay score ($r = -0.02$); however, when bigram tokens were partialed out, the correlation between type ratio and score was still statistically reliable ($r = -0.23$, $p < .001$). It is interesting that the number of different kinds of errors is a good predictor of score, whereas, if one controls for the variety of errors, the total number of errors predicts virtually nothing about score. This means that, all other things being equal, if two essays have four different kinds of errors, their scores will differ very little, even if one essay has a higher total number of errors than the other. It seems that the first instance of any error type is what counts against the score.

Figure 12.1 shows a graphical view of the relation between score and error variety. The x-axis shows holistic score (from 2 to 6, because there were very few essays with a score of 1 in the development set); the y-axis shows the number of low-frequency bigram types per 100 words in the essays. As the score increases, the number of error types decreases.

Variety is more important than the number of errors, but are some error types more costly than others? We computed a stepwise linear regression with the type ratios of the 21 generalized bigrams as predictors of the essay score. The best model used 16 of the bigrams and accounted for 23% of the variance in the score –

which seems quite good considering that, according to the holistic scoring rubric, the essay is being judged for organization of ideas and syntactic variety as well as what ALEK is trying to evaluate – control of language. In the regression model, the five most useful predictors involved agreement, ill–formed modals, ill–formed infinitive clauses, and ill–formed participles. These were followed by problems with confusable words and wrong words. The less costly errors involved problems with pronouns and with missing punctuation. Five of the bigrams did not contribute to the model: three of these capture typographical errors, typing "he" when "the" was clearly intended, typing two determiners in a row, or typing "you" instead of "your." Another primarily identifies "you" and "your" and "it" and "it's" confusion, which might be considered typographical errors. The last one, which is surprising given the strength of bigrams that identify problems with verbs, is a bigram that identifies when a modal is followed by "of" instead of "have" ("I would of left"). However, this error is extremely common, occurring hundreds of times in the essays, so perhaps the readers have simply gotten very used to it.

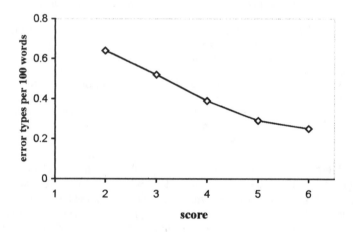

FIG. 12.1. The relation between holistic essay score and the number of error types per 100 words.

CONCLUSION

This work is best viewed as a proof–of–concept. For this study, precision was at 80%, which means that one out of every five errors that ALEK reported were false positives. The recurring problem has been with a mismatch between a system that was developed based on newspapers and tested on student essays. This occurs both with the training of the part–of–speech tagger and with the textual corpus that is used as the basis for the model of English. We are currently retraining the part–of–speech tagger and extending our filters to raise precision to a more acceptable level. We have also acquired a new corpus to use to build the model.

We do not, as yet, have statistics on recall — the percentage of errors in the essays that ALEK finds. We do know that recall is low for two reasons: (a) The system is tuned for high precision at the expense of recall, because we feel that missing some errors is less annoying than "identifying" an error in a perfectly well-formed construction; and (b) because ALEK only uses bigrams, it cannot identify an error that involves a long–distance dependency ("the <u>car</u> with the flat tires <u>are</u> .").

We return to the three questions that were posed in the opening of this chapter and provide answers. First, generalized low–probability bigrams are good indicators of a wide range of error types. The overall accuracy, however, should be improved to achieve at least 85% precision. Second, as a rule, these bigrams can be used to diagnose the error type accurately. In a few cases, where two different types are manifested by a single bigram, further processing will be required to distinguish between them. Finally, because the detected errors are reflected in the essay's score, this leads us to believe that the professional readers who score the essays consider these errors to be important.

REFERENCES

Chodorow, M., & Leacock, C. (2000). An unsupervised method for detecting grammatical errors. *Proceedings of the First Meeting of the North American Chapter of the Association for Computational Linguistics*, USA, 140-147.

Church K. W. & Hanks P. (1990). Word association norms mutual information and lexicography. *Computational Linguistics, 16*, pp. 23–29.

Francis, W., & Kučera, H. (1982). *Frequency analysis of English usage: Lexicon and grammar*. Boston: Houghton Mifflin.

Golding, A. (1995). A Bayesian hybrid for context–sensitive spelling correction. *Proceedings of the Third Workshop on Very Large Corpora*. USA, 39–53.

Leacock, C., & Chodorow, M. (2001). *Automatic assessment of vocabulary usage without negative evidence* (TOEFL Research Report RR–67). Princeton, NJ: Educational Testing Service.

Manning, C. D., & Schütze, H. (1999). *Foundations of statistical natural language processing*. Cambridge, MA: MIT Press.

Park, J. C., Palmer, M., & Washburn, G. (1997). Checking grammatical mistakes for English-as-a-second-language (ESL) students. *Proceedings of the Korean-American Scientists and Engineers Association (KSEA) Eighth Northeast Regional Conference & Job Fair*. New Brunswick, NJ: KSEA.

Ratnaparkhi, A. (1996). A maximum entropy part–of–speech tagger. *Proceedings of the Empirical Methods in Natural Language Processing Conference*, USA, 133-141.

Schneider, D. A., & McCoy, K. F. (1998). Recognizing syntactic errors in the writing of second language learners. *Proceedings of Coling–ACL–98*, Montréal, Canada, 1198-1204.

13

Automated Evaluation of Discourse Structure in Student Essays

Jill Burstein
ETS Technologies, Inc.
Daniel Marcu
University of Southern California/Information Sciences Institute

It has been suggested that becoming a strong writer is a blend of inherent ability and learned skills (Foster, 1980). Foster explained that writing includes both closed- and open-class capacities (Passmore, 1980). Closed-capacities are those skills that can eventually be mastered. In terms of writing, it is suggested that closed-class capacities would be skills such as spelling, punctuation, and grammatical form. Open-class skills, on the other hand, are those skills that are never completely mastered, and require imagination, inventiveness, and judgment. It is suggested that discourse strategy in writing is an open-class capacity.

There are many factors that contribute to overall improvement of developing writers. These factors include, for example, refined sentence structure, a variety of appropriate word usage, and strong organizational structure. Of course, mastery of the closed-capacities (grammar- and mechanics-related factors) is required if one is to be a competent writer. Some automated feedback capabilities for closed-class capacities do exist in standard word processing applications that offer advice about grammar and spelling. With regard to the open-class capacity, students can read about what the discourse structure of an essay should look like. A number of theoretical, innovative approaches for analyzing and teaching composition have been suggested (Beaven, 1977; Flower, Wallace, Norris, & Burnett, 1994; Foster, 1980; Myers & Gray, 1983; Odell, 1977; Rodgers, 1966). Yet, if we look in modern textbooks about writing style, we consistently find that the typical description of the structure of an essay discusses the five-paragraph strategy. These descriptions typically include references to these essay segments: (a) introductory paragraph, (b) a three-paragraph body, and (c) a concluding paragraph. They also include conventional advice explaining that compositions should contain a thesis statement, topic sentences for paragraphs, and concluding sentences. Certainly, this formula provides a practical starting point for the novice writer.

Although the available rules to explain discourse strategies appear to be limited in standard instructional materials, the potential for developing a rhetorically sophisticated piece of writing is open-ended. To become increasingly proficient, and to produce effective writing, the invention, arrangement, and revision in essay writing must be developed. Stated in practical terms, students at all levels, elementary school through post-secondary education, can benefit from practice applications that give them an opportunity to work on discourse structure in essay writing.

In traditional textbook teaching of writing, students are often presented with a "Revision Checklist." The Revision Checklist is intended to facilitate the revision process. This is a list of questions posed to the student to facilitate reflection on the quality of his or her writing. For instance, a checklist might pose questions such as the following: (a) Is the intention of my thesis statement clear? (b) Does my thesis statement respond directly to the essay question?, (c) Are the main points in my essay clearly stated?, and (d) Do the main points in my essay relate to my original thesis statement? If these questions are expressed in general terms, they are of little help; to be useful, they need to be grounded and need to refer explicitly to the essays students write (Scardamalia & Bereiter, 1985; White 1994).

This chapter discusses the potential of an instructional application that automatically provides feedback about discourse elements in student essays. Such a system could present to students a guided list of questions concerning the quality of the discourse strategy in their writing. For instance, it has been suggested by writing experts that if the thesis statement of a student's essay could be automatically identified, the student could then use this information to reflect on the thesis statement and its quality. In addition, this kind of application could utilize the thesis statement to discuss other types of discourse elements in the essay, such as the relation between the thesis statement and the conclusion, and the relation between the thesis statement and the main points in the essay. And, what if the system could inform a student that, in fact, the essay she wrote contained no thesis statement at all? This would be helpful information for students, too. Especially for the novice writer, information about the absence of expected discourse elements in an essay could be useful information for essay revision, so that the revised discourse structure of the essay is more likely to achieve its communicative goal.

TEACHING DISCOURSE STRATEGY IN ESSAY WRITING

A good high-level description of how composition instruction is handled in conventional textbooks is discussed by Foster (1980). Foster pointed out that conventional textbooks explain the writing process in terms of outlines, the writing of thesis statements, and careful editing. He illustrated further that these books tend to focus on the method of formulating a strong thesis statement, and using a clear body of text with well-supported ideas. The standard advice also includes guidance about punctuation, spelling, word choice, and common grammatical errors.

A number of web-based sites for writing instruction can be found, for both native and non-native English speakers. Some of the sites are associated with university writing laboratories or English departments, and offer the instruction for free. Alternatively, there are sites advertising software packages for writing instruction. These sites often offer some standard advice about how to structure one's essay. Sometimes the advice is explicit, and other times it can be inferred from a demo version of the application. Either way, it is similar in nature to the advice we find in conventional textbooks.

In the literature on the research relevant to the teaching of writing, there is considerable discussion about how to teach students about discourse strategies in essay writing. Although students can locate well-defined information about these aspects by referring to a grammar textbook, there are varying pedagogical approaches with regard to how discourse strategy in writing should be presented to students. Some of these approaches are more theoretical than others yet, the underlying message is similar. In earlier work researchers seem to discuss approaches that facilitate, through an iterative process, a student writer's ability to invent and arrange the discourse elements of an essay coherently, so that there is clear communication between the writer and the audience (Burke, 1945; D'Angelo, 1999; Flower, Hayes, Carey, Schriver, & Stratman, 1999; Rodgers, 1966; Witte, 1999). This is consistent with Bereiter and Scardamalia's (1987) theory of knowledge-telling mode and knowledge-transforming mode. The former relates to the more novice writer who discusses everything that he or she knows, but with little structure. This kind of writer is more writer-oriented. On the other hand, as writers become more developed, they take on the latter mode and their writing is more reader-oriented. The knowledge-transforming style of writing indicates a more expert writer, where more planning is evident in the writing.

USING COMPUTER-BASED INSTRUCTION TO IMPROVE WRITING QUALITY

A primary aspect of this chapter is a discussion related to the ways in which automated essay evaluation technology can be used to teach discourse strategies in essay writing. Our goal is to persuade the reader that providing automatic discourse-based feedback to students has the potential to help novice writers improve the quality of their writing. If the feedback of automatic systems is reliable, students could get additional practice, while instructors could be partially relieved of the total manual evaluation of students' writing during the semester.

Several research studies indicate that students can improve the quality of the discourse structure in their writing if given access to computer-based tools geared to working on this aspect of writing.

The Writer's Workbench software was an early application that provided feedback on a number of aspects of writing, including diction, style, spelling, and discourse structure (MacDonald, et al., 1982). With regard to discourse structure, the software located topic sentences in essays based on sentence location. In a study by Kiefer and Smith (1983) using Writer's Workbench, students had access to the following programs: SPELL (a program for spell checking), DICTION and SUGGEST (programs that offers advice about word choice and word substitution), and STYLE (a program that comments on sentence variety with regard to simple and complex sentence types). Results from the study indicated that students who used the tool outperformed students who did not, in terms of the clarity and directness of the writing. Kiefer and Smith concluded that the use of computer aids for the purpose of editing one's writing can help improve the overall quality of a text. What is of particular interest in this study is that part of the criteria on which the edited texts were judged was the strength of discourse elements, specifically, thesis statements and specificity of support. Presumably, the advice from the editing software helped improve the discourse strategy in the text for students who used the software.

Zellermayer, Salomon, Globerson, and Givon (1991) hypothesized that the particular contribution of the computer-based instruction is that it can provide guidance throughout the writing process that relates to the planning, writing, and revising stages. They point out that it is also not feasible for each student to have a personal human tutor over a prolonged period of time.

To test this hypothesis, Zellermayer et al. (1991) conducted a study to investigate if a computer-based 'writing partner' would improve the quality of the writing of novice writers, if the system provided a) memory support, b) guided stimulation of higher order processes, such as planning, transcribing, and diagnosing, and c) self-regulatory advice. In particular, the study examined which is most helpful as a computer-based instructional tool: a system that imposes guidance, or one where the guidance must be deliberately requested by the user. The reason that this study is relevant to this chapter is that the Writing Partner software that was used in the study expressly includes guidance that asks students to think about the rhetorical purpose and discourse schemata. Specific guidance questions in the application include the following: (a) Do you want your composition to persuade or describe? (b) What is the topic of your composition? (c) What are some of you main points? (d) Don't you have to explain some concepts? (e) Does this lead me to the conclusion that I want to reach?, and (f) Is your argument supported by data that is sufficient to convince a novice?.

The study was conducted using 60 students. The students, ages 13 to 15, were from the sixth and ninth grades of a kibbutz school near Tel Aviv, Israel. Students were randomly assigned to one of three groups: a) an unsolicited guidance group that wrote five training essays using a specially designed computer tool (Writing Partner), b) a solicited guidance group that wrote essays with a second version of the Writing Partner that provided guidance only on request, and c) a control group using only a word processor. All students were pretested, and then posttested 2 weeks after the end of the training period using a paper-and-pencil essay task.

The results of the study indicated that the students in the group that used the version of the Writing Partner with unsolicited advice showed significantly improved performance in the quality of the essays that they wrote during the study. This same effect was observed for this group for the posttest, when the students did not use the Writing Partner. Zellermayer et al. (1991) attributed this to internalization of relevant guidance provided in the Writing Partner. The study also indicated for this group that the finding was consistent across ability level.

Rowley and Crevoisier (1997) illustrated in their own research on evaluating MAESTRO, a cognitively-based writing instruction application, that MAESTRO improves the quality of student writing. They asserted that findings from studies, such as Zellermayer et al. (1991), contribute to the validation of the claim that computers can be useful partners in the writing instruction process.

To inform the design of MAESTRO, Rowley and Crevoisier (1997) used previous research findings from the R-WISE research program (Rowley, Miller, & Carlson, 1997). The R–WISE software was designed through the U.S. Air Force's Fundamental Skills Training Program as an adaptive, supportive learning environment for strengthening the critical skills associated with a number of writing tasks. The results of the R-WISE research indicated that over a 4-year program, students using R-WISE outperformed those not using the system on overall measures of writing quality. Improvements between one and two letter grades were reported.

Both the R-WISE and MAESTRO software include features that help students to develop the rhetorical and discourse structures in their writing. Rhetorical- and discourse-related concepts in these applications included the following: a) identification of topic, b) analysis of the thesis statement, c) organization of ideas into categories, and d) organization of the categories into an outline.

In an analysis of text coherence of student essays, O'Brien (1992) used Rhetorical Structure Theory (RST)-based analyses (Mann & Thompson (1989; see the later section on Rhetorical Structure Theory for a detailed description). In a case study that compares a native English speaker's writing performance in an examination to coursework performance, O'Brien showed how RST analysis can be used to identify incoherencies in text. She claimed that her findings are related to Bereiter and Scardamalia's (1987) models of knowledge-telling and knowledge-transforming in that the analysis illustrates how the text of the student essay is not reader-oriented. She asserted this because the reader is not provided with sufficient general information about the essay topic, or intertextual links to make the information in the essay easy to process.

O'Brien (1992) completed a detailed RST-based analysis of a student's classroom writing assignments compared to her writing on an examination. In this comparison, she indicated how the lack of certain RST relations in the student's classroom writing causes the text to be less coherent. For instance, one would anticipate the presence of text associated with the RST background relation in the introduction to an essay, where writer's often provide some background information to the reader. In the student's essay, readers noted that the material in the introductory section of the essay was questionably background information in that it was not helpful to a reader in understanding the remainder of the essay. Furthermore, the readers noted that none of the information later on in the essay related back to information in the introductory section. This was, in part, attributed to the fact that readers could not find a clear thesis statement in the introduction. This particular essay began by reporting lots of experimental findings related to the topic of the question, but never took a clear position. The readers associated this introductory text with the relation justification, indicating information related to support only. This study does not show direct evidence of how student writing improves using a computer-based aid, as do the studies of Zellermayer et al. (1991) and Rowley and Crevoisier (1997). However, the study suggests ways in which a text might be automatically evaluated from a rhetorical perspective, and accordingly, ways in which a system might provide rhetorical feedback to help students think about the discourse strategies they employed.

Because RST-based discourse parsers are now available (Marcu, 2000), theoretically, one could implement a method to identify automatically what O'Brien (1992) is able to find manually using RST relations. If instructional systems can reliably identify incoherencies in student essays that correspond to concrete rhetorical categories, this is a step toward helping the student fix such problems either collaboratively with an instructor or peers, or alone. Burstein, et al. (2001) and Burstein and Marcu (accepted) found that the use of automatically generated RST-based text structures contributed to the successful performance of a discourse structure classification algorithm.

AUTOMATIC DISCOURSE ANALYSIS FOR WRITING ASSESSMENT

As we discussed earlier, educators emphasize time and again that it is crucial that students produce coherent texts that are structured and organized so as to achieve the authors' high-level communicative goals. Many conventional textbooks posit that texts that have explicit thesis statements, conclusions, and well-developed supporting arguments are better than texts that do not contain these elements. Unfortunately, formalizing and operationalizing these concepts is not straightforward. If we want to write computer programs that identify thesis statements and supporting arguments, for example, in student essays, then we need to define unambiguously what these concepts mean. Unless we can define these concepts well enough so that essay evaluators agree systematically on their judgments with respect to these discourse elements, it is difficult to justify the utility of a program that automatically identifies instances of these elements in essays.

Let us assume that trained assessors are unable to agree on what are thesis statements are. If this is the case, it is obvious that thesis statements cannot be used to distinguish between good and bad essays and to provide students with useful feedback even when they are identified manually. In this scenario, identifying thesis statements automatically makes no sense either: a computer program that selects randomly any text fragment and labels it as thesis statement is as good as any human judge. (Fortunately, as we see in the Section titled "What are thesis statements?" the concept of thesis statement can be defined and exploited adequately both by human assessors and computer programs.)

Although the concepts of thesis statement, conclusion, and supporting argument have been the focus of much research in education and the teaching of writing, they have received little attention in discourse linguistics. The types of discourse elements that linguists have focused on cover a wide spectrum. For example, Grosz and Sidner (1986), Hirschberg and Nakatani (1996), and Passonneau and Litman (1997) relied on an intention-based classification of discourse elements. Hearst (1997) worked with discourse elements that subsume an informal notion of topic. Carletta et al. (1997) focused on transactions, that is, textual spans that accomplish a major step in a plan meant to achieve a given task. Mann and Thompson (1988) defined 22 discourse elements types in terms of intentional, semantic, and textual relations to other discourse elements in a text. These types include background, contrast, elaboration, justification, and so forth.

Some of the discourse elements used in discourse linguistics, such as topic and intentionally defined segments, seem to be too general to be useful in the context of essay scoring. Others, such as the wealth of discourse element types defined by Mann and Thompson (1988), seem to be too fine-grained.

In developing computer programs that automatically recognize essay specific discourse elements in texts, we have two choices:

1. We can start from scratch and develop a discourse theory and computer programs tailored to it.
2. We can take advantage of previous work in discourse linguistics and capitalize on existing theories and previously developed computer programs.

In the work described in this chapter, we chose the second alternative. We decided to use as backbone for our work the RST developed by Mann and Thompson (1988), for the following reasons:

1. RST enables one to analyze the discourse structure of a text at various levels of granularity. Because the rhetorical analysis of a text is hierarchical (see the Section titled, "Rhetorical Structure Theory – An Overview"), it captures both the discourse relations between small and large text spans and it makes explicit the discourse function of various discourse segments.
2. RST has been the focus of much work in computational linguistics. Recent advancements in the field have yielded programs capable of automatically deriving the discourse structure of arbitrary texts (Marcu, 2000). Taking advantage of these programs is less expensive than developing theories and programs from scratch.
3. Previous research in writing assessment (O'Brien, 1992) suggests that RST analyses of essays can be used to distinguish between coherent and incoherent texts and to provide students with useful discourse-level feedback.

RHETORICAL STRUCTURE THEORY — AN OVERVIEW

Driven mostly by research in natural language generation, RST (Mann & Thompson, 1988) has become one of the most popular discourse theories of the last decade. In fact, even the critics of the theory are not interested in rejecting it so much as in fixing unsettled issues such as the ontology of the relations (Maier, 1993; Rosner & Stede, 1992), the problematic mapping between rhetorical relations and speech acts (Hovy, 1990), and between intentional and informational levels (Moore & Paris, 1993; Moore & Pollack, 1992); and the inability of the theory to account for interruptions (Cawsey, 1991).

Central to RST is the notion of *rhetorical relation,* which is a relation that holds between two nonoverlapping text spans called nucleus (N) and satellite (S). There are a few exceptions to this rule: some relations, such as contrast, are multinuclear. The distinction between nuclei and satellites comes from the empirical observation that the nucleus expresses what is more essential to the writer's purpose than the satellite, and that the nucleus of a rhetorical relation is comprehensible independent of the satellite, but not vice versa.

Text coherence in RST is assumed to arise due to a set of constraints and an overall effect that are associated with each relation. The constraints operate on the nucleus, on the satellite, and on the combination of nucleus and satellite. For example, an evidence relation (see FIG 13.1) holds between the nucleus 1 and the satellite 2, because the nucleus 1 presents some information that the writer believes to be insufficiently supported to be accepted by the reader; the satellite 2 presents some information that is thought to be believed by the reader or that is credible to him or her; and the comprehension of the satellite increases the reader's belief in the nucleus. The effect of the relation is that the reader's belief in the information presented in the nucleus is increased.

Relation name:	EVIDENCE
Constrains on N:	The reader R might not believe the information
That is conveyed by the nucleus N to a degree	
Constraints on S:	The reader believes the information that is
Conveyed b the satellite S or will find it	
Credible.	
Constraints on	
N+S combination:	R's comprehending S increases R's belief of N.
The effect:	R's belief on N is increased.
Locus of effect:	N
Example:	[The truth is that the pressure to smoke in junior High is greater than it will be any other time of one's life:[1]] [we know that 3,000 teens start smoking each day.[2]]

FIG 13.1 The definition of the evidence relation in Rhetorical Structure Theory (Mann & Thompson, 1988, p. 251).

Rhetorical relations can be assembled into rhetorical structure trees (RS-trees) on the basis of five structural constituency schemata, which are reproduced in Figure 13.2 from Mann and Thompson (1988). The large majority of rhetorical relations are assembled according to the pattern given in Figure 13.2 (a). Fig. 13. 2 (d) covers the cases in which a nucleus is connected with multiple satellites by possibly different rhetorical relations. Fig. 13.2 (b), 2 (c), and 2 (e) cover the multinuclear relations.

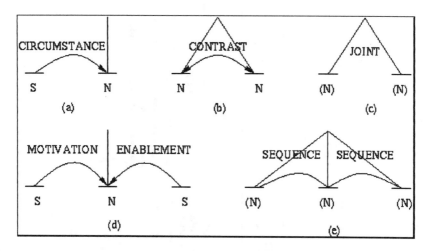

FIG. 13.2 Examples of the five types of schema that are used in Rhetorical Structure Theory (Mann & Thompson, 1988, p. 247). The arrows link the satellite to the nucleus of a rhetorical relation. Arrows are labeled with the name of the rhetorical relation that holds between the units over which the relation spans. The horizontal lines represent text spans and the vertical and diagonal lines represent identifications of the nuclear spans. In the sequence and joint relations, the vertical and diagonal lines identify nuclei by convention only because there are no corresponding satellites.

According to Mann and Thompson (1988), a canonical analysis of a text is a set of schema applications for which the following constraints hold:

- Completeness—One schema application (the root) spans the entire text.
- Connectedness—Except for the root, each text span in the analysis is either a minimal unit or a constituent of another schema application of the analysis.
- Uniqueness—Each schema application involves a different set of text spans.
- Adjacency—The text spans of each schema application constitute one contiguous text span.

Obviously, the formulation of the constraints that Mann and Thompson (1988) put on the discourse structure is just a sophisticated way of saying that rhetorical structures are trees in which sibling nodes represent contiguous text. The distinction between the nucleus and the satellite of a rhetorical relation is their acknowledgment that some textual units play a more important role in text than others. Because each textual span can be connected to another span by only one rhetorical relation, each unit plays either a nucleus or a satellite role.

Figure 13.3 displays in the style of Mann and Thompson (1988) the rhetorical structure tree of a larger text fragment.

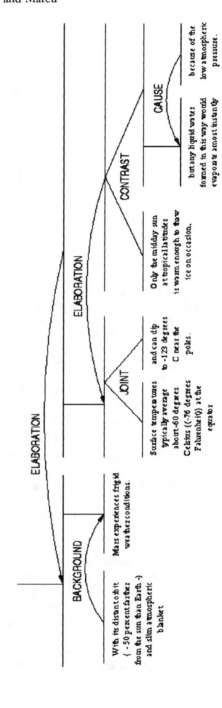

FIG 13.3: Example of RST tree.

In the next section, we discuss in detail how we use RST-specific features to automatically identify in texts discourse elements that are useful in the context of writing assessment.

TOWARD AUTOMATED ESSAY-BASED DISCOURSE FEEDBACK: DESIGNING AN NLP-BASED CAPABILITY FOR LABELING DISCOURSE STRUCTURE IN ESSAYS

Pedagogy with regard to the teaching of writing suggests that improvement in discourse strategies in essay writing can improve overall writing quality. The studies discussed in earlier sections related to the improvement of student writing using computer-aided instruction suggest that these instructional applications can be effective. It could be useful, then, to build on current computer-aided writing instruction by adding capabilities that automatically provide discourse-based feedback. If reliable, these systems could identify discourse elements in students' essays, such as thesis statement, main points, supporting ideas, and conclusion. The reliable identification of these elements would permit one to provide automatic feedback about the presence or absence of discourse element, the quality of each of there elements, and the strength of the connections between discourse elements in an essay.

In this section, we describe the development of a prototype application for the automatic identification of thesis statements in essays. A relatively small corpus of essays has been manually annotated with thesis statements and used to build a Bayesian classifier (see Burstein et al., 2001). The following features were included: sentence position; words commonly used in thesis statements; and discourse features, based on RST parses (Mann and Thompson, 1988; Marcu, 2000). The results indicate that this classification technique may be used toward automatic identification of thesis statements in essays.

(Annotator 1) *"In my opinion student should do what they want to do because they feel everything and they can't have anythig they feel because they probably feel to do just because other people do it not they want it.*
(Annotator 2) *I think doing what students want is good for them.* I sure they want to achieve in the highest place but most of the student give up. They they don't get what they want. To get what they want, they have to be so strong and take the lesson from their parents Even take a risk, go to the library, and study hard by doing different thing.
Some student they do not get what they want because of their family. Their family might be careless about their children so this kind of student who does not get support, loving from their family might not get what he wants. He just going to do what he feels right away.
So student need a support from their family they has to learn from them and from their background. I learn from my background I will be the first generation who is going to gradguate from university that is what I want."

FIG. 13.4 Sample student essay with human annotations of thesis statements.

What Are Thesis Statements?

A thesis statement is defined as the sentence that explicitly identifies the purpose of the paper or previews its main ideas. This definition seems straightforward enough, and would lead one to believe that even for people to identify the thesis statement in an essay would be clear-cut. However, the essay in Fig. 13.4 is a common example of the kind of first-draft writing that a system has to handle. Figure 13.4 shows a student response to the following essay question:

> Often in life we experience a conflict in choosing between something we "want" to do and something we feel we "should" do. In your opinion, are there any circumstances in which it is better for people to do what they "want" to do rather than what they feel they "should" do? Support your position with evidence from your own experience or your observations of other people.

The writing in Figure 13.4 illustrates one kind of challenge in automatic identification of discourse elements, such as thesis statements. In this case, the two human annotators independently chose different text as the thesis statement (the two texts highlighted in bold and italics in Figure 13.4). In this kind of first-draft writing, it is not uncommon for writers to repeat ideas, or express more than one general opinion about the topic, resulting in text that seems to contain multiple thesis statements.

Before building a system that automatically identifies thesis statements in essays, it is critical to determine whether the task is well-defined. In collaboration with two writing experts, a simple discourse-based annotation protocol was developed to manually annotate discourse elements in essays for a single essay topic. This was the initial attempt to annotate essay data using discourse elements generally associated with essay structure, such as thesis statement, concluding statement, and topic sentences of the essay's main ideas. The writing experts defined the characteristics of the discourse labels. These experts then annotated 100 essay responses to one English Proficiency Test (EPT) question, called Topic B, using a PC-based interface.

The agreement between the two human annotators was computed using the kappa coefficient (Siegel & Castellan, 1988), a statistic used extensively in previous empirical studies of discourse. The kappa statistic measures pairwise agreement among a set of coders who make categorial judgments, correcting for chance expected agreement. The kappa agreement between the two annotators with respect to the thesis statement labels was 0.733 ($N = 2,391$, where 2,391 represents the total number of sentences across all annotated essay responses). This shows high agreement based on research in content analysis (Krippendorff, 1980) suggests that values of kappa higher than 0.8 reflect very high agreement and values higher than 0.6 reflect good agreement. The corresponding z statistic was 27.1, which reflects a confidence level that is much higher than 0.01, for which the corresponding z value is 2.32 (Siegel & Castellan, 1988).

In the early stages of this project, it was suggested that thesis statements reflect the most important sentences in essays. In terms of summarization, these sentences would represent indicative, generic summaries (Mani and Maybury, 1999; Marcu, 2000). To test this hypothesis (and estimate the adequacy of using summarization technology for identifying thesis statements), an additional experiment was carried out. The same annotation tool was used with two different human judges, who were asked this time to identify the most important sentence of each essay. The agreement between human judges on the task of identifying summary sentences was significantly lower: the kappa was 0.603 (N = 2,391). Tables 13.1 and 13.2 summarize the results of the annotation experiments.

Table 13.1 shows the degree of agreement between human judges on the task of identifying thesis statements and generic summary sentences. The agreement figures are given using the kappa statistic and the relative precision (P), recall (R), and F values (F), which reflect the ability of one judge to identify the sentences labeled as thesis statements or summary sentences by the other judge.[1] The results in Table 13.1 show that the task of thesis statement identification is much better defined than the task of identifying important summary sentences. In addition, Table 13.2 indicates that there is very little overlap between thesis and generic summary sentences: Just 6% of the summary sentences were labeled by human judges as thesis statement sentences. This strongly suggests that there are critical differences between thesis statements and summary sentences, at least in first-draft essay writing. It is possible that thesis statements reflect an intentional facet (Grosz and Sidner, 1986) of language, while summary sentences reflect a semantic one (Martin, 1992). More detailed experiments need to be carried out though before proper conclusions can be derived.

TABLE 13.1
Agreement between human judges on thesis and summary sentence identification.

Metric	Thesis Statements	Summary Sentences
Kappa	0.733	0.603
P (1 versus 2)	0.73	0.44
R (1 versus 2)	0.69	0.60
F (1 versus 2)	0.71	0.51

[1] Precision=total agreed upon thesis sentences between human 1 & human 2 ÷ total human 1 thesis sentences; R= total agreed upon thesis sentences between human 1 & human 2 ÷ total human 2 thesis sentences; F = 2 * P * R / (P + R).

TABLE 13.2

Percent overlap between human labeled thesis statements and summary
sentences.

	Thesis statements vs. Summary sentences
Percent Overlap	0.06

The results in Table 13.1 provide an estimate for an upper bound of a thesis
statement identification algorithm. If one can build an automatic classifier that
identifies thesis statements at recall and precision levels as high as 70%, the
performance of such a classifier will be indistinguishable from the performance of
humans.

A BAYESIAN CLASSIFIER FOR IDENTIFYING THESIS
STATEMENTS' DESCRIPTION OF THE APPROACH

A Bayesian classifier was built for thesis statements using essay responses to one
essay-based test question: Topic B.

McCallum and Nigam (1998) discussed two probabilistic models for text
classification that can be used to train Bayesian independence classifiers. They
described the multinominal model as being the more traditional approach for
statistical language modeling (especially in speech recognition applications), where a
document is represented by a set of word occurrences, and where probability
estimates reflect the number of word occurrences in a document. In using the
alternative, the multivariate Bernoulli model, a document is represented by both the
absence and presence of features. On a text classification task, McCallum and
Nigam showed that the multivariate Bernoulli model performs well with small
vocabularies, as opposed to the multinominal model which performs better when
larger vocabularies are involved. Larkey (1998) used the multivariate Bernoulli
approach for an essay scoring task, and her results are consistent with the results of
McCallum and Nigam (see also, Larkey & Croft 1996, for descriptions of
additional applications). In Larkey (1998), sets of essays used for training scoring
models typically contain fewer than 300 documents. The vocabulary used across
these documents tended to be restricted.

Based on the success of Larkey's (1998) experiments, and McCallum and
Nigam's (1998) findings that the multivariate Bernoulli model performs better on
texts with small vocabularies, this approach would seem to be the likely choice
when dealing with small data sets of essay responses. Therefore, this approach was
adopted to build a thesis statement classifier that can select from an essay the
sentence that is the most likely candidate to be labeled as the thesis statement.

In the experiment, three general feature types were used to build the classifier:
sentence position, words commonly occurring in thesis statements, and RST labels
from outputs generated by an existing rhetorical structure parser (Marcu, 2000).

The classifier was trained to identify thesis statements in an essay. Using the multivariate Bernoulli formula, shown later, this gives us the log probability that a sentence (S) in an essay belongs to the class (T) of sentences that are thesis statements. Performance was improved when a Laplace estimator was used to deal with cases where the probability estimates were equal to zero.

$$\log(P(T|S)) = \log(P(T)) + \sum_i \begin{cases} \log(P(A_i|T)/P(A_i)), \\ \text{if S contains } A_i \\ \log(P(\overline{A_i}|T)/P(\overline{A_i})), \\ \text{if S does not contain } A_i \end{cases}$$

In this formula, P(T) is the prior probability that a sentence is in class T, $P(A_i|T)$ is the conditional probability of a sentence having feature A_i, given that the sentence is in T, and $P(A_i)$ is the prior probability that a sentence contains feature A_i, $P(\overline{A_i}|T)$ is the conditional probability that a sentence does not have feature A_i, given that it is in T, and $P(\overline{A_i})$ is the prior probability that a sentence does not contain feature A_i.

FEATURES USED TO CLASSIFY THESIS STATEMENTS

Positional Feature

It was found that the likelihood of a thesis statement occurring at the beginning of essays was quite high in the human annotated data. To account for this, one feature was used that reflected the position of each sentence in an essay.

Lexical Features

All words from human annotated thesis statements were used to build the Bayesian classifier. This list of words is referred to as the thesis word list. From the training data, a vocabulary list was created that included one occurrence of each word used in all resolved human annotations of thesis statements. All words in this list were used as independent lexical features. Stop words decreased the performance of the classifier, so a stoplist was not used.

Rhetorical Structure Theory Features

RST trees were built automatically for each essay using the cue-phrase-based discourse parser of Marcu (2000). See the previous section on RST for a detailed description of an RST tree. Each sentence in an essay was associated with a feature that reflected the status of its parent node (nucleus or satellite), and another feature that reflected its rhetorical relation. For example, for the last sentence in Figure 13.3, we associated the status satellite and the relation elaboration because that sentence is the satellite of an elaboration relation. For sentence 2, we associated the status nucleus and the relation elaboration because that sentence is the nucleus of an elaboration relation.

We found that some rhetorical relations occurred more frequently in sentences annotated as thesis statements. Therefore, the conditional probabilities for such relations were higher and provided evidence that certain sentences were thesis statements. The *Contrast* relation shown in Figure 13.2, for example, was a rhetorical relation that occurred more often in thesis statements. Arguably, there may be some overlap between words in thesis statements, and rhetorical relations used to build the classifier. The RST relations, however, capture long distance relations between text spans, which are not accounted by the words in our thesis word list.

Evaluation of the Bayesian Classifier

Performance of the system was estimated using a six-fold cross validation procedure. Ninety-three essays labeled with a thesis statement by human annotators were partitioned into six groups. (The judges agreed that 7 of the 100 essays they annotated had no thesis statement.) Six times the data were trained on five sixths of the labeled data and performance was evaluated on the other 1/6 of the data.

The evaluation results in Table 13.3 show the average performance of the classifier with respect to the resolved annotation (Alg. wrt. Resolved), using traditional recall (R), precision (P), and F value (F) metrics.[2] For purposes of comparison, Table 13.3 also shows the performance of two baselines: the random baseline classifies the thesis statements randomly; while the position baseline assumes that the thesis statement is given by the first sentence in each essay.

TABLE 13.3
Performance of the thesis statement classifier.

System vs. system	P	R	F
Random baseline wrt. Resolved	0.06	0.05	0.06
Position baseline wrt. Resolved	0.26	0.22	0.24
Alg. wrt. Resolved	0.55	0.46	0.50
1 wrt. 2	0.73	0.69	0.71
1 wrt. Resolved	0.77	0.78	0.78
2 wrt. Resolved	0.68	0.74	0.71

Note: P = precision; R = recall; F = F values; wrt. = with regard to; Alg. = algorithm.

---

[2] P = total agreed upon thesis sentences between 1 human reader & Alg. ÷ total human reader thesis sentences; R= total agreed upon thesis sentences between 1 human reader & Alg./ Alg. Thesis sentences; F = 2 * P * R / (P + R).

DISCUSSION

The results of this experimental work indicate that the task of identifying thesis statements in essays is well-defined. The empirical evaluation of the algorithm indicates that with a relatively small corpus of manually annotated essay data, one can build a Bayes classifier that identifies thesis statements with good accuracy. The results compare favorably with results reported by Teufel and Moens (1999) who also used Bayes classification techniques to identify rhetorical arguments such as *aim* and *background* in scientific texts, although the texts in this essay-based study were extremely noisy. Because these essays are often produced for high-stakes exams, under severe time constraints, they are often ungrammatical, repetitive, and poorly organized at the discourse level.

Identifying thesis statements correctly is key to developing automatic systems capable of providing discourse-based feedback. The system described in this section identifies with relatively high accuracy thesis statements in student essays.

In more current research, new classification methods are being evaluated to classify additional discourse elements; specifically, main points, supporting evidence, conclusions, and irrelevant text. Results indicate that these new approaches can be used to identify these additional features, especially in cases where agreement is strong between human annotators for these categories (Burstein and Marcu (accepted.)

POTENTIAL DIRECTIONS OF AUTOMATED DISCOURSE FEEDBACK FOR WRITING INSTRUCTION

In this chapter, we illustrated that pedagogically and practically-speaking, the development of writers' discourse strategies in essay writing is critical to the overall improvement of writing quality. We showed that research on the teaching of writing assumes that discourse strategies are key to a writer's development. We also presented studies that are consistent with this view, especially with respect to novice writers.

As researchers who work closely with teachers, we realize that a problem in the classroom is finding time to evaluate student writing. The invention of automated essay scoring technologies is now being used in classrooms for assessment and instruction and has given teachers the ability to assign additional writing in the classroom. The technology can provide students with immediate feedback on a writing assignment. Beyond the holistic essay score, teachers have expressed considerable interest in more specific feedback about their student's essays, both in terms of grammaticality (see Leacock and Chodorow, Chapt. 12 this volume) and discourse coherence.

As evidence of the current interest in a capability that can automatically provide discourse-based feedback to students, we provide some reactions to a prototype of an enhanced version of the thesis identification software described earlier. The enhanced prototype labels several discourse elements, including the following: (a) thesis statements, (b) main points, (c) supporting ideas, (d) conclusions, and (e) irrelevant text. These elements were based on discussions from several focus groups with writing instructors. A goal of each focus group was to listen to the instructors' feedback to inform the development of our automated discourse analysis capability.

During a number of discussions with various focus groups, writing instructors were shown a software prototype that read in a student essay, and automatically labeled the following discourse elements in the essay: thesis statement, topic sentences, supporting evidence, conclusion, and irrelevant information. Based on the application they viewed in the demo, the focus group participants suggested these possible applications:

1. They believed that expected discourse elements that were absent from texts should be identified as "missing."
2. Along the same lines of pointing out to students the discourse errors in their essays, instructors asserted that a discourse analysis tool should show students the irrelevant information in their essays. In other words, the application should indicate the parts of the text that did not contribute effectively to the essay.
3. The writing instructors indicated that the application should provide an evaluation of the quality of the discourse structures in an essay. Accordingly, one kind of advice might be for the system to rate the strength of the thesis statement in relation to the text of the essay question.
4. Another kind of evaluation that most instructors wanted to see in the application was the relationship among the discourse elements in the essay. For instance, how related were the thesis statement and the conclusion? And, were the main points in the essay related to the thesis statement?
5. Teachers suggested another potential application in which students would have the ability to label their intended thesis statement. The system would then make a selection to identify the text of the thesis statement. If the application agreed with the student, then this might be an indication of the clarity of the intended thesis statement. If the system disagreed with the student's selection, it could tell the student to review the intended thesis statement with an instructor.

Generally speaking, writing teachers expressed a strong interest in capturing the student's voice. Although students often cover the required "topic" of the essay item, they do not always write to the task. Persuasive, informative, and narrative modes of writing lend themselves to different kinds of rhetorical strategies. If the discourse profile of an essay could be captured (i.e., "Does an essay written in a particular mode have all the expected discourse elements?"), then the information about the discourse might be used to evaluate if the essay was written to task. Given the identifiable discourse elements in an essay, a system might be able to answer questions like the following: "Is this really a 'persuasive' essay?" or "Does its discourse structure resemble more a 'narrative' essay type?" In this way, such a system would be getting closer to identifying the writer's voice.

Once any of these potential applications is developed, it would have to be evaluated in the environment where it is intended to be used. Discourse analysis of student essays is available through Criterion^{SM}'s CRITIQUE writing analysis tools (see http://www.etstechnologies.com/criterion). Ultimately, studies showing improvement in students' writing performance with these applications will confirm their effectiveness as instructional tools.

REFERENCES

Beaven, M. H. (1977). Individualized goal setting, self-evaluation, and peer evaluation. In C. R. Cooper and L. Odell (Eds). *Evaluating Writing: Describing, Measuring, Judging.* Urbana, IL: National Council of Teachers of English (pp.135-153).

Bereiter, C., and Scardamalia, M. (1987). *The psychology of written composition.* Hillsdale, NJ: Lawrence Erlbaum Associates, Inc.

Burke, K. (1945). *A Grammar of Motives.* Prentice-Hall, New York.

Burstein, J., & Marcu, D. (Accepted). Using machine learning to identify thesis and conclusion statements in student learning. *Computers and the Humanities.* Kluwer Academic Publishers. Dordrecht, The Netherlands.

Burstein, J., Marcu, D., Andreyev, S. & Chodorow, M. (2001). Towards automatic classification of discourse elements in essays. *Proceedings of the 39th annual meeting of the Association for Computational Linguistics.* France, pp. 90-92.

Carletta, J., Isard A., Isard S., Kowtko J., Doherty-Sneddon G., & Anderson A. H. (1997). The reliability of a dialogue structure coding scheme. *Computational Linguistics, 23,* 13-32.

Cawsey, A. (1991). Generating interactive explanations. *Proceedings of the Ninth National Conference on Artificial Intelligence* (AAAI-91), (USA) 1, 86-91.

D'Angelo, F. J. (1999). The search for intelligible structure in the teaching of composition, In L. Ede, (Ed.). *On writing research: The Braddock Essays 1975-1998.* New York: Bedford/St. Martins. (pp. 51-59).

Flower, L., Hayes, J. R., Carey, L., Schriver, K., & Stratman, J. (1999). Detection, diagnosis, and the strategies of revision. In L. Ede, (Ed.). *On Writing Research: The Braddock Essays 1975-1998,* New York: Bedford/St. Martins. (pp. 191-228).

Flower, L., Wallace, D. L., Norris, L., and Burnett, R. E. (1994). *Making thinking visible: Writing, collaborative planning and classroom inquiry.* Urbana, IL: National Council of Teachers of English.

Foster, D. (1980). *A primer for writing teachers: Theories, theorists, issues, problems.* Upper Montclair, NJ: Boynton/Cook Publishers, Inc.

Grosz B. and Sidner, C. (1986). Attention, Intention, and the Structure of Discourse. *Computational Linguistics, 12,* 175-204.

Hearst, M. A. (1997). "Texttiling: Segmenting text into multi-paragraph subgoric passages." *Computational Linquistics, 23,* 33-64.

Hirschberg, J. & Nakatani, C. (1996). A prosodic analysis of discourse segments in direction-given monologues. *Proceedings of the 34th annual meeting of the Association for Computational Linguistics (ACL-96)*, USA, 286-293.

Hovy E. H. (1990). Unresolved issues in paragraph planning. In R. Dale, C. Mellish, & M. Zock (Ed.), *Current research in natural language generation* (pp. 17-45). New York: Academic.

Kiefer, K., & Smith, C. (1983). Textual analysis with computers: Tests of Bell Laboratories computer software. *Research in the Teaching of English, 17*, 201-214.

Krippendorff, K. (1980). *Content analysis: An introduction to its methodology.* Thousand Oaks, CA: Sage.

Larkey, L. (1998). Automatic essay grading using text categorization techniques. *In Proceedings of the 21st Annual International Conference on Research and Development in Information Retrieval (SIGIR 98)*, 90-95, Australia.

Larkey, L., & Croft, W. B. (1996). Combining classifiers in text categorization. *In proceedings of the 19th International Conference on Research and Development in Information Retrieval (SIGIR 96)*, 289-298, Switzerland.

MacDonald, N. H., Frase, L. T., Gingrich P. S., & Keenan, S. A. (1982). The writer's workbench: computer aids for text analysis. *IEEE Transactions on Communications. 30*, 105-110.

Maier, E. (1993). The extension of a text planner for the treatment of multiple links between text units. *Proceedings of the Fourth European Workshop on Natural Language Generation (ENLG-93)*, Italy, 103-114.

Mani, I. & Maybury, M. (1999). *Advances in automatic text summarization.* Cambridge, MA: MIT Press.

Mann, W. C. & Thompson, S. A. (1988). Rhetorical structure theory: Toward a functional theory of text organization. *Text, 8*, 243–281.

Marcu, D. (2000). *The theory and practice of discourse parsing and summarization.* Cambridge, MA: MIT Press.

McCallum, A. & Nigam, K. (1998). A comparison of event models for naive bayes text classification. *The AAAI-98 Workshop on "Learning for Text Categorization"*, USA, 41-48.

Myers, Miles & Gray, James.(1983). *Theory and practice in the teaching of composition.* Urbana, IL: National Council of Teachers of English.

Moore J. D. & Pollack M. E. (1992). A problem for RST: The need for multi-level discourse analysis. *Computational Linguistics, 18*, 537-544.

Moore J. D. & Paris C. L. (1993). Planning text for advisory dialogues: Capturing intentional and rhetorical information. *Computational Linguistics, 19*, 651-694.

O'Brien, T. (1992). Rhetorical structure analysis and the case of the inaccurate, incoherent source hopper. *Applied Linguistics, 16*, 442-482.

Odell, L. (1977). Measuring changes in intellectual processes as one dimension of growth in writing. In Cooper, C. R. and Odell, L. (Eds). *Evaluating writing: Describing, measuring, judging.* Urbana, IL: National Council of Teachers of English (pp. 107-134).

Passmore, J. (1980). *The philosophy of education*. New York: Cambridge University Press.

Rodgers, P. Jr. A discourse-centered rhetoric of the paragraph, *College Composition and Communication,,* 17, 2-11.

Passonneau R. & Litman D. (1997). Discourse segmentation by human and automated means. *Computational Linguistics, 23,* 103-140.

Rosner D., & Stede, M. (1992). Customizing RST for the automatic production of technical manuals. In R. Dale, E. Hovy, D. Rosner, & O. Stock, (Eds.), *Aspects of automated natural language generation* 6th *international workshop on natural language generation* (pp. 199-214). Heidelberg, Germany: Springer-Verlag.

Rowley, K., Miller, T., & Carlson, P. (1997). *The influence of learner control and instructional styles on student writing in a supportive environment.* Paper presented at the annual meeting of the American Educational Research Association, Chicago, IL.

Rowley, K. & Crevoisier, M. (1997). MAESTRO: Guiding students to skillful performance of the writing process. *Proceedings of the Educational Multimedia and Hypermedia Conference,* Canada.

Scardamalia, M. & Bereiter, C. (1985). Development of dialectical processes in composition. In D. R. Olson, N. Torrance, & A. Hildyard (Eds), *Literacy, language, and learning: The nature of consequences of reading and writing.* New York: Cambridge University Press.

Siegel S. & Castellan, N. J. (1988). *Nonparametric statistics for the behavioral sciences.* New York: McGraw-Hill.

Teufel, S. & Moens, M. (1999). Discourse-level argumentation in scientific articles. *Proceedings of the ACL99 Workshop on Standards and Tools for Discourse Tagging.*

White E. M. (1994). *Teaching and Assessing Writing.* San Francisco: Jossey-Bass.

White E.M. (1994). *Teaching and assessing writing.* San Francisco: Jossey-Bass.

Witte, S. (1999). Topical structure and revision: An exploratory study. In L. Ede (Ed.). *On writing research: The Braddock Essays 1975-1998.* New York: Bedford/St. Martins.

Zellermayer, M., Saloman, G., Globerson, T., & Givon, H. (1991). Enhancing writing-related metacognitions through a computerized writing partner. *American Educational Research Journal,* 28, 373-391.

SUBJECT INDEX

AUTHOR INDEX

L

Landauer, T. 33, 55, 64, 67, 68, 89,
    152, 153, 160, 161, 165, 167,
    173, 180
Langer, L. A. 48
Larkey, C. S. 55, 223
Larson, M. S. 4
Lauer, J. 45
Leacock, C. xv, 227
Lewis, C. 128
Lewis, D. D. 56, 57, 61
Linn, R. L. 4, 8. 25
Litman, D. S. 215
Livingston, S. A. 128
Lu, C. 28, 35

M

MacCaffery D. F. 8
MacDonald, N. H. xiv, 212
Maier, E. 216
Mani, I. 222
Manzo, K. K. 8
Marcu, D. 115, 117, 118, 121, 122,
    214, 216, 220, 222, 224, 227
Margolis, M. J. 35
Maron, M. E. 57
Masand, B. 68
Mathews, J. 3, 17
Maybury, E. M. 222
Mayer, R. E. 35, 37
McCallum, A. 223
McCoy, L. F. 196, 209
Meons, M. P. 122
Messick, S. 147, 164, 168
Meyer, P. R. 125, 130, 147
Miller, T. 213, 214
Mislevy, R. 37
Moens, M. 227
Moffet, J. 9, 11
Moore, J. D. 216
Mugele, R. 45
Mullis, I. V. S 48
Myers, C. 7, 12
Myers, M. 10

N

NAEP 9
Nakatani, C. 215
Nanda, H. 130
National Council of Measurement in
    Education 24, 33, 75
National Council of Teachers of
    English and the International
    Reading Association, 7
Newman, S. E.
Nichols, P. D. 36
Nigam, K. 223
Norris, L. 211

O

O'Brien, T. 213, 214, 216
O'Neil, H. F. 32
Odell, L. 209
Olson, J. 51
Osmundson, E. 32

P

Page, E. B. xii, 4, 28, 36, 43, 44, 46,
    49, 50, 101, 102, 125, 145, 148,
    151-155, 165-168, 170, 173, 174,
    177, 180, 181
Palacio-Cayetano, J. 36
Palmer, M. 196, 208
Pardl, E. M. 9
Paris, C. L. 216
Park, J. C. 196, 208
Passonneau, R. 215
Paulus, D. 4, 44
Penfield, R. D. 178, 179, 180
Petersen, N. S. 28, 36, 46, 145, 148,
    153, 154, 166, 168, 173, 176,
    99180
Pollack, J. 216
Ponte, J. M. 56
Powers, D. 149, 161, 162, 168
Putnam, R. D. 3, 6